ENCOUNTER
WITH GOD

ENCOUNTER WITH GOD

*An Introduction to
Christian Worship and Practice*

DUNCAN B. FORRESTER
J. IAN H. McDONALD
GIAN TELLINI

Second Edition

T&T CLARK
EDINBURGH

T&T CLARK LTD
59 GEORGE STREET
EDINBURGH EH2 2LQ
SCOTLAND

First edition 1983
Second edition 1996

ISBN 0 567 08505 8

British Library Cataloguing-in-Publication Data
A catalogue record for this book is available from the British Library

Typeset by Waverley Typesetters, Galashiels
Printed and bound in Great Britain by Bell & Bain, Glasgow

CONTENTS

PREFACE TO THE FIRST EDITION

'Are you interested in Liturgy?' an old woman asked Dean Inge. 'No, Madam, neither do I collect butterflies,' the Gloomy Dean replied. But if liturgy properly understood focuses and interacts with the whole of life it cannot be only the esoteric hobby of a few, and if worship indeed is a central activity of the Church, the study of worship should have a significant place in departments and faculties of theology and in seminaries and centres of ministerial formation. Since theology, like worship, is a function of the whole Church rather than the preserve of an elite, Christians who take their faith and its practice seriously should constantly be reviewing and discussing their worship as part of the ongoing interaction between theology and practice which is integral to the Christian Faith. This introductory textbook is offered in the hope that it will stimulate, provoke and encourage profitable study and reflection on worship, rooted both in theology and practice, on the part of theological students and seminarians, clergy and lay people of various traditions.

The writing of this book was stimulated by the experience of teaching worship to lively, responsive and varied groups of students in the ecumenical context of Edinburgh University's Faculty of Divinity. Most, but not all, of these students were preparing for the ministry of Presbyterian or Anglican churches, but students from other traditions and with different motivations leading them to the study of worship also made distinctive and valuable contributions to the discussions out of which this book has arisen. We wish to thank our students for comments, challenges, questions and suggestions which have played no little part in carrying forward our thinking on worship and shaping this book.

Encounter with God has three particular emphases. In the first place, it is written with the conviction that the study of worship today must be ecumenical. The modern convergence in the theology and practice of worship is based on the realization that the major ecclesiastical traditions share more in terms of the principles and structure of worship than was commonly realized when the various traditions were studied and practised in virtual isolation from one another. Now we can, and must, take a broader view which is full of possibilities for the renewal of worship and the restoration of Christian unity.

Secondly, we have made the complementarity of Word and Sacrament the pivot of our argument. In the past even when the theological principle was affirmed, practice often denied it. For example, in churches which gave to their ministers great freedom in the conduct of worship, much attention was devoted in theological education to homiletics while the principles of worship were often given perfunctory treatment. As a consequence worship sometimes degenerated into nothing but the preliminaries to the sermon, and sacramental life became impoverished. In churches of the 'catholic' tradition, on the other hand, it was not un-common for seminaries to devote a major part of their time to liturgy but to inculcate the view that preaching and the ministry of the Word were little more than appendages. This unhealthy polarization is clearly reflected in many textbooks. We have tried to do something to redress the balance and hope we have suggested some ways in which this fundamental principle of the theology of worship may be adequately expressed in practice.

In the third place, we believe that worship should be studied primarily theologically. Karl Barth was right to say of the adage *Lex orandi, lex credendi*, 'this saying is not simply a pious dictum, but one of the most intelligent things that has ever been said about method in theology'. It is as important for theology that it takes seriously both worship and the questions it generates as it is that the study of worship should understand itself as a theological discipline. Some may feel that we have given too little attention to the history of liturgy, but we have restricted the space devoted to historical matters advisedly, because we feel it necessary to stress that the study of worship is not a form of antiquarianism – and, besides, the necessary historical information is easy to come by elsewhere.

The three authors brought varied experience and background to teaching in Edinburgh and the writing of this book. Tellini was a Roman Catholic priest working on Eastern liturgies in Rome before becoming an Anglican and teaching in various theological colleges. He now divides his time between teaching, in Edinburgh University, serving as a parish priest, and working on the Scottish Episcopal Church's Liturgical Commission. McDonald was a parish minister of the Church of Scotland before teaching Religious Education in a college of education and developing special expertise in the New Testament and in homiletics. Forrester was ordained in the Church of South India where an interest in worship was aroused which he further developed while chaplain of a new English university. It should not be beyond the capacity of a moderately competent textual critic to work out which author has had primary responsibility for which parts of the book. Each section has been revised after discussion, but we have not sought uniformity of style and although we have substantial agreement on our approach to the theology of worship, we are still debating vigorously among ourselves some of the positions presented in these pages. We hope that those who read and use this book will join in the debate, recognizing its importance for the future vitality of the worship and theology of the Church.

DUNCAN FORRESTER
J. IAN H. McDONALD
GIAN TELLINI

New College
University of Edinburgh
Easter, 1983

PREFACE TO THE SECOND EDITION

The authors are deeply gratified that the first edition of this book has been found helpful by so many and that a second edition has been called for. They have taken the opportunity to add three new chapters: on 'Worship and Christian Practice' (Duncan Forrester), 'Becoming a Christian' (Gian Tellini) and 'Christian Formation' (Ian McDonald). Other chapters have been revised, some of them quite radically. Gian has added some stirring thoughts on the theology of worship, and we are happy to include a section on 'New Developments in Homiletics' by Jolyon Mitchell, who lectures on the Theology and Ethics of Communication at Edinburgh University. A fellow of the College of Preachers, he has worked as a BBC World Service and Radio 4 producer and journalist. It is our hope that this enhanced volume will meet the needs of students studying the worship and theology of the Church, including preaching and Christian formation. We also hope that it will commend the study of this vital area of ministry to a wider readership.

The authors are grateful for the help received in the preparation of this edition of the book: particularly to Jolyon and Clare Mitchell and to Jenny McDonald for reading the proofs and making helpful suggestions; and also to the editors of T&T Clark for their interest, skill and guidance.

IAN MCDONALD
(*on behalf of all the contributors*)

New College
University of Edinburgh
November, 1995

CHAPTER 1

WORSHIP AND CHRISTIAN PRACTICE

People worship. For most people ritual in some form or other has importance in their lives. They may not recognize that worship expresses the meaning they find in life, and offers consolation, encouragement and challenge. But the rituals of everyday life, the ceremonies at marriage or at a death, or the observances of civil society, like Remembrance Sunday, or university graduations, mean a great deal to people. Worship relates to belief and meaning, and also to practice and social order. It is this interaction between worship, which is itself a form of practice, and Christian belief and practice which is the central concern of this book.

The oldest archaeological evidence suggests that worship in some form or other occupied a central place in the activity of people from the dawn of history, and the modern world is full of shrines, temples, mosques, churches, gospel halls, meeting houses: places where activity relating to the holy, what Rudolph Otto spoke of as the *mysterium tremendum et fascinans*, takes place. But is it not true that in the West, at least, society has become secular, worship has less and less of a recognized place, and fewer and fewer people take part in worship, at least as traditionally understood? Yet although the formal expressions of Christian worship may play a less significant role in most Western societies than once they did, these very societies are not as free from worship as might appear at first glance. There are, of course, nations in the West where Christian worship continues to hold a central place, as if to mock the sociologists' generalizations about secularization – Poland and the United States are cases in point. And even when few seem to attend worship frequently, large numbers of people feel the need to mark the great turning points of life – birth, maturity, marriage,

death – with Christian rituals or 'rites of passage', which give
meaning to these transitions and allow them to be understood
in the context of eternity. The rituals of civil religion are also
alive and well. Worship continues, in a multitude of forms, some
of them bizarre, others but vain repetitions of rituals which
seem to have lost their significance long ago. Worship is not
just a hobby of a few, like squash or model railways: an astonish-
ingly large proportion of humankind takes part in worship with
at least some glimmering awareness of its significance. And this
despite the fact that worship in modern societies often seems
strangely anomalous – a quaint museum-piece, or a furtive and
surreptitious activity indulged in by little curious cliques of
cranks and 'cognitive dissidents'.

It is not easy to suggest an adequate definition of worship, or
of *Christian* worship. One description of Christian worship
might be the answer to the first question in the Westminster
Shorter Catechism (1648): 'Man's chief end is to glorify God
and enjoy Him for ever.' This speaks of Christian worship as
ascribing to God the glory that is properly his and delighting in
encountering God. It also suggests that worship is a central,
characteristically human, and virtually universal activity.
Worship, encountering God, for Christians is the pivotal and
most important thing in human life, that which focuses and
enriches the whole of life, the giving of meaning to existence,
the purpose for which people were made.

The very word 'worship' in English is odd. Basically it means
the recognition and celebration of worth, value, goodness,
holiness, wherever such qualities are to be found. In England
they still retain the archaic usage of referring to 'His Worship
the Mayor'. And in the 1662 Anglican Prayer Book the groom
says to the bride, 'With my body I thee worship' – he recognizes
and celebrates her worth and value, her lovableness. And this
he does not only in words – the words of lovers are sometimes
pretty incoherent, but words are still important – but also with
the body, in action. The love that this worship celebrates is
expressed and strengthened in bodily acts; it is something that
involves the whole personality. The kiss, the cuddle, gazing
silently into one another's eyes, coitus – these are just some of
the bodily ways in which love shows itself. And lovers, like
worshippers (indeed the argument is that they are very much
the same), use symbols that are charged with rich meaning: the
bunch of flowers, the ring, the gift of perfume. In such symbolic

acts a lover recognizes and celebrates the love and worth of the partner. They communicate with one another in verbal, bodily and symbolic ways, and their communication both shows that love is there, and deepens, enlarges and strengthens the love between them.

But the English word 'worship' has been narrowed in meaning down the years, so that today it is rarely used except to refer to set times of formal ritual. This is misleading, in as far as it suggests that worship is a distinct, specialized part of life; just as medical care takes place in clinics and surgeries and hospitals, so worship takes place in churches and mosques and temples. At one level this is quite true. There are times and places for public worship, and most people draw a pretty clear distinction between what goes on in these times and places, and the rest of life. But this narrow sense needs to be complemented by a broader understanding of worship. Christian worship is the offering of the whole of life; our relationship to God cannot be confined in one compartment of our lives. Times of service are important if we are to offer the service of our lives; the special times sustain and deepen the constant relationship.

Worship as Practice

That strange activity called 'worship' stands at the heart of Christian practice. You cannot understand the Christian life without reference to worship, and Christian worship must be understood as a form of practice, an activity in which one participates rather than something one observes or contemplates. Worship is the distinctive activity of the people of God. In worship God is encountered and glorified, God's purposes are discerned, however faintly, and God's people are nourished and strengthened for service. Worship is not just part of Christian practice, but it is the centre without which everything else falls apart, the place from which we may extrapolate the other dimensions of Christian practice, the part that clarifies and sustains the rest. In worship we are in touch with the life of heaven, and despite the incompleteness and imperfection of earthly worship, God can and does use for God's glory and the good of humankind our frail and stumbling efforts to worship God.

Worship, then, is something that we do. 'Religion, like art, *lives* in so far as it is performed', wrote the anthropologist Victor

Turner.[1] Christian faith can only live if it is enacted both in times of worship and in life. It is a doing that involves the whole person, the head just as much as the heart. In worship we use symbols, and words, and gestures in complex patterns of behaviour which communicate meaning. The philosopher Wittgenstein wrote that 'Language did not emerge from some kind of ratiocination . . . Children do not learn that books exist, that armchairs exist, etc. – they learn to fetch books, to sit in armchairs, etc.'[2] So in worship we learn by doing, by acting, by re-enacting the story of the community. The pioneer anthropologist, R. R. Marrett, said that what he called 'savage religion' was 'something not so much thought out as danced out'.[3] How religion is 'danced out' in worship, and how this relates to thought about God, theology, and the practice of the community of faith and individual believers are main concerns of this book.

Worship as Relationship

One of the commonest misunderstandings of worship is to regard it in an impersonal way. When this happens worship is seen as a mechanical or magical process in which worshippers ensure their salvation or happiness by manipulating supernatural forces. But Christian worship, as Edward Schillebeeckx has so strikingly affirmed, is an encounter, a meeting:

> Religion is . . . essentially a personal relation of man to God, of person to person; a personal encounter or a personal communing with God. It is precisely in this that the essential condition for a life truly centred on God consists. It is because God lovingly takes the initiative and comes down to meet man in grace that man lives in a condition of active and immediate communication with the one who, in this relationship, becomes the 'living God'. The act itself of this encounter of God and man, which on earth can only take place in faith, is what we call salvation. On God's part this encounter involves a disclosure of himself by revelation, and on the part of man it involves devotion to God's service – that is religion.[4]

[1] Victor Turner, *The Anthropology of Performance*, New York 1986, p. 48.

[2] L. Wittgenstein, *On Certainty*, G. E. M. Anscombe and G. H. von Wright (eds.), New York 1969, p. 62e.

[3] R. R. Marrett, *The Threshold of Religion* (1909), p. xxxi, quoted in Tom F. Driver, *The Magic of Ritual*, San Francisco 1991, p. 84.

[4] Edward Schillebeeckx, *Christ the Sacrament of the Encounter with God*, London 1963, p. 4.

If worship is an encounter between God and people, this must be reflected in the quality of relationships between the worshippers and their attitude to their neighbours. It is right and proper to emphasize that worship is the recognition and celebration of the glory and worth of God. This should have a priority in our understanding of worship as a human activity. But it is also true that worshippers experience an affirmation of their own worth and value to God. They come to worship aware of their sins; they confess them and experience the forgiving grace and love of God, the divine confirmation that, despite all, they are loved with an infinite love, and are of incalculable value to God.

Worship, then, should be an encounter with God in which we enjoy him. It shows, even in the midst of oppression, poverty and the bleakest of circumstances, the delight of keeping company with God, in whom all true joys are to be found. This applies, of course, to the whole of the Christian life. But worship, if it percolates through the whole of life as it should, is still the time set aside for loving attention to God. In the best of families time needs to be kept for doing things together, for enjoying one another, for talking, for playing together. Of course, these times are not the *whole* of the family relationship, but without them the relationship may wither. We need, in other words, to make time for God, jealously guarded time, in which we give loving attention to God, that the whole of our lives may be lived as a loving encounter with God.

Worship is enjoying *God*. We do not 'enjoy ourselves' in worship, indeed the very opposite, for in worship our attention is directed away from ourselves, to God and to our neighbour. In worship we look at ourselves honestly and confess our sins; then as forgiven sinners we can cease to be absorbed by self and open out to God and God's glory, and to the neighbour and that neighbour's needs. C. S. Lewis in his autobiography, *Surprised by Joy*, describes how as a young man he was engrossed with his own inner workings. He constantly and morbidly scrutinized his motivation, his attitudes, his feelings as if these were matters of supreme moment. Conversion drew him out of himself; he became far more open to other people, far more sensitive to their feelings, because he was now open to God. Worship should encourage the capacity for open, mature, confident and honest relationship. Sin, according to a phrase beloved by Augustine and Luther, is being *incurvatus in se*, turned in on oneself. C. S. Lewis, like many others, found an amazing release from this obsession with self when he was given the capacity of enjoying God and his neighbour. Understanding worship as an encounter with God should save us from the traps of over-concentration on our own inwardness, and of being obsessed with the minutiae of liturgy and the details of worship as if these things were important in themselves. They are simply aids, which ought to be unobtrusive, to the glorification and enjoyment of God by his people.

In the encounter, God takes the initiative. God has promised to be with people whenever two or three are gathered in God's name. God keeps promises! Encounter involves the whole person, body, mind and spirit. And in encounter love is expressed, sustained and nurtured.

Worship and Faith

It is frequently held that an articulate belief, or the ability to subscribe to a creed or confession, is in some way the necessary qualification for taking part in worship. The creed is felt to be like an entrance exam; only those who pass can belong in the worshipping community. To worship without having worked out exactly what you believe, to this way of thinking, is dishonest and lacking in integrity.

This position depends on a typically modern confusion between faith and belief, as Wilfred Cantwell Smith suggests, arguing that faith

> is an orientation of the personality, to oneself, to one's neighbour, to the universe; a total response; a way of seeing whatever one sees and of handling whatever one handles; a capacity to live at a more than mundane level; to see, to feel, to act in terms of a transcendent dimension. Belief, on the other hand, is the holding of certain ideas.[5]

But it is not enough to say that while an intellectually formulated belief is not a requirement for worship, faith in Cantwell Smith's sense is. For worship is radically misunderstood if it is seen as the joyful expression of the confident, unclouded faith of the community and all its members. The sole requirement for taking part in worship is some element of hunger, of desire for truth and for reality. For faith and belief as well are nurtured

[5] Wilfred Cantwell Smith, *Faith and Belief*, Princeton 1979, p. 12.

and shaped in worship, and find their expression and fulfilment in worship. And often enough it is in worship that faith is born, so that in certain traditions people will speak of the Lord's Supper as a 'converting ordinance'.

Worship and Theology

Down the ages the experience of worship has called for theological explication. Sometimes this has been no more than elaborate explanations for practices and symbols which arose accidentally or in rather strange circumstances. But it has also been true that much great theology has been the attempt to interpret practices in worship and relate them to the deposit of faith in the Bible. Neither the doctrine of the Trinity nor orthodox christology can be simply read off the pages of the Bible. Doctrinal formulation has to relate the faith to changing cultural contexts, it is true; but even more urgent is the task of relating the practices and formulations used in worship to the tradition of faith. How could Christians worship Jesus as divine (as they did from a very early stage) and still be monotheists? Thus, christology arose very largely as an explanation of how Christians worship. Likewise, baptism was administered in the three-fold name before there was any agreement that the Holy Spirit was a separate *hypostasis*, let alone a formulated doctrine of the Trinity. These, and other, doctrines emerged out of consideration of what is said and done in worship; the experience of worship demands theological explication.

We can properly think of worship *as* theology. Worship in all its forms and elements is laden with theological insights, some of which are rarely brought to verbal expression: theology is acted out, expressed in practice. Worship is the vehicle of theology, communicating far more effectively than learned treatises ever can. Thus, Methodists and Lutherans have felt particularly strongly that the hymns used in worship communicate the faith in a way that people can appropriate. Many Roman Catholics felt that the changes in the mass enjoined by the Second Vatican Council involved a change in the 'faith once delivered to the saints', and that the change in the language of worship from Latin to the vernacular separated them from their fellow Catholics who worshipped in other languages. The 1662 Prayer Book was, and is, one of the theological standards of the Church of England – an authoritative repository of the teaching of the Church which many Anglicans felt was not at the mercy of cultural and theological fashions as the Alternative Book was believed to be.

We can think of theology *as* worship. Anselm, for instance, believing that theology is faith seeking understanding and that faith is inseparable from worship, wrote some of his most significant works of theology in the form of prayer, of dialogue between God and the theologian. Much classical theology is in the form of sermons, bearing all the marks that they were originally delivered in the context of worship. For centuries it was assumed that theological lectures should start with prayer, because theology is done in the presence of the living God, and should therefore be reverent as well as rigorous. The Orthodox Churches, in particular, maintain a lively conviction that theology should be doxology, that it should lead people to give praise to God, that it should flow naturally and unselfconsciously into worship.

In a sense theology provides a test of worship, and worship provides a test of theology. Theology should properly be the friendly critic of worship and preaching, seeing part of its function as the encouragement of honesty and integrity in the church's worship and proclamation. There is nothing wrong in seeing worship as a kind of theological laboratory, on the assumption that authentic theology should 'ring true' in the worship of God's people. This is not to suggest that worship and theology are, or ought to be, indistinguishable from one another, or that there should always be complete harmony between them. Worship, like the canon of scripture, is a kind of repository of insights, images and convictions, some of which appear to die, and others of which go dormant for centuries until in altered circumstances, there is what Austen Farrer called a 'rebirth of images'. Worship and theology are both explorations into the ultimate mysteries of life; it would be strange (and rather dull!) if they were always in step with one another. One may in worship, for example, rejoice to join 'with angels and archangels and all the company of heaven', while as a theologian having great difficulty in working out whether one believes in angels, or what we mean by heaven. But if after careful consideration we feel that the existence of angels must be stoutly denied, and that heaven is simply the fruit of false consciousness, then in honesty we should attempt to remove all such language from our orders of worship. To move between worship and theology convinced that both are orientations towards the same mysteries is exhilarating and productive in both areas. It is also true that worship provides some significant tests of theological positions – can they be prayed or preached? Do they lead into worship? Do they engage reverently as well as rigorously with mysteries which are to be adored, explored, and lived out in practice?

The old epigram *lex orandi lex credendi*, the law of praying and the law of believing, points to the truth that the doing of theology and the practice of worship should be held together for the health of each.[6] Karl Barth called the epigram 'one of the most profound descriptions of the theological method'.[7] What is at issue here is not simply the relationship between an academic subject, Christian theology, and the practice of worship, but the proper orientation towards truth. Michael Polanyi, scientist, philosopher and seminal Christian thinker suggests that worship stimulates, provokes and encourages enquiry; it points towards the truth, and sustains serious seekers after truth; but it only indicates in paradoxical and fragmentary ways the nature of the truth which 'we see in a mirror dimly', until at the last we encounter the truth 'face to face' (1 Corinthians 13:12). Polanyi's concern is with the relationship of worship and enquiry in general. He suggests that all forms of disciplined enquiry are nourished, held to their task, and pointed steadily towards the truth by worship:

> It resembles not the dwelling within a great theory of which we enjoy the complete understanding, nor an immersion in the pattern of a musical masterpiece, but the heuristic upsurge which tries to break through the accepted frameworks of thought, guided by intimations of discoveries still beyond our horizons. Christian worship sustains, as it were, an eternal, never to be consummated hunch; a heuristic vision which is accepted for the sake of its irresolvable tension. It is like an obsession with a problem known to be insoluble, which yet follows against reason, unswervingly, the heuristic command, 'Look at the unknown!' Christianity sedulously fosters, and in a sense permanently satisfies man's craving for mental dissatisfaction by offering him the comfort of a crucified God.[8]

---

[6] See P. de Clerck, '*Lex orandi lex credendi*: Sens originel et avatars historiques d'un adage équivoque', in *Questions Liturgiques et paroissiales*, 59 (1978), pp. 193–212; E.T., *Studia Liturgica*, and Geoffrey Wainwright, *Doxology*, London 1980, pp. 218–83.

[7] Karl Barth, *The Humanity of God*, London, 1961, p. 88.

[8] Michael Polanyi, *Personal Knowledge*, London 1962, p. 199.

Worship is a way of dwelling in truth, which should encourage a passion to explore the mysteries of life.

Worship and Ethics[9]

Our relationship to God and our relationship to our neighbour are interdependent. We cannot cultivate a close and loving relationship with God in worship while we are being manipulative or exploitative in our relationship to our neighbour. The Sermon on the Mount puts it thus: 'So if you are offering your gift at the altar, and there remember that your brother has something against you, leave your gift there before the altar and go; first be reconciled to your brother and then come to offer your gift' (Matthew 5:23–24). If Christian worship is isolated from the spheres of politics and economics (the way relationships within society are structured), it loses its authenticity and easily becomes the opium of the people, a cover for injustice and oppression, or an irrelevance. Archbishop Trevor Huddleston reminded us of this when he commented that many Christians are so concerned with the real presence in the Eucharist that they forget the real presence of Christ in the needy neighbour. Indeed we have been reminded recently by Jose Miranda and others that for many of the prophets the real worship of God is the doing of justice, not ritual nor sacrifices. Hence they see worship misused as an alternative to ethical behaviour, a distraction from the service of the neighbour, a disguise for injustice and oppression, and constantly liable to degenerate into idolatry.

Others, like the American theologian Tom Driver, emphasize the capacity of ritual to liberate and transform.[10] In worship, they argue, an alternative world is manifested which, by its very existence, challenges 'the real world'. Ritual is concerned as much with transformation as with order and continuity. It can challenge the present order by presenting the order that is to come. And yet the reality of worship continues to be profoundly ambiguous. Totalitarian regimes this century have tended to prohibit evangelistic and educational activity on the part of the Church, and to strive to control preaching, but to regard the worship that goes on within a recognized church building as

---

[9] This section draws on Duncan Forrester's article 'Ecclesiology and Ethics: A Reformed Approach', *The Ecumenical Review* 47/2 (1995), pp. 148–54.
[10] Tom F. Driver, *The Magic of Ritual*, San Francisco 1991.

relatively inoffensive. There have even been suggestions that the Nazis, so far from being worried by the movement for liturgical renewal, secretly encouraged it on the grounds that it made church people less concerned with the political, social and economic processes around them.[11] But, contrariwise, both the Nazi and the communist dictatorships were at pains to develop alternative secular forms of worship and rituals to wean the people away from the Church: evidence of the continuing power and influence of worship over behaviour and belief.[12]

But how, in a deeply divided world, can we worship so that the situation is challenged and transformed? Camillo Torres, the Colombian priest who died as a guerrilla, believed that in a society as profoundly unjust and divided as Colombia it was impossible for the mass to be properly celebrated. Hence, he said, 'I took off my cassock to be more fully a priest', and gave up celebrating mass.[13] In a very different context, Ulrich Duchrow asks whether a Church which 'is divided among active thieves, passive profiteers and deprived victims' is indeed the body of Christ, capable of celebrating the Eucharist.[14] But we must recognize that we are not yet in the Kingdom for which we pray. Worship is for those seeking that kingdom and its justice, and is superfluous for those who have already arrived, for in the New Jerusalem, there is no need of a temple. Worship, after all, is for sinners, not for those who trust in their own righteousness, as we are reminded by the parable of the Pharisee and the publican. And in worship we find God's forgiveness and the grace of new beginnings.

But we need to recover today ways in which worship may be a healing, transforming, effective sign of community and of hope, as well as a place in which division and hostility are overcome. If in worship we find the true nature of Christian community and experience a little of the Kingdom that is to come, prefiguring the life of that Kingdom, we are encountering something that is sharply at variance with the way of the world. In a sense we are playing out the roles appropriate to the Kingdom and expressing fundamental ethical commitments. The Johannine saying,

[11] See Dermot A. Lane, *Foundation for a Social Theology*, Dublin 1984, pp. 143–44, 182.

[12] See especially Christel Lane, *The Rites of Rulers: Ritual in Industrial Society – The Soviet Case*, Cambridge 1981; and David I. Kertzer, *Ritual, Politics and Power*, New Haven 1988.

[13] J. Gerassi (ed.), *Camillo Torres: Revolutionary Priest*, Harmondsworth 1979, p. 9.

[14] U. Duchrow, *Global Economy*, Geneva 1987, p. 137.

'The bread which I shall give for the life of the world is my flesh' surely implies that the body broken on the cross and the bread broken and shared among believers are both for the life of the world. To share that bread involves quite specific commitments to the hungry neighbour and to the needs of the world. Thus, it is not only legitimate but also necessary to explore the theology and the ethics of what happens and what is said in Christian worship.

Worship and Community

Worship is the activity of the people of God. It is not something that people do in isolation; even when praying on one's own one is praying with the Church. Worship is not something people watch, a kind of stage-show laid on for an audience, nor is it something they listen to, like a lecture. Rather it is something that they *do*, and do *together*. It is the central activity of the Christian fellowship which creates as it expresses, friendship with God and with our neighbours. In worship we are in fellowship with the faithful on earth and in heaven. We learn the profound interdependence of which the writer of the Letter to the Hebrews wrote when he said, of the great saints of the past, 'they, without us, shall not be made perfect' (Hebrews 11:40).

Christian worship expresses and makes community in which hostilities and divisions are overcome. The poor and the weak have a special place in the community. If they are despised or maltreated the nature of the Church as 'members one of another' is denied:

> Two visitors may enter your meetings, one a well-dressed man with gold rings, and the other a poor man in grimy clothes. Suppose you pay special attention to the well-dressed man and say to him, 'Please take this seat,' while to the other poor man you say, 'You stand over there, or sit here on the floor by my footstool,' do you not see that you are discriminating among your members and judging by wrong standards? Listen, my dear friends: has not God chosen those who are poor in the eyes of the world to be rich in faith and to possess the kingdom he has promised to those who love him? And yet you have humiliated the poor man (James 2:2–6).

And Paul warns the Corinthian Christians, few of whom 'are wise by any human standard, few powerful or of noble birth' that when they shame the poorer members at the Lord's table 'it is not the Lord's Supper that you eat' (1 Corinthians 11:20).

In worship the stories that are formative of the community are retold, re-enacted, recalled and meditated upon. The story of the community of faith is grafted together with the personal stories of the worshippers. When the kings of the old Anglo-Saxon kingdoms of England were converted to Christianity, they looked afresh at their personal and dynastic histories as represented by the genealogies. These traced their descent back many generations to the old Norse gods – Thor, and Wodin and so on. Then, rather than renouncing their stories, denying their history and assuming an entirely new identity, the Anglo-Saxon kings simply extended their genealogies backwards, so that now, as Christians, they traced their descent through the Norse gods to the patriarchs of the Old Testament and back to Adam. They had grafted their stories into the new salvation-history, and assumed a Christian identity without a total repudiation of the old. Every believer has to relate the personal story to the story of the community of faith, and worship is one of the crucial places where this grafting takes place.

In the Jewish Passover a central part of the ritual is when the youngest child present asks four questions:

> Why does this night differ from all other nights? For on all other nights we eat either leavened bread or unleavened bread; why on this night only unleavened bread?
>
> On all other nights we eat all kinds of herbs; why on this night only bitter herbs?
>
> On all other nights we need not dip our herbs even once; why on this night must we dip them twice?
>
> On all other nights we eat either sitting or reclining; why on this night do we all recline?

The reply from the elders comes in terms of the story of the first Passover and of God's deliverance of his people from Egypt, the story which they are ritually re-enacting, and the story which tells the child and the whole gathering what it means to be a Jew, who they are. The great story of God's people dovetails with their personal stories:

We were Pharaoh's slaves in Egypt, then the Lord our God brought us forth with a mighty hand and an outstretched arm. And if the Holy One, Blessed be He, had not brought our forefathers forth from Egypt then we, our children, and our children's children, would still be slaves in Egypt.

So, even though all of us were wise, all of us full of understanding, all of us elders, all of us knowing the Torah, we should still be under the commandment to tell the story of the departure from Egypt. And the more one tells the story of the departure from Egypt, the more praiseworthy he is.[15]

That is precisely what happens at the Passover feast. They tell again the old story, they sing and pray about it, but above all they re-enact the first Passover, appropriating afresh the story of God's deliverance and making it live in contemporary experience. They glimpse in the story who they are, where they belong, and what their destiny is.

In worship we look back. In order to understand ourselves and our times we must hear again and relate ourselves to the stories of God's dealings with God's people. We need constantly to repossess our past as something that is still operative and influential in the present. And in this process we see where we 'fit in'. But worship would quickly become maudlin, wistful and disabling if it were simply concerned with the past. It also looks towards the future and encourages hope and expectation, for the God who meets us in the present and dealt with us graciously in the past is also the God who will be with us in the future, when all worship will find its fulfilment and culmination in the immediate presence of God. And in the present in worship and in life we act out the roles of the coming Kingdom. W. H. Auden is reputed to have said: 'Human beings are by nature actors, who cannot become something until they have pretended to be it.'[16] In this profound sense, Christian worship is a pretence, a form of play-acting.

All down the ages Christians have recognized that in worship they are *doing* something of ultimate importance, celebrating the mystery of God's love and grace. They have experienced the excitement and the challenge of encountering the living God, and found that their thirst for God was both satisfied and challenged by their worship in Spirit and in truth. They would

---

[15] N. N. Glatzer (ed.), *The Passover Haggada, with English Translation, Introduction and Commentary*, New York 1969, pp. 21–23.

[16] Cited in Driver, *op. cit.*, p. 79.

agree with Karl Barth who said that 'Christian worship is the most momentous, the most urgent, the most glorious action that can take place in human life'.[17]

FURTHER READING

Tom F. Driver, *The Magic of Ritual*, New York 1991.
Geoffrey Wainwright, *Doxology*, London, 1980.
David I. Kertzer, *Ritual, Politics and Power*, New Haven 1988.
Edward Schillebeeckx, *Christ the Sacrament*, London 1963.
D. B. Forrester, 'Ecclesiology and Ethics: A Reformed Approach', *The Ecumenical Review*, 47/2 (1995), pp. 148–54.

FOR DISCUSSION

1. What is the place of Christian worship in modern secular societies?
2. How should worship relate to the doing of theology?
3. Explore some of the ways in which the Church in its worship *is* a social ethic.

---

[17] K. Barth, cited in J.-J. von Allmen, *Worship: Its Theology and Practice*, London 1965, p. 13.

CHAPTER 2

THE ROOTS OF CHRISTIAN WORSHIP

In 1966, Louis Bouyer argued that, though one of the most original creations of Christianity, Christian worship did not spring up '*from a sort of spontaneous generation, fatherless and motherless like Melkizedech*'; in discussing Christian worship, one must search for its roots; in recounting its genesis and development, one must strive to understand it in its proper context.[1]

When Louis Bouyer wrote those words, the idea that the roots of Christian worship were to be found mainly, though not exclusively, in Judaism was still a controversial one. Today it is no more so. Progress in biblical studies and in the comparative study of liturgy has shown not only the artificiality of the dichotomy between the Old and the New Testament, but also the continuity between the worship of the Old Testament and that of the New.[2]

The Concept of Worship in the Old Testament

Scholars have been known to discern the existence of two distinct theologies of worship in the Old Testament. The first of these theologies would be overwhelmingly based on the liturgy of the Temple in Jerusalem and therefore heavily dependent on the role of the Levitical priesthood. The second of these theologies would be mainly based on the wider platform of everyday life and would therefore appear to be much more people-orientated.

---

[1] L. Bouyer, *Eucharist: Theology and Spirituality of the Eucharistic Prayer*, Notre Dame, Indiana 1968, p. 15.
[2] *Ibid.*, p. 19.

A priesthood-orientated theology of worship

According to some texts,[3] it would appear that the Holy One of Israel could be encountered only in his own Temple in Jerusalem. It was in the Temple's sanctuary that the glory of the Lord was said to reside, rather than in the people of Israel as a whole. In these texts, we are confronted with a sharp distinction and separation of the 'sacred' from the 'profane'. To give but one example, the book of Ezekiel decrees to the last cubit the shape and measurement of the Temple seen by the prophet in his vision. The basic architectural plan of this Temple is that of the Temple of Solomon. Few but significant departures are nevertheless taken from this basic architectural plan. Every time this happens, it is to emphasize the separation of the sacred from the secular and to safeguard from defilement both the holiness of God and the holiness of his dwelling-place.[4] Divine laws are set out concerning those who are to be admitted to the Temple and those who are excluded from the sanctuary. Of all Levitical priests, only the sons of Zadok are allowed to draw near to the Lord and minister to him. The king may come as far as the gateway and the people must remain outside. When they approach the sanctuary, the sons of Zadok are enjoined to wear special linen garments which they are then to remove and leave behind in the holy place 'lest they communicate holiness to the people with their garments' (Ezekiel 44:19).

According to these texts, the highest possible worship can be rendered to the Lord only on his own altar in his own Temple. With or without the limitation to the sons of Zadok which is peculiar to the book of Ezekiel, the priests are the unique 'personae' of this worship by the Lord's own decree. The people can be said to worship only in a secondary and derivative sense, and that only by attending from afar. When 'drawing near' (that is when offering sacrifice), the priests must perform their worship according to absolute, immutable and indispensable rules promulgated by God himself. The objects used in the performance of worship are themselves invested with special holiness: the vestments, the vessels and even the furniture. As a consequence, they must not be touched by

[3] Cf. e.g. Ezekiel 40–46: Numbers 1:50–54; 3:5–10; 4:15; Leviticus 1–7; 2 Chronicles 5:5; 13:10–12; Zechariah 14:16–20.
[4] T. Chary, *Les Prophètes et le culte à partir de l'Exil,* Paris–Tournai 1955, pp. 4–16 and 276.

unauthorized hands. God's unapproachable transcendence is stretched to the limit and the manner of the Lord's presence in his Temple is understood quite literally in spatial terms. The basic unworthiness of all human beings is clearly stated, access to God being guaranteed only in terms of the sacred rites performed by a hierarchy of mediation. Failing to observe the universal cultic law, even on the part of the Gentiles, would incur the most severe penalties such as drought on the land or even plague.

A people-orientated theology of worship

According to other texts,[5] worship would appear to be a kind of 'spiritual sacrifice' leaving little room for outward ritual observances seen as an end in themselves. It must be stressed that in this context 'spiritual' is not to be taken as synonymous with 'anti-materialistic'. The worship advocated by these texts is not one of withdrawal from the world. On the contrary, it is seen essentially in the faithful discharge of one's duties of brotherhood and solidarity towards one's fellow Israelites. It consists of obedience to the voice of the Lord and of faithfulness to his covenant. It means caring for the hungry, the thirsty, the widow, the orphan, the stranger, the destitute and the oppressed, for the sake of the Lord. The arena of this kind of worship is as wide as that of life itself. According to these texts, worship is not the cult of an unapproachable God, but a celebration of Immanuel, 'God-who-is-with us'. Access to the transcendent God is not brought about by a priestly hierarchy of mediation. On the contrary, the whole of the chosen People understands itself as called to become the place where the glory of the Lord dwells: a holy, royal nation of priests spreading God's Word not by means of sacred ceremonies, but by their lives. The worship advocated by these texts is clearly people-orientated. No hard and fast separation exists between the sacred and the profane. In its original and primary sense, worship refers to the life and belief of a whole nation, a life and a belief that have immediate practical and social consequences. In a secondary and derivative sense, worship may then be said

[5] Cf. e.g. Exodus 19:5–6; Deuteronomy 10:12–22; Psalms 50:7–23; 51:17–19; Amos 2:6–8; 5:12–5, 21–25; Hosea 6:4–10; 8:11–14; Isaiah 1:10–17; 56:6–8; 60 and 61; Micah 6:6–8; Jeremiah 7:1–12, 22–23; Zechariah 8:14–23 and 1 Samuel 15:22–23.

to refer also to outward moments of prayer and encounter reflecting, alongside all the other aspects of ethical and practical behaviour, an indispensable inner ('spiritual') attitude to the God who speaks and acts according to an eschatological plan.

Unity and diversity in the Old Testament

From the publication in 1885 of Wellhausen's 'Prolegomena to the History of Israel', biblical scholars have engaged in a recurrently flaring debate over the precise nature of the prophets' attitude to the worship of the Temple in Jerusalem. As E. Heaton wrote, the controversy 'has generated more heat than light', mainly because of an unreadiness to credit the biblical writers and redactors with the impartiality of which we are not always capable ourselves.[6] Suffice it to say here with J. P. Hyatt that a substantial consensus is being gathered today around the opinion according to which 'the ultimate Biblical and prophetic view is not that cultic worship can be completely dispensed with'.[7] In the first place, prophets appear regularly on both sides of the argument. In the second place, as R. Daly points out, 'the very criticism of the prophets makes sense only on the supposition that they believed not only in the idea of sacrifice but also in its practical efficacy'.[8]

If the two theologies of worship we discerned in the Old Testament are not mutually exclusive, how can they be successfully made to relate to each other? Heavily influenced by the liberal *Religionsgeschichte* school, some scholars thought that the priest-centred theology of worship was the original one and that the 'spiritual sacrifice' theory was a later Hellenistic development.[9] A corrective to this theory was more recently supplied by others who showed how the idea of 'spiritualized cult' went well back into Old Testament times.[10] On the other hand, some scholars argue that the priest-centred conception

---

[6] E. W. Heaton, *His Servants the Prophets*, London 1949, pp. 78–79.
[7] J. P. Hyatt, *The Prophetic Criticism of Israelite Worship* in H. M. Orlinsky (ed.), *Interpreting the Prophetic Tradition*, New York 1969, p. 210.
[8] R. J. Daly, *The Origins of the Christian Doctrine of Sacrifice*, London 1978, p. 23.
[9] Cf. e.g. H. Wenschkewitz, *Die Spiritualisierung der Kultusbegriffe in Alten Testament: Tempel, Priester und Opfer in Neuen Testament*, in Angelos 4 (1932), pp. 70–281.
[10] Cf. H.-J. Hermisson, *Sprache und Ritus im alt-israelischen Kult: Zur Spiritualisierung der Kultbegriffe in Alten Testament*, Wissenschaftlichen Monographien zum Alten und Neuen Testament 19, Neukirchen-Vluyin 1965, pp. 156–60. Cf. also R. E. Clements, *The Idea of the Divine Presence in Ancient Israel*, Oxford 1965, especially chapter 7.

of worship, faithfully reflected in the vocabulary of the Septuagint, was due more to the corrupt ideal of worship at the times of the post-exilic Temple than to the biblical texts themselves.[11]

A similar and more attractive theory is that of T. Chary, who argues that there were indeed initially in the Old Testament not one but two understandings of worship of which Jeremiah and Ezekiel were the forefathers. These two understandings did to a large extent run in opposite directions, Ezekiel and his followers having broken away from the tradition of the early prophets to introduce into the history of Israel a new and potentially dangerous factor, as Deutero-Zechariah and the pre-Maccabean section of the book of Daniel show. The concentration of worship in the Temple of Jerusalem and the rise of a distinctly priestly-orientated mentality greatly contributed to the stressing of the Ezekiel-based theology of worship at the expense of that theology of worship which was characteristic of pre-exilic times. The balance had shifted. The emphasis was now on sacrificial worship rather than the imparting of the Torah; but this shift was due more to the practical abuses condemned so totally and effectively by all the prophets than to any real elements in the theology of Ezekiel himself. Though heavily outweighed by the priest-centred strand, the Jeremiah-based theology of worship did not die out completely, but continued with the Wisdom literature and the 'psalms of the poor', to merge eventually with the previously more successful Ezekiel-based strand in the uneasy harmony of the Maccabean section of the book of Daniel in the second century BC. The harmony reached at this point was an uneasy one because it was no more than a vision of hope for the future, a vision of perfect worship in which the ritual element would find complete resonance in the lives of a People embracing all nations, races and tongues. The people would then be truly a People of Saints gathered around the 'Holy of Holies', a term deliberately signifying in the opinion of the ancient rabbis both a Temple and the person of the coming Messiah Son of Man.[12]

As anyone in Israel, a priest or not, was seen above all as the subject of God's revelation and covenant, it would be misleading to call the People of God a 'democracy'. Since it was

[11] Cf. S. Marsili, *La Liturgia, momento storico della salvezza*, in *Anamnesis*, (AA.VV.), vol. 1, Torino 1974, p. 38.
[12] T. Chary, *op. cit.*, pp. 265–74.

principally through an encounter with the living God that correct ethical behaviour was seen to ensue, it would be equally misleading to point exclusively to the moral issue: justification by works was never a doctrinal theme in either Testament. Without falling into either trap, Chary's thesis takes nevertheless into serious account the clash between a strongly priest-orientated theology of worship and what might be called rather misleadingly a more 'democratic' and 'ethically minded' view. It throws new light on W. Eichrodt's masterly account of the distinctive character of the priestly tradition's understanding of God and his dealings with man and the world, of the place of man in creation and of the meaning and purpose of history.[13] In his comparative study of the priesthood across times and cultures, L. Sabourin showed that 'no serious investigations of Old Testament institutions can be conducted unless due attention is also paid to the streams of tradition which led to the texts as we have them'. He warned us that this applied particularly to the study of the evolution of the Old Testament priesthood, 'since the redaction of the texts which are likely to be informative depend largely on the priestly circles being investigated'. For him it was clear, for example, 'that the varying biblical interpretations of the Levitical status reflect historical ambitions and rivalries', and that 'some texts set forth a program of action, others sanction, justify or explain what has already taken place'.[14] Without incurring such strictures, Chary successfully explains the evolution of the concept of worship in the Old Testament with due care to both texts and traditions. Though still not widely known, Chary's thesis is no doubt the most satisfactory theory to be advanced so far.

The Concept of Worship in the New Testament

In approaching the question of what theology of worship – if any – is contained in the New Testament, we are again confronted with the usual, familiar difficulties of exegesis. On the one hand the Gospels in general and the Synoptics in particular are the almost exclusive source of information on the life and teaching of Jesus. On the other hand, the Gospels are not the most ancient of New Testament writings. Moreover, all these

---

[13] Cf. W. Eichrodt, *Theology of the Old Testament*, vol. 1, London 1961, pp. 392–436.
[14] L. Sabourin, *Priesthood: A Comparative Study*, Leiden 1973, p. 102.

writings, including the most ancient such as the Pauline epistles, are dependent upon a stream of preaching and theologizing the growth of which predates the writings themselves. As R. Daly points out, although the chronology of the New Testament is by now fairly well established and the lines of theological growth are becoming increasingly recoverable, not enough work has as yet been done to allow even the best exegesis to avoid altogether the circularity of arguments.[15] Happily, the different New Testament sources, though starting from different points, appear so to converge on the subject of worship as to suggest basic agreement. A proper exegetical study would have to take very seriously the complexities of both New Testament chronology and theological growth. No adequate study of the New Testament theology of worship has appeared to date. In these pages, we must therefore be tentative, relying on the apparent unanimity of the primary sources rather more heavily than we would otherwise choose.

The Synoptic Gospels and the Book of Acts

The Gospels of Matthew and Luke portray Jesus' respect for the Temple by putting on his lips traditional expressions of contemporary Jewish piety. In the Gospel of Luke, Jesus is made to refer to the Temple as 'my Father's house' (Luke 2:49). In both the Gospel of Matthew and the Gospel of Luke, Jesus refers to the Temple as the 'house of God' (Matthew 12:4; Luke 6:4). In the Gospel of Matthew, Jesus quotes Psalm 48:2–3 and refers to Jerusalem as the city where God the great King has chosen to dwell (Matthew 5:35). All three Synoptic Gospels portray Jesus as going to the Temple; he is never said to have prayed there or to have offered sacrifices (Matthew 21:14–23; Mark 12:35; Luke 19:47; 21:37). Mark and Luke show us Jesus' preference for praying alone and in secret (Mark 1:35; 6:46; Luke 5:16; 6:12; 11:1), and Matthew makes him enjoin his disciples to do likewise (Matthew 6:5–6). Matthew seems to imply that Jesus felt a stranger to the Temple, and that the Church, based on the confession of Peter, should also be a stranger to it (Matthew 17:24–27. Cf. also Matthew 16:16–18 in the light of Malachi 3:5).

Jesus' real attitude to the worship of the Temple and his championing of the 'spiritual cult' (foreshadowed in Matthew

[15] R. J. Daly, *op. cit.*, pp. 53–54.

9:13), is particularly evident in the account all three Synoptic Gospels give of the episode of the cleansing of the Temple and of the trial of Jesus. It is made perfectly clear that the action of the cleansing of the Temple was directed against the priests and the masters of the Law and not against the merchants and money-changers by making Jesus quote publicly Isaiah 56:7 and Jeremiah 7:11. The clearest and most reliable account of Jesus' trial before the Sanhedrin, paralleled in Matthew and Luke, is to be found in the Gospel of Mark (Mark 14:55–64). After many accusations that could not be made to stand up in court, Mark 14:58 gives us the one accusation on the basis of which Jesus was condemned to death: 'We heard him say, "I will destroy this temple that is made with hands, and in three days I will build another, not made with hands."' Since the Septuagint had reserved the expression 'made with hands' to refer exclusively to idols, calling the Temple of Jerusalem a temple made by hands was tantamount to denouncing all Temple practices as idolatrous. This was something the ancient prophets had never done. Challenged to reply to these accusations, Jesus remains obstinately silent (Mark 14:61). Directly challenged by the high priest, Jesus not only admits to being the Messiah, but actually quotes Daniel 7:13. In doing so he identifies himself with the Son of Man around whom the new temple-community was to be built and who therefore would spell the end of the old Temple cult (Mark 14:61b–62). No further evidence is needed and Jesus is condemned. His crime, the crime for which he was condemned to die, was not that he had claimed to be the Son of God (in a post-Nicaea sense), but that he had blasphemed against the Temple, the most sacred of Jewish institutions.

This interpretation of the Synoptics is confirmed by the Acts of the Apostles, chapters 5 and 6. Stephen fiercely criticizes the worship of the Temple, quotes Exodus 32:4–6, Amos 5:25–27, Isaiah 6:1, and ends by referring to the Temple as an idolatrous artefact; upon which he is immediately put to death as his Master was, and for the same reason.

The Pauline epistles and Hebrews

The Greek translation of the Old Testament, the Septuagint, uses *leitourgein* and cognate words not less than 173 times to refer to the priestly worship of the Temple. In the New

Testament, *leitourgein* and cognate words are used only fifteen times. Apart from one quotation in the Gospel of Luke referring to the cultic role of the Levitical priesthood in Jerusalem (Luke 1:23) and a quotation in the book of Acts which it is practically impossible to interpret correctly without having recourse to other books of the New Testament (Acts 13:2), *leitourgein* and cognate words appear entirely in the Epistles: three times in the Epistle to the Romans, once in 2 Corinthians, twice in Philippians and seven times in the Epistle to the Hebrews. From these we may safely discard for our purposes two passages from the Epistle to the Hebrews referring to the cultic role of the Levitical priesthood in Jerusalem (Hebrews 9:21 and 10:11), two passages from the same Epistle referring to the angels' ministry to God (Hebrews 1:7–14) and one passage from Romans referring to civil magistrates as 'ministers of God' (Romans 13:6). Of the remaining passages, the two from Romans and the two from Philippians refer respectively to the *leitourgia* of Paul (Romans 15:16; Philippians 2:17) and the *leitourgia* of Christians (Romans 15:27; Philippians 2:30); the one passage from 2 Corinthians refers only to the *leitourgia* of Christians; the three from Hebrews to the *leitourgia* of Christ (Hebrews 8:1–2, 6). In all these passages, *leitourgein* and cognate words are deliberately used in a polemical sense and directed to show, by way of contrast and antithesis, that the *leitourgia* of Christians is primarily a life of service to others. On the basis of these texts, we may safely conclude that:

1. Christ is the key-foundation stone of a new Temple not made by hands and composed of living beings.

2. Christ is the high priest of this new kind of worship, the *leitourgōs tōn hagiōn* (where *tōn hagiōn* is deliberately left to signify both the new temple and the people of which the new temple is composed).

3. Christ's *leitourgia* was and is one of obedience to God and service to others.

4. Through their obedience to God and service to others, Christians are empowered to be with Christ one priest, one altar and one victim.

5. Like Christ's, the *leitourgia* of Christians is indeed a 'liturgy of life'.

The theme of the priestly sacrificial community as the new 'spiritual temple' is particularly strong in the Epistle to the

Hebrews. In Hebrews 10:22, the readers of the Epistle are given a last solemn exhortation to 'draw near', that is to participate in Christ's high-priestly sacrificial activity, and verses 23–25 spell out what this sacrificial activity consists of, namely Christian life itself lived in community. Commenting on this passage, R. Daly is in no doubt that 'living the Christian life has taken over the atoning function of the sacrificial cult' and that therefore 'the deliberate sin of Hebrews 10:26 for which "there no longer remains a sacrifice for sins" would seem to be the separating of oneself from the only sacrificial action that now has any validity: Christian life itself'.[16]

The New Temple theology of the Epistle to the Hebrews finds confirmation in the theology of the Pastorals (e.g. 1 Timothy 3:15; 2 Timothy 2:20–22; Titus 2:14), that of the Deutero-Pauline corpus (e.g. Ephesians 2:19–22) and also in those strictly Pauline passages referring to the Christian community as God's dwelling in the Spirit (e.g. 1 Corinthians 3:9–17; 6:15–19; 2 Corinthians 6:16). Further impressive confirmation of this interpretation is to be found in those passages in which Paul expands his ideas on Christian service as 'liturgy of life'[17] and in particular in the pastoral section of the Epistle to the Romans (Romans 12:1–15, 35).

The First Letter of Peter

Quite apart from the question of its authorship, the First Letter of Peter deserves here a special mention. Though a very practical letter, it constitutes a valuable summary of Christian theology.

The purpose of the letter is clear and uncontroversial: to give strength and hope to a Church persecuted for its beliefs. From the very beginning of the letter we learn, somewhat obliquely, that God has a provident purpose (1:2) by which the readers were chosen to receive salvation and to be obedient to the Lord Jesus. The salvation the readers received consists of a new birth as children of God through the resurrection of Christ from the dead (1:3–9). In searching and inquiring for this salvation, the prophets foretold the sufferings of Christ and the grace those sufferings would bring (1:10–12), but the

---

[16] *Ibid.*, p. 73.

[17] Cf. R. Corriveau, *The Liturgy of Life: A Study of the Ethical Thought of St. Paul in His Letters of the Early Christian Community*, Studia 25, Brussels–Montreal 1970, pp. 155–80.

fullness of the salvation brought by Christ will not appear until
the day of the final judgement (1:13). Christ was destined from
the foundation of the world to be the Lamb without blemish
(1:19–20). The readers are therefore exhorted to make a
habit of obedience (1:14): obedience to God means love and
service to the brethren (1:22). The gift of the new birth is not
enough. Like babes, the readers need the nourishment of the
milk of spiritual integrity: now that they have tasted the
goodness of the Lord, that milk will help them to grow up to
salvation (2:1–3).

Obedience and spiritual integrity are the secret of the
growth to salvation which the readers receive as a gift in Christ
Jesus. It is at this point in the letter that Jesus is called the
living stone rejected by men but chosen by God to be the
foundation-stone of his new temple. The readers are invited to
'draw near' and 'be built' like living stones into a spiritual
house, to be a holy priesthood and to offer spiritual sacrifices
acceptable to God through Jesus Christ (2:4–5). Others dis-
obeyed the word of God and for this they shall be punished.
The readers, on the contrary, since they obeyed the word of
God, are a chosen race, a royal priesthood, a holy nation,
God's own people: in other words, being united with Jesus in
obedience to God's word and purpose, they are with him one
temple and one priesthood. The *purpose* of this new priesthood is that the readers might declare the wonderful deeds
of him who called them out of darkness into his marvellous
light (2:6–10); the *way* in which this new priesthood is to be
exercised consists of the discharge of one's duty to others (2:11–
13, 12). Christ suffered to lead us to God (3:18). In baptism,
the readers have died with Christ (3:21). They must therefore
arm themselves with the same resolution as Christ had: to
obey the will of God even if this means suffering and death
(4:1–2).

The full revelation of Christ, the letter says, is now close
(4:7). In the meanwhile, each one of the priestly body, having
received his or her gift for a purpose, must use it efficiently: like
good stewards responsible for all these different graces of God,
they must put themselves at the service of others, that in all this
God may receive the glory which, through Jesus Christ, is his
due in the world (4:8–11). Christ suffered for all who are prepared to accept the grace of the new priesthood. The sufferings
of the readers are a share in the suffering of Christ: a blessing

and a privilege (4:12–16). Yet, the letter warns, the judgement which is upon all will begin with the judgement of the household of God (4:17). So even those whom God allows to suffer must trust themselves to the constancy of the creator and go on doing good, that is go on offering to God as his new temple and his new priesthood the worship of a good life in Christ (4:19 and 3:16).

Paul's familiar theme of the new temple is firmly connected with the concept of the new priesthood. Both themes are then clearly expounded in a way which is strongly redolent of the Pauline ideal of Christian service as a liturgy of life: all in all, a striking confirmation of our interpretation of the New Testament theology of worship.

The Johannine literature

The theology of Christian community as the new temple, greatly developed in Paul and Hebrews and confirmed by 1 Peter, is more clearly articulated in the Johannine literature than in the Synoptics.

For the Synoptics, the Temple was the *hierón*, or the place where God could be met. For the Gospel of John, the Temple was the *naós*, or the place where God dwells. The very first chapter of the Gospel of John states that the Word pitched his tent among us (1:14). Commenting on this verse, R. Brown writes: 'When the Prologue proclaims that the Word made his dwelling among men, we are being told that the flesh of Jesus Christ is the new localisation of God's presence on earth, and that Jesus is the replacement of the ancient Tabernacle.'[18] According to Brown, the theme of 'replacement' is the recurrent theme of the first ten chapters of the Gospel of John. In chapters 2–4, we have the replacement of Jewish institutions and Jewish religious views: the replacement of the water for Jewish purifications in turning of water into wine at Cana and in the announcement of the new birth in water and the Spirit, the replacement of the Temple in the episode of the purification of the place where God dwells and, finally, the replacement of worship at both Jerusalem and Gerizim in the episode of the Samaritan woman. Chapters 5–10 are dominated by Jesus' action and discourses on the occasion of religious feasts: the replacement of the Passover with the new Manna

[18] R. E. Brown, *The Gospel according to John*, vol. 1, New York 1966, p. 33.

from heaven, the replacement of the feast of Tabernacles with the new water and the new light coming from Jesus, the new Temple, and the replacement of the festival of Dedication with the consecration of the Messiah Son of God as the new Temple's altar.[19]

The Gospel of John is widely recognized to be more concerned with making theological points than with the details of chronology. In order to make a theological point, it places the episode of the cleansing of the Temple at the very beginning of Jesus' public life and ministry: the cleansing of the Temple and its replacement with the person of Jesus himself may well have happened historically just before Jesus died, but the whole of his life and ministry cannot be understood except in the light of that replacement. The Gospel of John is also the only Gospel to put on Jesus' lips Zechariah 14:21 rather than Jeremiah 7:11 and Isaiah 56:7: in the new Covenant there shall be no trader in the house of the Lord because there shall then be a new Temple, a new altar, a new sacrifice, a new priesthood, new worship, new light and new life-giving water.

In view of the centrality of the Temple theme in John, we should stress with R. Daly the importance of John 19:34–37. He writes: 'John's witness in 19:35 pushes us to a clearer awareness that Jesus is the new temple, that he alone is the source of living water (i.e. faith), and that by drinking (believing in Jesus) we also become sources of living water for others.' The whole of that passage – Daly maintains – should be seen in the light of John 10:17 (where Christ's sacrificial self-giving is seen to be both perfectly voluntary and done in loving obedience to God), John 13:1–15 (where the washing of the feet is seen as an act of service for us symbolizing Christ's readiness to die for others and impelling us to do the same for the sake of our brethren) and of 1 John 3:16 (where we are exhorted to lay down our lives for the brethren in imitation of Christ's self-giving). In so doing, Daly successfully removes any remaining doubt that 'the same intimate association between the sacrifice of Christ and the sacrifice of Christians which we found in Paul and Hebrews is also richly witnessed to in the Johannine writings'.[20]

The book of Revelation is often dismissed as an unhelpful source for the theology of worship in the New Testament.[21]

[19] *Ibid.*, pp. CXL–CXLI.
[20] R. J. Daly, *op. cit.*, p. 77.
[21] *Ibid.*, p. 82.

Since the greater part of the book consists of allegories to which we have long lost the key, this judgement may prove to be too severe. With regard to the last section of the book of Revelation, not enough attention is often paid to the parallels with the books of Isaiah, Ezekiel and Zechariah in which the themes of light and water, so characteristic of the Johannine literature, are also highly prominent. To use the familiar language of Hans Küng, in its last two chapters the book of Revelation is aware that 'the Church as it is' is not yet either 'the Church as it should be' or 'the Church as it shall be'. The real down-to-earth Church is still a place harbouring the cowardly, the faithless, the polluted, murderers, fornicators, sorcerers, idolaters and liars as well as the holy (21:8). The Christian 'ecclesia' is not yet altogether the Temple embracing all people and all nations giving to God the pure worship of their spotless lives. The Lamb who died is indeed the lamp of the new Temple (21:22–24) and the fountain of the water of life, but that life does not as yet flow freely in the midst of a city in which no one practises abomination and falsehood (21:27–22, 2a). Firmly planted in the midst of the city, the tree of life does not yet produce its fruits each month. The leaves of that tree are not yet properly used for the healing of the nations (22:2b). All the familiar themes of the Johannine literature are present in these two last chapters, backed in even greater profusion by references to Isaiah, Ezekiel and Zechariah in which the same themes appear. Since the evil-doer is still doing evil and the filthy is still being filthy here on earth (22:11), true worship will not take place in its entirety until such time as the real, down-to-earth practicalities of the Christian life will be observed, and observed by all (22:3). A clear parallel exists between Revelation 22:8 and John 19:35. The judgement of Revelation 22:10–15 is extended to the Christian community as well as to the world at large. A more down-to-earth statement of the nature of true worship would be hard to find, and so would a more striking confirmation of the overall teaching of the New Testament on the subject.

Worship, the Fathers and the Early Christian Writers

No survey of the roots of Christian worship, however brief, should forget to make reference to the ways in which the early Church understood the subject in the light of the teachings of the Bible.

There is no doubt that for the majority of the Church's Fathers and early writers the sacrifice expected of Christians was that of obedience to God. In certain cases, the sacrifice of obedience would take the form of partaking in the cup of Christ by actually laying down one's life in witness to the Gospel.[22] In more ordinary cases and in direct opposition to the sacrificial system of the Old Testament, the only perfect and well-pleasing sacrifices Christians undertook to offer were those 'of prayer and giving of thanks, when offered by worthy people'.[23] The early Church understood this 'spiritual sacrifice' in the most concrete of terms. So Clement of Alexandria (before AD 215) could write that the sacrifice which the Church offered was that of the 'composite incense' of which the ancient Law spoke and which, in the new Covenant, 'is brought together in our songs of praise by purity of heart and righteous and upright living grounded in holy actions and righteous prayer'.[24]

A strongly incarnational theology led the early Church to see the perfect temple of God in the 'spiritual being'.[25] Individual Christians became such a temple when they acted justly throughout their lives and therefore gave God 'uninterrupted worship in His own temple, that is in their own bodies'.[26] The community of such individuals, and not a building, was for them, collectively, the true house of prayer and worship.[27] In this sense, the individual Christians were seen as 'the chosen stones well fitted for the divine edifice of the Father'.[28]

For the Church's Fathers and early writers, the 'spiritual sacrifice' of Christians was a bloodless sacrifice,[29] offered on an altar which was both Christ and the company of believers.[30] At the turn of the fifth century, Augustine (AD 354–430) could therefore write that 'the whole redeemed city, that is to say the congregation or the community of the saints, is offered to God as our sacrifice through the great High Priest, who offered himself in his passion for us, that we might be members of his

---

[22] Cf. e.g. The Martyrdom of Polycarp, chapter 14.
[23] Justin Martyr, *Dialogue with Trypho*.
[24] Clement of Alexandria, *Stromata*, book VII, chapter 6, paragraph 34.
[25] The Epistle of Barnabas, chapter 14.
[26] Irenaeus of Lyons, *Evangelical Demonstrations*, n. 96. Cf. also Ignatius, *Epistle of the Ephesians*, chapter 15, and the Epistle of Barnabas, chapter 16.
[27] Justin Martyr, *Dialogue with Tryphon*.
[28] Ignatius, *Epistle of the Ephesians*, chapter 9.
[29] Athenagoras, *Plea for the Christians*, chapter 13.
[30] Ignatius, *Epistle to the Magnesians*; Polycarpus, *Epistle to the Philippians*, chapter 4.

glorious head, according to the form of a servant'.[31] Augustine argued that, since 'true sacrifices are works of mercy to ourselves or others, done with reference to God', it followed that 'this is the sacrifice of Christians: we, being many, are one body with Christ' and that therefore 'this is also the sacrifice which the Church continually celebrates in the sacrament of the altar, known to the faithful, in which she teaches that she herself is offered in the offering she makes to God'.[32]

Not surprisingly, the early Church was often accused of 'impiety' or religiouslessness.[33] 'Why have they no altars, no temples, no consecrated images?', well-meaning pagans asked themselves.[34] In their answer, the early Church turned these accusations into proud boasts. So Minucius Felix (third century AD could write that 'the victim fit for sacrifice is a good disposition, and a pure mind, and a sincere judgement . . . Therefore those who cultivate innocence supplicate God; those who cultivate justice make offering to God; those who abstain from fraudulent practices propitiate God; those who snatch human beings from danger slaughter the most acceptable victim. These are our sacrifices, these our rites of God's worship: thus, among us those who are most just are those who are most religious.'[35] Thus, Origen (AD 253–54) could argue against Celsus: 'We regard the spirit of every good man as an altar from which arises an incense which is truly and spiritually sweet-smelling, namely the prayers ascending from a pure conscience . . . The statues and gifts which are fit offerings to God are the work of no common mechanics, but are wrought and fashioned in us by the Word of God . . . In all those, then, who plant and cultivate within their souls, according to the divine word, temperance, justice, wisdom, piety, and other virtues, these excellences are the statues they raise, in which we are persuaded that it is becoming for us to honour the model and prototype of all statues: the image of the invisible God . . . By far the most excellent of all these (statues) throughout the whole of creation is that image of our Saviour who said, "My Father is in me."'[36]

[31] Augustine, *City of God*, book X, chapter 6.
[32] *Ibid.*
[33] Cf. Justin Martyr, *The First Apology*, chapters 5 and 6; Athengoras, *Plea for the Christians*, chapters 4, 10, 12, 13 and 27.
[34] Minucius Felix, *Octavius*, chapter 10.
[35] *Op. cit.*, chapter 32.
[36] Origen, *Against Celsus*, book VIII, chapter 17.

The early Church was often accused also of atheism, that is of
the absence of belief in the State gods, and therefore of sub-
version and civil disobedience. The accusation, the Fathers
argued, was deeply unjust: absence of belief in the State gods
did not at all involve any such consequences. So Tertullian
(after AD 220) could firmly state that Christians everywhere did
indeed 'invoke on behalf of the safety of the emperors a God
who is everlasting, a God who is real, a God who is living . . . We
already pray for the emperors, that they may have a long life, a
safe rule, a family free from danger, courageous armies, a
faithful senate, loyal subjects, a peaceful world, all that Caesars
and the common people, pray for'. Since however, 'these things
I cannot pray for from any one else than from him from whom
I know I shall get them', I, 'who on account of his teaching am
put to death', can only offer to God the best fat victim which
God himself commanded: 'prayer arising from a pure body,
from an innocent soul, from the Holy Spirit'.[37]

From the already quoted Minucius Felix (third century AD)
we learn that Christians were thought 'to threaten conflagra-
tion to the whole world, and to the universe itself' and to
'mediate its destruction' in the hope of substituting 'a life of
want, hard work and hunger' with 'a blessed and perpetual life
after death'.[38] In their eagerness to reply to such accusations,
the Fathers and the early Christian writers afford us further
insights into the kind of 'spiritual worship' they were advocating. They stressed that Christians, like others in the Empire,
were dutiful citizens, deeply involved in the complex fabric of
their concrete historical, social, cultural and political environment. Their religion was not one of destruction or escape. So
in the Epistle to Diognetus we can read (third century) that
'inhabiting Greek as well as barbarian cities, according as the
lot of each of them has determined, and following the customs
of the natives in respect to clothing, food and the rest of their
ordinary conduct', Christians displayed as their only distinguishing mark 'their wonderful and paradoxical method of
life'. They dwelled in their own countries, 'but simply as
sojourners'. As faithful citizens, they shared all things with
others, yet they endured 'all things as foreigners'. They did
good, yet they were 'punished as evil-doers'. To sum up all in
one word, 'what the soul is in the body, that are Christians in

[37] Tertullian, *Apologeticus*, chapter 30.
[38] Minucius Felix, *Octavius*, chapters 10, 11 and 12.

the world'.[39] Rather less prudently and in a way hardly calculated to reassure the authorities, Tertullian similarly argued that Christians were solid citizens and friends of the Empire. He pleaded that the proof of this was in the fact that 'nearly all the citizens you have in nearly all the cities are Christians . . . We are but of yesterday, yet we have filled all that is yours, cities, islands, fortified towns, country towns, centres of meeting, even camps, tribes, classes of public attendants, the palace, the senate, the forum; *we have left you only your temples*'.[40]

Broadly speaking, the theology of worship of the Fathers and early Christian writers contains and reflects all the familiar themes of the New Testament theology of worship: the worship of Christians is both 'spiritual' and 'perfect' not because it is free from material, social, this-worldy elements, but precisely because it presupposes an involvement in the affairs of this world as total and unreserved as the involvement of the Incarnate Word. As christology and soteriology developed, they were increasingly brought to bear upon the concept of Christian worship, as in Irenaeus (bishop of Lyons from AD 177–78) and Hippolytus (AD 235), and above all Origen (AD 253–54), who most eloquently taught that the whole of Christian life was a sacrifice and whose main concern it was therefore to show how the Church and indeed the whole world are called to share in the sacrifice of Christ.[41]

The early Fathers and Christian writers are remarkably consistent in their teachings on the subject of Christian worship. Yet, as so often the theology of worship of the early Church contained the seed of its own destruction. Clement of Rome, who did not hesitate to teach that true sacrifice was a life according to the will of God,[42] was the first solitary voice to uphold strict regulations on the subject of worship and to teach that priestly worship should be offered at the appropriate time, in the appropriate places, by appropriate persons, lay worship being bound by the laws pertaining to lay people.[43] In making this claim, Clement made recourse to the very Old Testament

[39] The Epistle to Diognetus, chapters 5 and 6.

[40] Tertullian, *Apolegeticus*, chapter 37.

[41] Irenaeus, *Against Heresies*, book IV, chapters 30 and 31. For Hippolytus and Origen, see R. Daly, *op. cit.*, pp. 98–100 and 122–27.

[42] Cf. Clement, *The First Epistle to the Corinthians*, chapters 10 and 31. The attribution to Clement of Rome is not certain.

[43] *Ibid.*, chapters 18, 35 and 52.

regulations which the other Christian writers were so busy proving to have been superseded, the most notable among these being the so-called Epistle of Barnabas.

After the establishment of Christianity as the only permitted religion within the Roman Empire under Theodosius I (AD 371), the flood-gates of the Church were open to all kinds of barely-Christianized attitudes. Human nature was soon to do the rest, since attempting to tame the sacred comes more easily to a human being than allowing oneself to be swept up by it. In practical terms, the original freedom of Christian worship soon turned into the ossification of liturgical forms.[44] By the beginning of the fifth century, the private house where the Church met[45] had universally become the *ecclesia (Église, Iglesia, Chiesa, Eglwys)* or *kyriakón* (kirk, church): the house of God, a temple filled with sacred objects the most important of which was the stone altar of sacrifice standing in a 'sanctuary' reserved for the ordained and separated from the rest of the building by the 'tetravela'[46] – a cloth-screen designed to insure, as John Chrysostom himself (AD 354–407) explained,[47] that no profane eye would set its gaze on the 'sacred mysteries' (cf. Exodus 36:35–36). Within that sanctuary there would be placed seven ceremonial candlesticks as a latter-day 'menorah': a perfect outward reconstruction of the Temple whose veil (Matthew 27:51) was torn from top to bottom.[48] Under the onslaught of such practices, the teaching of the earlier Fathers was soon to be overlaid by all kinds of *ex post facto* theologies. Throughout these changing times, the Church continued to teach that Christian worship was worship 'in spirit and in truth': charity should not prevent us from asking ourselves what, if anything, was understood by that.

---

[44] For this, see e.g. K. Latte, *Römische Religiongeschichte*, München 1960, p. 62.
[45] Cf. e.g. 1 Corinthians 16:19
[46] Cf. Duchesne (ed.), *Liber Pontificalis*, vol. 2, p. 120.
[47] John Chrysostom, *Homilies on the Epistle to the Ephesians*, hom. 4.
[48] For this, see S. Marsili, *La Liturgia, momento storico della salvezza*, in *Anamnesis* (AA.VV.), vol 1, Torino 1974, pp. 53–58.

FURTHER READING

R. K. Yerkes, *Sacrifice in Greek and Roman Religious and Early Judaism*, London 1953.

R. J. McKelvey, *The New Temple: The Church in the New Testament*, London 1969.

R. Corriveau, *The Liturgy of Life: A Study of the Ethical Thought of St. Paul in His Letters to the Early Christian Communities*, Studia 25, Brussels–Montreal 1970.

R. J. Daly, *The Origins of the Christian Doctrine of Sacrifice*, London 1978.

P. F. Bradshaw and L. A. Hoffman (eds.), *The Making of Jewish and Christian Worship*, Notre Dame 1991.

FOR DISCUSSION

1. How far does our idea of God influence our worship?
2. Does it make sense today to speak of holy places and holy things?
3. What inferences for a renewed understanding of the Lord's Supper, if any, may be legitimately drawn from the biblical and early patristic understanding of the nature of Christian worship?

CHAPTER 3

IN SPIRIT AND
IN TRUTH

The word *worship* comes from the Anglo-Saxon *weorthscipe* that, in turn, comes from a root meaning *to honour*. In our context therefore, *worship* should mean *the act of paying divine honour to God.*

Let it be said from the outset that this word can be confusing to Jews and Christians alike. Its New Testament Greek equivalent is *proskynesis*, meaning originally the action of falling down to the ground in an attitude of humble submission before someone 'worthier' than ourselves, but in the context of religious ceremonies it was used mainly by pagans, who approached their gods in fear and trembling.[1] The favourite New Testament words for the same thing were on the contrary the Greek equivalents (*douleia* and *latreia*) of the Old Testament Hebrew words for *service* (*sheret* and *'abodah*). For Jews and Christians alike, therefore, *worship* should be not so much the act of *paying honour* to God as the *service* we are to offer in terms of his final purpose, individually and collectively, through the manner and quality of our lives (including, of course, our practices of devotion).

The words, actions and gestures we use in our worship are so familiar to us that as a rule we tend not to question either their nature or their effectiveness. The ways of our worship are not by and large the product of our own discoveries as individual worshipping communities, but a precious inheritance from the past handed down to us by tradition. Some sociologists would say that they are part of the common sense world of everyday life, of what everybody knows, and therefore part of a social stock of assumed and unchallenged knowledge. Often enough,

[1] For the attitude of Christians, see e.g. Irenaeus of Lyons, *Evangelical Demonstration* 96.

when asked why we should act in such ways, our answer would be a vague assertion that the Church has behaved in this way for a long, long time: because of its obvious connection with the sacred, worship is often thought to share in the very unchangeability of God.

All too often we assume that what we do now means to us what it meant to our forefathers. We have no real guarantee that worship as set out in the liturgical books, worship as proposed by the cultic officials, worship as explained by theologians, and worship as lived by the congregations are in fact one and the same thing. The truth is that no form of worship, not even that of the New Testament, mirrors the essence of worship perfectly and for all times. As Hans Küng remarks with regard to the theology of the Church, 'a delicate balance must be struck between the unthinking conservatism of a *dead* past, an attitude which is unconcerned with the demands of the present, and the careless rejection of the *living* past, an attitude which is all too concerned with the transitory novelties of the present'.[2] To remain true to itself, Christian worship must always allow itself to be conditioned anew by history; it must always be both a call and a response within constantly changing historical situations.

The history of the Christian Church in its complex pattern of growth and decay, renewed understanding, forgetfulness and betrayal provides ample material for the construction of a theology of worship. The embarrassment is one of riches. The problem is one of method. The danger is not that we might pervert truth, but that we might forget that all human knowledge, including theology, is provisional by definition. The truth of the God who gives himself to his people should never be confused with statements about it. As Karl Barth wrote, theology will always be 'a thinking, an investigation and an exposition which are relative and liable to error',[3] since all theology can do is 'attempt to understand, expound, see, hear, state, survey, co-ordinate and present the theoretical meaning and the practical consequences of an encounter-dialogue which must be experienced before it is talked about'.[4]

Some theologians have attempted to solve the methodological impasse by attributing to the worship of their Church an

[2] H. Küng, *The Church*, London 1971, pp. 4–6, 13–14.
[3] K. Barth, *Dogmatics in Outline*, London 1966, p. 11.
[4] *Ibid.*, p. 9.

artificial kind of changelessness the better to judge individual
historical developments on the basis of their conformity with
the supposed archetype of the ancient liturgical books. The
certain knowledge that Christian worship is constantly conditioned anew by history and culture should dissuade us from
treading this path. Other theologians have adopted as their
touchstone a system of confessional theology built without
much reference to either liturgical documents or historical fact.
The perennial quarrels between the Catholics and Protestants
of old should be enough to dissuade us from following in
these footsteps. Yet other scholars have chosen to engage in a
purely phenomenological study of the history of religions in an
attempt to find a minimum common denominator. Without
wishing to criticize the appropriateness of this method in other
fields of study, one can only lament its exclusive application in
theological research.

On the understanding that the paramount reality of Christian
experience is that God speaks to us in the here-and-now, we
shall attempt to construct an organic and coherent framework
(theology) within which we might understand more deeply a
particular phenomenon (worship) from the vantage point of
the faith of the Church and in the light of our commitment
and action in the world of today.

Christian Worship

The Psalms and Prophets of the Old Testament taught us that
God takes no delight in the sacrifice of bulls and rams. The
New Testament teaches us that God takes no particular delight
in our liturgical endeavours. Christian worship is worship in
spirit and in truth. It is not so much a question of time and
place and even less a question of correct words and suitable
ceremonies, but above all a question of the right attitude of
openness, surrender and obedience to God in a life consecrated
to his purpose.

Worship in spirit and in truth is not disembodied; it is not
divorced from everyday experience. In spiritual worship, the
real God encounters and addresses the real human being, and
the real human being is made able to respond in the power of
the Spirit. True worship is not escape from the temporal, but
communion between the human and the divine. As God
encounters us with his Word, we are identified with God's

purpose and are made able to consecrate our existences to his will. In themselves, liturgical words and gestures are neither good nor bad. They are not transparent and therefore may hide and veil what truly lies behind them. Being unable to carry by themselves a meaning of their own, they can only *point* to a reality greater than themselves. As such, they are never condemned in the Scriptures. We are so built that, without outward expression, spiritual realities cease to be present and to have meaning for us. Worship can only be conducted in the human tongue, according to human ways. Even before a word is on our mouth, the Lord knows it altogether, and since we do not understand the tongue of angels, God addresses us in our own language.

The word 'tradition' (in the Greek, *parádōsis*) refers to a process whereby something is offered, handed over to us. For the community of faith, what is primarily offered and handed over to us is the reality of God himself as a gift of love ('parádōsis', in the singular). About this fundamental fact, there is a variety of 'traditions' ('parádóseis, in the plural), some of which are expressed in liturgical form and none of which exhausts the meaning of God's self-gift. In giving to us both himself and his power to transform what is still imperfect, God speaks. Our role in worship is that of obedience to God's spoken Word.

In speaking of worship, we often forget that nothing can be added to or taken away from God's purpose. The response of the Church is not a condition for the ultimate coming of the Kingdom. The Kingdom will come whatever we do or fail to do. By grace, we are called to give embodiment to the Kingdom and to share in God's creative, redeeming and fulfilling activity. If we refuse to co-operate, the loss will be ours and not God's. When we approach God in worship, we do so only too aware of our needs. Our needs are always fulfilled, though not always according to the measure of our expectations. As St. Augustine writes, 'no one will think he did a benefit to a fountain by drinking or to the light by seeing'.[5] Strictly speaking, God does not need our worship either in terms of what we do in our churches or in terms of what we do with our lives. It is we who need to worship, so that we might attain to the unity of the faith, to mature manhood, to the measure of the stature of the fullness of Christ (Ephesians 4:13–14).

[5] Augustine, *City of God*, book 10, chapter 6.

According to the same Epistle, the experience of Christians
is that 'the God and Father of our Lord Jesus Christ chose us
before the foundation of the world to be his children'. God's
empowering call is not only to satisfaction, but also to mission.
The teaching of the Old Testament Prophets, reinforced by the
New Testament, is unequivocal on this subject: life must feed
our worship as worship must feed our life. What we do when we
worship has no value if the Word has no resonance in the
quality of our existence. In all kinds of ways, God makes known
to us, his Church, 'the mystery of his will, according to the
purpose which he set forth in Christ as a plan for the fullness of
time, to unite all things in him, things in heaven and things on
earth'. It is our belief that, within this will and purpose, 'we who
first hoped in Christ have been destined to live for the praise of
God's glory' (Ephesians 1:3–14). Worship is therefore both a
personal and a corporate encounter with God. The Word of
God is spoken and we are renewed for the service of his
Kingdom. The initiative is God's, the power is God's: ours is
only the response of a life transformed by the Spirit. Our
experience shows the truth of what the Bible teaches: if in a
strict sense the word 'worship' refers primarily to what happens
when we gather to pray, in a wider sense it embraces the whole
of our lives.

The worship in spirit and in truth which is characteristic of
Christians should be governed by these three simple principles:

1. Christian worship and Christian life are indissolubly linked
   together.
2. A corporate activity needed by us and not by God, Christian
   worship is both the moment and the consequence of an
   encounter in which God gives himself to his people as a gift of
   love, reveals to them his will for the world, demands and
   empowers a response, and consecrates to his purpose the life of
   the whole community of faith.
3. Therefore, before it is seen as an activity of people towards God,
   Christian worship should be seen as an activity of God directed
   towards those whom God has chosen to live and work to his
   praise and glory.

The Worship of Jesus the Christ

Among others, S. Marsili teaches that our salvation has a
historical dimension and contains three distinct moments. The

first moment was one of prophecy and announcement. In it there was disclosed the eternal love of God with which the Father, who wishes all people to be saved, chose us as his own children in his dear Son (1 Timothy 2:4; Ephesians 1:4; 2 Timothy 1:9). The second moment was that of the fullness of time. The time of preparation being over, the Word, now Incarnate, was himself the bearer of the good news of the present event of salvation. In this second moment, the Word of salvation becomes 'reality in people', that is 'flesh' (John 1:14). It was the moment in which the grace given to us from eternity was actualized in the appearing of our Saviour (2 Timothy 1:10). In the Word made flesh, the reality of salvation found its two constitutive elements: perfect at-onement with God and the fullness of worship. The third moment, the moment in which we live, is both the result and the perpetuation of the second moment: the 'time of Christ' continues into the 'time of the People of God'. Made one with Christ, his at-onement is our at-onement, his worship is our worship. When God addresses us in worship we can respond because we are one Body with Christ, the one high priest. Christ's priesthood makes of him the primary source of our worship. In worship, we respond to God *in* Christ, *with* Christ, *through* Christ, because we have been made one Body with him. When two or three are gathered together, there is the Church. There is also her Lord, the Incarnate Word. The Word which is announcement, proclamation and call to salvation is made present. The call is heard and the power to respond is given.[6] As E. Brunner remarks, 'an exchange takes place here that is wholly without analogy in the sphere of thinking. The only analogy is the encounter between human beings, the meeting of person with person'.[7]

In worship, Christ is our only Mediator. We are with him one priest, one altar, one victim. His self-offering is our self-offering, his obedience our obedience, his priesthood our priesthood. His response is our response. As Scripture says, we are crucified with Christ: since our life is hidden with Christ in God, it is no longer we who live, but Christ who lives in us, and the life we now live in the flesh we live by faith in the Son of God who loved us and gave himself for us (Galatians 2:20).

[6] Cf. S. Marsili, 'La liturgia, momento storico della salvessa', in *Anamnesis*, vol. 1, Torino 1974, pp. 88–92.

[7] E. Brunner, *Truth as Encounter*, London 1964, p. 114.

In the person of Jesus, the people of Palestine met the God who called them. In him, they met the human being who responded to God with the perfect answer. In his life, they saw the perfect example of the response of God required of them. As the Epistle to the Philippians says, 'though he was in the form of God, he did not count equality with God a thing to be grasped, but emptied himself, taking the form of a servant, being born in the likeness of men', and 'being found in human form he humbled himself and became obedient unto death, even death on a cross' (Philippians 2:6–8). Because of his obedience and in fulfilment of the prophecies of Isaiah, Christ is the perfect servant and the perfect worshipper of God (in the Hebrew, '*ebed YHWH* means both). In him, we have the perfect high priest. From the Epistle to the Hebrews we learn that 'when he appeared as the high priest of the good things that have come, then through the greater and more perfect tent (which is his Body) he entered once and for all into the Holy Place, taking not the blood of goats and calves, but his own blood, thus securing an eternal redemption'. We learn that 'he entered not a sanctuary made with hands, a copy of the true one, but into heaven itself, now to appear in the presence of God on our behalf', and that, therefore, 'he is truly the mediator of the new covenant' (Hebrews 9:11–24): subjectively, because of his obedience, and objectively because of his very being in whom the fullness of God was pleased to dwell. In him, as the ancient Easter liturgy sings, 'heaven and earth are joined in one, and man is reconciled to God'.[8] He is therefore the 'bridge' as well as the 'bridge-maker' (in the Latin, *pontifex*, that is 'high priest').

The belief of the Church is that the fullness of deity dwells bodily in Christ and that from his fullness we have all received, grace upon grace (Colossians 2:9; John 1:16). We therefore believe that through the high priesthood of Jesus the life of God has become our life and that, through the Incarnation of the Son, God has now a human face. Through Christ the high priest, all have now direct access to grace and are made able to 'draw near' and offer their existence as a service of love and a spiritual sacrifice. We are now a new temple, a spiritual house built of living stones to be a holy priesthood (1 Peter 2:5). Hans Küng writes: 'Christians do not stand on the threshold of the temple like impure people begging for grace, in fear and trembling': they are themselves the new temple of which Jesus is the cornerstone, so that 'the decisive factor in their new situation is not the barrier that divides them from God, but the fellowship which links them to God through Christ'.[9]

The fellowship which links us to God through Christ is the fellowship of the Holy Spirit. It is through the mediation of the Holy Spirit that the mediation of Christ the high priest bears its fruit within us. Since we do not know how to pray as we ought, the Spirit himself, who dwells in us, intercedes with us and helps us in our weakness (Romans 8:26–27). We are strengthened with might through the Spirit in our inner being so that through the power at work within us, God is able to do far more abundantly than all that we ask or think (Ephesians 3:16–20): when we worship, we worship in, with and through Christ the high priest in the unity and power of the Holy Spirit.

The doctrine of the objective mediation of Christ the high priest (common to many of the Greek Fathers) and the doctrine of the mediation of the Spirit soon disappeared both from Western theology and Western liturgical formularies. As A. J. Jungmann explained, this was due to an excessive reaction to the dangers of Arianism in Europe.[10] Europe was saved from Arianism, but the price paid for that rescue was a serious perversion of the understanding of worship. From a joyous encounter with God through Christ and in the fellowship of the Holy Spirit, worship became the action of an impure people begging for grace and offering from afar, in fear and trembling and by means of human mediators, due homage of praise interspersed with repeated entreaties for a forgiveness already offered by God to all who would care to accept it. Neither Catholics nor Protestants are free from this indictment and no truly Christian theology of worship can be constructed until the two forgotten doctrines – the mediation of Christ and the mediation of the Holy Spirit – are reinstated not only in our books, but first and foremost in the consciousness of the People of God.

The Worship of Christ's Body

A human being can perceive God only by means of something created. It may be a word, a sentence or a poem. It may be a

[9] H. Küng, *op. cit.*, p. 373.
[10] J. A. Jungmann, *Pastoral Liturgy, passim.*

sculpture, a painting or a piece of music. It may be a natural
occurrence such as a storm in the mountains, the becalming of
the sea, a sunrise or a sunset. It may be, and it often is, another
human being.

In this sense, the very person of the Incarnate Word was the
highest possible means of God's presence to us. Since the flesh
and blood of Jesus cannot be met in this fashion today, the
Church which is Christ's Body is called into being as a living
temple of God's presence. As E. Schillebeeckx teaches, this is
what we mean when we say that the Church is called to be the
earthly sacrament of the *primordial* Sacrament which is Jesus the
Christ. We may choose not to respond to God's call. Even when
we respond, our answer is never complete. To be faithful to
God's Word, the Church has to be renewed day by day.

In the last chapter we said that where two or three are
gathered together, there is the Church and there is her Lord:
to be the Body of Christ on earth, the Church needs to meet for
both prayer and action. When the Church meets for prayer, the
meeting must be so ordered as to facilitate both the encounter
between God and his People and the empowering that ensues
from it. The words, the sounds, the actions and the gestures
that compose our worship must be directed to this end without
trace of self-indulgence or complacency. To achieve this end,
the leader in worship must pay attention to the Word of God as
well as to the laws of human nature.

The God of our faith took humanity seriously enough to
become flesh and to pitch his tent among the pilgrim people.
No truly viable theology of worship can be constructed without
a more extensive theological anthropology than we possess to
date: anyone who takes the human less seriously than the divine
can do so only at his or her risk and peril. The work needed in
this direction is of staggering proportions.

Worship, Theology and Anthropology

Open a book on theological anthropology and what will you
find? A cogent demonstration of how sinful we are and of how
much we are in need of redemption. So far, so good. But very
often you will also find little or nothing about human
phenomenon as such or about the consequences of the fact
that God created us male and female and gave us corporeal
existence in a world that has not yet reached its final goal.

Many disciplines, both old and new, are dedicated to the study of human beings: philosophy, history, psychology, sociology, anthropology, biology, physiology and medicine, economics and politics to mention but a few. The stated scope of theology is to view everything rationally in the light of God's revelation. Theological anthropology (the study of human beings from the point of view of theology) could therefore be defined as 'the attempt of human beings to attain self-understanding through reflection in the light of God's revelation'. The purpose of all search for knowledge is self-understanding. The purpose of theological anthropology should therefore be to understand ourselves, in the light of God's revelation, as human beings in the concrete circumstances of our existence. Viewing the human phenomenon in the abstract would not be enough.

In Christianity, the human phenomenon can only be interpreted christologically. Christ is the first-born of the new creation (Colossians 1:15). Are we not meant to attain to the full measure of the stature of Christ (Ephesians 4:13)? Without such a christological understanding of the human phenomenon, the life and mission of the Church would be impaired. So would its worship, the power-house of our growth.

According to A. Cuva, within the context of theological anthropology the human phenomenon should be approached from a *dynamic-functional* as well as from a *static-ontic* point of view.[11]

From a *dynamic-functional* point of view, a human being should be approached in the light of his or her four basic functions:

1. The *theological* function. Though long fallen into disuse, the word 'theological' still best expresses the meaning to be conveyed here: the first and most fundamental function of a human being is that of entering by grace into a living relationship with God.

2. The *social* function. After one's relationship with God comes, in order of importance, one's relationship with other human beings. We are social animals that cannot fully 'be' except in relationship with others (the *gender* function should be considered as an important subsection of the social function).

---

[11] A. Cuva, 'Linee di antropologia liturgica', in *Nel decennale dell Costituzione 'Sacrosanctum Concilium'*, Rome 1974, pp. 1–31.

3. The *historical* function. Living by grace in freedom, a person is called to realize himself or herself in time and space and to bring his or her contribution to the history of the world in terms of God's ultimate design of salvation.

4. The *cosmic* function. Our role as human beings in the cosmos is one of responsibility to the rest of creation. Theology teaches us not only that we must respect everything that God brings into being, but also that creation as a whole is waiting with eager longing for the revealing of the children of God, when it will be set free from its bondage to decay and obtain the glorious liberty of the children of God (Romans 8:18–22).

From a static-ontic point of view, the human phenomenon should be approached under two fundamental aspects:

1. The *oneness* of a human being. Against the false dichotomy or trichotomy of *body and soul* or *body, soul* and *spirit*, biblical theology teaches us that a human being, male or female, is a single and unique psycho-physical unit.

2. The *bodiliness* of a human being. Since we are a single psycho-physical unit, body and soul (or body, soul and spirit) are but two 'aspects' of one and the same reality. Contemporary theological anthropology must rehabilitate the *bodily* and look upon a human being as a *person incarnate*.

In the light of the above, is it legitimate to speak of a branch of theological anthropology that might be called *liturgical anthropology*? Human beings have felt the need to ritualize for as long as they have been on this earth. Should it not be legitimate therefore to study also the manner in which ritualization is and/or should be done? Though very few theologians have as yet bothered to go down this road, when put like that the question answers itself. There should be a theological discipline called liturgical anthropology and, in short, its purpose should be the study of *homo liturgicus*.

What is *liturgy*? The Second Vatican Council defines it as 'the work of Christ's priesthood in which our sanctification (i.e. our growth to the full measure of the stature of Christ) is signified and effected by means of visible signs and through which the Body of Christ, both Head and members, exercises the wholeness of its public worship'. As good a definition as any, and one that has the great advantage of not trying to reduce what happens in the liturgy to the sole activity of the people of God.

According to Ambrosius Verheuil[12] there is in the liturgy a double direction: a descending and an ascending line. The descending line dominates in the catechetical part of the liturgy, such as in the Service of the Word, and in sacramental rites. The most characteristic thing of Christian liturgy is the celebration of our Redemption: God invites us and calls us together through the redeeming Word of the Proclamation, and this Redemption is pre-eminently expressed and actualized for us in the sacraments. Redemption comes to us solely through the initiative of God the Father, who sent his Son to earth as the visible form of the Father's love. In the catechetical part of the liturgy and in the sacraments God invites us to faith through his Word and, through Christ, focuses on us his redeeming action and comes to enrich his people with divine life.

The ascending line dominates in the praise and thanksgiving whereby the community of faith gives its answer to God's saving action on it. The liturgy of prayer as an act of human beings always comes second, because it can only be an answer, but the ultimate purpose of God's saving action on the Church is to make it possible for it to ascend to him in true praise and thanksgiving.

The liturgy in its totality is both the act of God and the act of the Church. It is therefore fundamentally a dialogue, a divine word and a human answer, a wonderful exchange of gifts whereby God gives to us himself and his divine life and we, empowered by him, give to him every fibre or our bodies and every moment of our existence.

This double movement is present in all parts of the liturgy. The two movements must be distinguished, but certainly not separated. It is not as if God first came to us in Christ and we, having been set on the right path by him, can then ascend to God, so to speak, on our own steam. The two aspects are inextricably interwoven, realized together at all moments, in whatever section of the liturgy: God is continually descending to us and we are continually ascending to him.

The liturgy is therefore a meeting between God and human beings. It is an 'encounter with God', not yet entirely direct, but in the great meeting point that is Christ. It is not yet a meeting 'face to face' either, but a meeting under the veil of signs in which God reveals himself to us and makes known his will.

---

[12] Cf. A. Verheuil, *Introduction to the Liturgy*, London 1969, pp. 17–19.

A. Verheuil gives this provisional definition of liturgy (provisional because as yet incomplete): 'a personal meeting, under the veil of signs, of God and his Church and with the total person of each one of its members, in and through Christ and in the unity of the Holy Spirit'.[13] From this definition, Verheuil develops in more detail five basic aspects of the liturgy:

1. The *theocentric* character of the liturgy: the liturgy is a personal encounter with God.

2. The *christocentric* character of the liturgy: the encounter takes place in and through the Mediator Christ.

3. The *ecclesial* character of the liturgy: the encounter does not take place primarily with individuals, but with the living community of the Church.

4. The *sign* character of the liturgy: the encounter does not take place directly, but through the veil of 'signs with power'.

5. The *bodily* character of the liturgy: it addresses itself to the whole person and invites to worship the whole human being in the dual unity of both body and soul.

Because of the *sign* and *bodily* character of the liturgy, liturgical anthropology should pay great attention to the anthropological laws of language. Human beings can express meaning not only with words, but also with gesture, posture and sign and invariably do so at their most effective by means of a combination of the two. We can therefore speak of a *liturgical* language as a sub-section of *religious* language.

Religious language, and therefore *a fortiori* liturgical language, can only be the language of a specific community situated in a specific socio-temporal context and will in consequence be subject to the dynamism regulating the cultural evolution of community itself.[14] As the community evolves, has new experiences and faces new challenges, the language of its worship must evolve with it and reflect the thus modified network of relationships between its members. If it does not evolve in this way, the language of worship will become detached from the actual circumstances of our existence and behind the times in terms of the evolution of human languages.

Liturgy is for human beings, and not the other way round. No benefit comes to God from our worship, of which we are the only beneficiaries. The liturgy must therefore reach us in our

[13] *Ibid.*, p. 13.
[14] A. Cuva, *op. cit.*, p. 17.

real lives. That is what the liturgy is for. It must be therefore both expression and exercise of the human condition. In full respect of the human person, the liturgy must value and augment *all* human values. Its mode of expression must be accessible to people living in the here-and-now and reflect the conditions of the times in which we live. Liturgical celebrations must be the celebrations of a specific assembly of which they are meant to be the concrete expression. If it does not do so, the liturgy will be at once both de-humanizing and de-humanized. Cut off from everyday life and from the world in which we live, the liturgy will be exposed to the danger of alienation.

However, to say that liturgy is for people and that it must link up with today's life does not mean that today's liturgy must take its measures from the modern world. Liturgy is for people, but it cannot resign itself to be as we still are. We should never forget that in the liturgy God lowers himself to our level to lift us up to his (see the *theocentric* character of the liturgy). The proper balance must be found between these two complementary exigencies without ever losing sight of either.

The *sign* character of the liturgy also presents its own demands. Sign-making activity is a universal religious phenomenon. The presence of signs may be found in all religions. They form a religious category of their own and are a legitimate and useful way to present and consider a religion, even if the signs themselves may point in different directions.[15] In fact, it may well be said that human beings are the creators of rituals. For human beings, the creation of rites capable of expressing adequately those things they deem most important is like a second nature.[16] The importance of the study of symbolic language in the liturgy cannot be underestimated.[17] The signs we adopt in the liturgy must be such as to make it possible for God's Word to reach us in the concreteness of our existence. They must be based on the authentic experience of the worshipping community, respect all genuine human values and promote them

[15] M.-D. Chenu, 'Anthropologie et liturgie', in *La Liturgie d'apres Vatican II*, Paris 1967, p. 54.
[16] E. Kennedy, 'The Contribution of Religious Ritual to Psychological Balance', *Concilium* 2.7, Feb. 1971, pp. 53–58.
[17] Cf. A. Vergote, 'Symbolic Gestures and Actions in the Liturgy', *Concilium* 2.7, Feb. 1971, pp. 40–52; E. Kennedy, *op. cit.*; A. Greeley, 'Religious Symbolism, Liturgy and Community', *ibid.* pp. 59–69; and G. Tellini, 'Of Symbols, Worship and the Word', in C. Robertson (ed.), *Singing the Faith*, Norwich 1990.

by engendering commitment to God's eschatological plan for creation.

Conclusion

It is a recognized characteristic of childhood, and therefore of immaturity, to see oneself and one's immediate needs, supposed or true, as the centre of the universe. Small infants and very young children firmly believe that all their wants will be satisfied by careful manipulation of their parents. This childish trait is nowhere more apparent than in the popular conception of worship.

Many cultures, past and present, have chosen to believe that, by accurately performing the appointed rituals, the gods might be made to be favourably influenced towards us and make them to bestow on us the benefits that are the object of our desires. If it was not for this self-centred reason, to what purpose should one bother to supplicate the gods? This is not what Christian worship is about.

In the first place, the word *worship* should be considered to have two distinct, if correlated meanings. In the wider sense, it should mean the *leitourgia* of one's life as expressed in Romans 12. In the narrower sense, it should be considered to refer to the moment, in the Greek (*kairós*) in which, in and through Christ and in the power of the Spirit, God encounters his people, transforms them with his power and sets them free to be Christ's Body in the world. In this second, narrower sense, the worship of the gathered community (that is the *liturgy*) is the moment (that is the *kairós*) in which God re-announces and re-actualizes the *mystery of Christ* (that is, his eternal plan of salvation) through the *mystery of the Church* (that is, through the earthly reality of the Body of those who are called to become the chosen instruments of the coming of God's kingdom).[18]

Hans Küng puts it most beautifully in these words:

> The Church does not derive its life only from the work which Christ did and finished in the past, nor only from the expected future consummation of his work, but from the living and efficacious presence of Christ in the present. Christ is present in the entire life of the Church. But Christ is above all present and active in the *worship of the congregation* to which he called us in his Gospel, and

---

[18] Cf. G. Tellini, 'Of Time, Calendars and Lectionaries', in D. Gray (ed.), *The Word in Season*, Norwich 1988, pp. 60–62.

into which we were taken up in baptism, in which we celebrate the Lord's Supper and from which we are sent again to our work of service in the world. In this congregation there occurs in a special way God's service to the Church and the Church's service to God. Here God speaks to the Church through his word, and the Church speaks to God by replying in its prayers and its songs of praise. Here the crucified and risen Lord becomes present through his word and his sacrament, and here we commit ourselves to his service: by hearing the Gospel in faith, by confessing our sins, by praising God's mercy and by petitioning the Father in Jesus' name, by taking part in the meal of the Lord who is present among us and by providing the basis for our service of one another by our public confession of faith and by praying for one another. *This is fundamentally where the Church is, where the Church, the community, the congregation, happens.*[19]

In both its wider and its narrower sense, worship is the one response required by God. In its narrower sense, it is the moment in which the Church *happens*.

In our worship, God encounters us through a system of visible, physical, material means. The need for such means stems from our nature as whole persons. Such means are used in worship *because we need them,* and not because God is supposed to delight in them in any way. They must be vehicles *both* of God's call to us *and* of our answer to God. In other words, they must be *realized human salvation,* that is means of pardon and grace. They must be the visible, historical and concrete actualization of the Word. They must be *eikónes tōn pragmátōn* (Hebrews 10:15): earthly signs charged with the power of a reality that totally transcends them. These signs charged with power (i.e. *symbols*) are *not* in themselves worship. Yet without them worship is impossible. Neither are the symbols which we use in worship in any way unique. They are only one of the *many* ways in which God concretely reaches ordinary men and women, grafts them into the Mystery of Christ, and transforms them into a chosen race, a royal priesthood (1 Peter 2:9), that is in the Body of those who offer to the consuming fire of God, with reverence and awe, the acceptable worship of brotherly love (Hebrews 12:28; 13:1), *having themselves become* a sacrifice of praise continually offered to God (Hebrews 13:15).

[19] H. Küng, *op. cit.*, pp. 234–35.

FURTHER READING

A. Greeley, 'Religious Symbolism, Liturgy and Community', *Concilium* 2.7, 1971, pp. 59–69.

E. Kennedy, 'The Contribution of Religious Ritual to Psychological Balance', *Concilium* 2.7, 1971, pp. 53–58.

G. Tellini, 'Of Symbols, Worship and the Word', in C. Robertson, *Singing the Faith*, Norwich 1990.

A. Vergote, 'Symbolic Gestures and Actions in the Liturgy', *Concilium* 2.7, 1971, pp. 40–52.

A. Vergote, 'La realisation symbolique dans l'expression cutuelle', *La Maison Dieu*, f.111 (1972), pp. 110–31.

FOR DISCUSSION

1. How far is it desirable, or even possible, for modes of liturgical expression to remain unchanged through the centuries?

2. If no civilization or culture is naturally Christian, is it important that the Church develops a cathechesis and a consequent pattern of formation in matters both human and liturgical? How can it do this?

3. Does the liturgy presuppose conversion? If so, is the liturgy primarily for those who believe? How can it go beyond the stage of the seeker or cathechumen?

4. In what sense may the Church be called the earthly sacrament of Jesus Christ, the Primordial Sacrament?

CHAPTER 4

WORD AND SACRAMENT

We understand worship as being an encounter with God, which can be illumined by analogies with encounters among human beings. An encounter takes place between people; it is inter-subjective. In the strict sense we cannot encounter things, or even animals, but only personal beings or (to use C. S. Lewis's term) a God who is 'beyond personality'. The whole Christian understanding of God and his dealings with people rules out an understanding of worship which is less than a personal meeting. Christian worship is not awe in face of an irresistible and unresponsive Power, nor is it the attempt to manipulate by magic or placate by offerings remote deities or the forces of nature.

Christian worship is an 'I-Thou', not an 'I-It', relationship. But immediately we must qualify these words. As they stand they effectively express the personal nature of Christian worship, but they would allow one to understand worship as 'the flight of the alone to the Alone'. In fact, Christian worship is always a communal affair, and that in two senses. First, as we argue elsewhere in this book, all prayer and all worship is the worship of the Church. The individual worshipping is never alone but always joining at least spiritually with the whole Church on earth and with 'angels and archangels and all the company of heaven'. We come to God as '*our* Father' even when we worship alone – a good reminder that we bring our neighbours and our fellows with us when we come before God. At the heart of Christian worship is the worship of the congregation, the fellowship of those who encounter God together, God in one another and one another in God. Prayerful believers who abstract themselves from the worship of the congregation, like the UN Secretary General Dag Hammerskjöld, are distinctly anomalous, as W. H. Auden noted in his introduction to Hammerskjöld's remarkable book of thoughts, *Markings*.[1] The norm must be participation in congregational worship 'both as a discipline and as a refreshment', as well as an awareness of participation in the fellowship of the saints. In the second place, Christian worship is communal because it is participation in the life of the Holy Trinity. God himself, in trinitarian theology, must be understood on the model of a fellowship rather than an isolated individual person. In worship we encounter the Father, our Father, through Jesus Christ. In other words, he offers our worship; he is, as it were, our spokesman; he gives access to the Father; we share in his encounter as Son with his Father. That is why prayer is normally addressed to the Father 'through Jesus Christ our Lord'. And our capacity to worship and our inclination to worship are the work of the Spirit, moving us towards and encouraging us in the *mysterium tremendum* of an encounter with the living God.

At the human level an encounter is not a superficial or momentary meeting but an engagement at depth in which each becomes aware of the mystery of the other. Real encounter always involves an element of mystery: not a contrived and artificial mystery but the authentic mystery that is integral to personality and only reveals itself to love: above all, the tender, reliable covenant-love of which the bible speaks. And encounter is not a partial matter, but a meeting with whole people. The disembodied voice we hear on the radio may thrill, delight, infuriate or instruct us; we become aware of the speaker's thoughts and style of speaking; but we do not encounter the person. To watch an athlete breaking a record or a great orator speaking on television may be a fuller experience, but it is still far short of an encounter. Even to see an actor or a musician perform – while it may be an enriching, or infuriating, or depressing experience, while it may deepen our understanding of the human condition or delight our senses and may even enrich our capacity for understanding and sensitive relationships – it is not an encounter with the actor or musician as a person. For people are complex as well as mysterious – the two are not unconnected – and there is more to the actor than his acting, and to the musician than his playing. Of course, human meeting is often very partial, with people shielding much of

[1] London 1964.

themselves from others, or acting a part rather than opening themselves to an encounter at depth with the other. But real encounter is lasting and deep, and involves the whole person, not just some qualities, aspects or dimensions.

The encounter with God in Jesus Christ, which is Christian worship, is not the hearing of a disembodied voice but a meeting with the incarnate Word, with the one who expresses in his being and his works the very heart of God, who is God's complete and adequate communication to humanity. Nor is Christian worship a matter of 'naked signs', of sacramental acts and symbols which magically ensure a meeting with transcendent powers, in isolation from words, the Word, or speech. No, Christian worship is rather the encounter with the living, speaking Lord who is himself both the living Word and the primordial sacrament. If worship is understood as encounter, Word and Sacrament belong together. They are complementary; both are necessary, for they interpret and illumine one another and neither in itself is complete or adequate. God has chosen Word and Sacrament as the two-dimensional locus of his encounter with his people, and to separate them, or neglect one in favour of the other, is to invite an incomplete encounter and an inadequate understanding of God and how God relates to people.

Almost all the Churches are today rediscovering the vital unity of Word and Sacrament and seeking to express it more adequately in their worship. But it still remains true that many in the Reformed and Lutheran Churches regard worship as essentially preaching, with the rest of the service seen as no more than the preliminaries to the sermon. And there are still seminaries and faculties of theology where detailed attention is given to training in homiletics but very little time is devoted to the principles of liturgy, so that clergy who have almost complete freedom in the construction and content of public worship have a very sketchy preparation for this vital part of their role. In Roman Catholic and some Anglican seminaries, on the other hand, the ministry of the Word has sometimes been treated as a rather unimportant postscript to liturgy. Students have been given detailed instruction in the history and practice of the Church's liturgy (but seldom much theology of worship), while the training in homiletics has been rudimentary. Even some current textbooks reflect and perpetuate this unfortunate split between the Word and the

Sacrament, so that one can go through books such as *The Study of Liturgy*[2] and gain the impression that the ministry of the word, and preaching in particular, played no part in the worship of Christendom down the ages. And many books on homiletics proceed with sublime disregard of the fact that preaching is an integral part of Christian worship and cannot properly be considered in isolation from this context.

The present book regards the unity of Word and Sacrament as a fundamental principle of Christian worship, which has been rediscovered by modern theology of all traditions but still has to penetrate fully into the practice of the Churches' worship and the education of clergy and all who lead the worship of God's people. The recovery, in practice as well as in theology, of the complementarity of Word and Sacrament involves cross-fertilization and mutual enrichment between the two great traditions, the one emphasizing the place of the Word, and the other the centrality of the sacraments, and must be a major contribution to the ecumenical renewal of worship, which is surely at the heart of the revitalization of the Church and Christian faith and practice.

The Word

Christianity understands worship as the encounter with God's Word; speech and hearing are indispensable to the authenticity of this meeting; God becomes really present with his people in his Word. And according to Augustine, in a phrase beloved of the Calvinist Reformers, a sacrament itself is a verbum visible, a visible word. In worship we hear the Word of God addressed to us, calling us, encouraging us, challenging us, forgiving us, nourishing us, uplifting us, strengthening us. All this implies that we must have, as it were, a sacramental understanding of the Word in worship, just as we must understand the sacraments as encounters with the God who addresses us in his Word.

As Karl Barth has observed, the Word meets us in a three-fold form: in preaching (which is discussed in chapter 5), in scripture and as the Word incarnate, Jesus Christ, to whom the scriptures bear witness.[3] Clearly, scripture is an important element, and one which requires careful handling. Scripture always points beyond itself: 'We do the Bible a poor honour',

---

[2] SPCK, 1978.
[3] *Church Dogmatics* 1/1, Edinburgh 1936, pp. 98–140.

writes Karl Barth, 'and one unwelcome to itself, when we directly identify it with this something else, with revelation itself.'[4] To avoid such verbal idolatry is important, but it is also necessary to have a clear idea of how scripture functions in the believing community and how it speaks as Word. A historical perspective allows us a useful point of entry.

(i) Scripture and worship in ancient Israel and Judaism

The practice of worship is strongly reflected in the Old Testament scriptures as we know them. Indeed, the recital of sacred tradition at Israel's religious festivals was an important part of the process whereby the traditions of Israel were shaped and developed. One function of scripture is to give authoritative guidance for worship, cult and ritual; another is to narrate the story of salvation in the context of worship. It has, therefore, an important interpretative function for the worshippers:

> Give ear, O my people, to my teaching;
> incline your ears to the words of my mouth!
> I will open my mouth in a parable;
>   I will utter dark sayings from of old,
> things that we have heard and known,
>   that our fathers have told us.
> We will not hide them from their children,
>   but tell to the coming generation
> the glorious deeds of the Lord, and his might,
>   and the wonders which he has wrought. (Psalm 78:1–4)

Ritual, story, interpretation, revelation . . . : these important elements in the worship of Israel are not only the direct concern of scripture; they also serve, in conjunction with scripture, to involve the worshippers in the divine mystery and in the inner, contemporary meaning of worship. Psalm 116, for example, is the liturgy used by the person who has come to the Temple to pay his vow and make a thank-offering to Yahweh. It is particularly appropriate to one who has been very ill and who promised in his distress to fulfil just such a vow on his recovery. Notice the loving response of one who finds his prayers answered, the recollection of his distress, the celebration of God's mercy, and the paying of the vow itself. The liturgy makes personal to the worshipper the relationship between Yahweh and Israel (cf. Deuteronomy 26:5–10).

[4] *Op. cit.*, p. 126.

Diversity is particularly noticeable in post-exilic Judaism, not least in the place given to scripture. To the priests in the temple tradition (cf. the Sadducees in Jesus' day), the Books of Moses formed the Torah, the essential and only scripture. For them, scripture prescribed and interpreted the cult, and directed the way of the worshippers. In these terms, the priest was the teacher of Israel. The destruction of the Temple by the Babylonians, however, led to new religious developments. The absence of Temple worship in Babylon gave an impetus to the editing, study and standardizing of the Torah as scripture, and called into being a new, or at least greatly enlarged, class of scribal experts in the Torah and written tradition. The rise of the synagogues in post-exilic Judaism provided centres for the discussion and study of the Torah as a continuing duty, allied to the saying of prayers. The scribal teachers (later, rabbis) regarded scripture as essentially the Torah, but admitted the Prophets and later the Writings as authoritative commentary on the Torah, interpreting and applying it to the daily lives of the people. That, too, was the function of the rabbis' sayings, the 'tradition of the elders' on which the Pharisees of Jesus' day placed so much emphasis. Indeed, so important was the interpretation and application of scripture to the rabbis that it could even be said that the modern commentary which related directly to the contemporary situation was more important than the ancient text considered in isolation.

Another broad grouping might be characterized as sectarian, the Essenes of Qumran being the most accessible example. Here, the worship took place within monastic communities, which had their own distinctive cultic practices (especially washings or baptisms); and scripture, not confined to the Books of Moses, was copied, studied and interpreted in relation to the community which believed that it had a special role to play in the Last Days. Such eschatological beliefs governed all aspects of their life. Their scriptural interpretation was designed to reveal the hidden meaning which the text held for them, standing as they believed at or near the completion of God's mighty works in Israel. They wrote commentaries on the scriptures with this purpose in mind. A characteristic procedure was to cite the scripture text (sometimes with modifications) and add an exposition, usually introduced by 'interpreted, this concerns ...' or some similar formula.[5]

[5] 'Midrash' (commentary) could be both explicit and implicit; see G. Vermes, *The Dead Sea Scrolls in English*, Harmondsworth 1962.

It must not be thought that such radically creative procedures were found only in sectarian Judaism. Because the traditions of Israel were constantly interpreted and applied in the living context of community worship and practice, new meaning was constantly being found in them. It was said that every word of scripture had seventy aspects,[6] so there was plenty of new meaning to be discovered by each generation! Hence, the literature expanded. Deuteronomy is just such a recasting of the ancient laws; the Priestly Code is a further example. The book we call Isaiah encapsulates a lengthy tradition of prophetic exposition. Chronicles recasts the historical tradition; apocalyptists and sectarians were similarly expansive, and so on. Finally, the rabbis closed the canon, the list of books recognized as scripture and hence regulative of faith and life. (The precise date when they did so is unknown – certainly later than Jamnia, *c.* AD 95: the priestly tradition had closed its canon many centuries previously.) But the expansion of meaning necessary to a living community was not halted or 'put on ice' by such action. The rabbinic tradition of authoritative exposition continued and was itself encoded in Mishnah and Talmud.

How can we sum up scripture and its relation to worship in ancient Israel and Judaism? Emerging from and operating within worshipping communities, scripture reflects and is shaped by their worship in many respects. It also regulates and informs continuing worship. It relates and interprets the story of God's wonders in the history of the people, and enjoins recital of them in worship. It enshrines and encapsulates the truth given to Moses but rediscovered in new ways from generation to generation. It helps Israel to walk in God's ways and to trust for the future. Hence, while it prescribes ritual and liturgical action, it can also attack Temple and cult when they do not truly reflect God's will and purpose for his people. Designed to speak a contemporary Word to the believing community, it continues to do so through commentary and renewed application. Of course, the dangers were immense: such as legalism, pedantry, and openness to external influence (e.g. hellenizing). But such dangers were not exclusive to Judaism. The resilience of the Jewish biblical tradition is well attested by its history since biblical times.

[6] See I. Epstein, *Midrash Rabbah I* (Genesis), Freedman and Simon (eds.), London 1939, p. xi.

(ii) Scripture and worship in the early Christian tradition

Christian worship has always had a scriptural dimension: the Old Testament was there from the beginning; both in Hebrew and in Greek translation (the Septuagint, second century BC). Although the scriptural canon was open-ended in the first century, all inspired writing was recognized as useful for teaching the truth and refuting error ... (2 Timothy 3:16). So where did Christian use of scripture in worship differ from the Jewish?

In the Jewish Christianity of the early days, the difference was not too marked. The brethren worshipped in the Temple and were to be found in the synagogues until such times as they were declared *personae non gratae*. Why? The root cause is found at the core of the Christian position: belief in Jesus as Messiah and Lord. If this was understood in a limited way, the Christians might have remained a sect within Judaism – albeit an extremely heterodox one. But as soon as Jesus' Lordship was interpreted in a radical way, so that the foundations of Judaism were shaken at their most vital points – Law, Temple, nation-hood – then the possibility of compromise was ruled out. After initial hesitation, the salvation that Christ offered was made open to all believers, without distinction of race, sex or status. In Christ, the New Age had been established; the Old was swept away. The End-time had come into the midst of history. Here was a new 'eschatological community', and it was wholly Christocentric, centred on the Word.

Such a position was of immense consequence for scriptural interpretation. It is true that the Old Testament has an expectation of the future: whether the coming forth of a 'shoot from the stump of Jesse', or 'the Day of the Lord', or Elijah the Prophet, or 'one like a son of man', or the servant of the Lord ... But the early Christians did not limit their interest in the scriptures to the exposition of such passages. Because they regarded Jesus the crucified and risen Christ, as the fulfilment of all God's work through Israel, they believed that all the scriptures testified to him. As the Jesus of the Fourth Gospel says to his fellow Jews, 'You search the scriptures because you think that in them you have eternal life; and it is they that bear witness to me; yet you refuse to come to me that you may have life' (John 5:35f.). Jesus as the Christ was therefore the starting point of their scriptural interpretation. They read the Old

Testament in the light of their Christian faith and found it responding in innumerable ways to their interrogation. It was as if the motifs which coalesced in Christ were prefigured in varied and fragmentary ways in the story of God's previous dealings with Israel. Hence Paul can take the notion of Moses' veil and use it to suggest that the splendour of the old covenant was a fading splendour (2 Corinthians 3:13) – not because there is anything in the Mosaic tradition to suggest this, but because Paul *knows* that 'what once had splendour' (i.e. the religion of the old covenant) 'has come to have no splendour at all, because of the splendour that surpasses it' (2 Corinthians 3:10). For Paul, this was not a tortuous or far-fetched argument: it was nothing other than 'the open statement of the truth' (2 Corinthians 4:2), as the truth was revealed in Christ. The cycle of interpretation began with Christ, read the Old Testament in the light of Christian faith, and then found the scriptures witnessing to the finality and completion that Christ represented. Such interpretation was integral to Christian worship and essential to evangelism among the Jews. Not for nothing did Paul spend three sabbaths in the synagogue at Thessalonica, arguing from the scriptures and 'explaining and proving that it was necessary for the Christ to suffer and to rise from the dead, and saying, "This Jesus, whom I proclaim to you, is the Christ"' (Acts 17:3).

This Christo-centrism was not a merely intellectual stance, a kind of hermeneutical game played on the chequer-board of Judaistic biblical usage. It permeated the whole Christian community, which resonated to the crucified-and-risen Christ. The relational aspect came to the fore in community life and worship: 'where two or three are gathered together in my name, there am I in the midst of them'. The new community was nothing less than 'the temple of the living God' (2 Corinthians 6:16), separated alike from the old community with its faded glory and from the paganism of the nations, but above all enjoying the welcome of God who was a Father to them, his sons and daughters.

In fact, scripture and worship inter-relate in several ways here. The worship and community life are informed by scripture. Because Christ came 'not to destroy the Torah but to fulfil it', the Christians could use and adapt Jewish psalms and liturgies; hence the 'psalms and hymns and spiritual songs' (Colossians 3:16, Ephesians 5:19), the great hymnic utterances in Revelation, and the Odes of Solomon, 'the earliest Christian Hymn-book'.[7] Hence, too, the doxologies, the use of 'Amen', and the great confessions: Cullmann has observed, 'All these old confession formulae have this in common, that they are Christocentric and that they stress the *present Lordship of Christ*'.[8] Christian prophets, too, would inject scriptural lessons and interpretations into the service of worship, as the Spirit moved them; a criterion of genuine prophecy was again Christo-centrism.[9]

This Christo-centrism was only possible by reason of a strong deposit of tradition about Jesus the Christ; both his teaching and the apostolic witness to his life, death and resurrection. One can see it in operation when Paul explicitly cites a 'word of the Lord' to correct error in his churches. Paul's use of the tradition of the last supper (1 Corinthians 11:23–26) is particularly informative. He stresses the chain of tradition, records the action at the meal and its purpose in a concise and careful way, and enlarges freely on the points he wants the Corinthians to understand in particular. However, from our point of view, the most significant fact is that Paul cites dominical tradition as the complete model for Christian practice, to be imitated and applied in the contemporary situation. Here we have Christian tradition already possessing a prescriptive function. And the apostle himself was con-sciously contributing to a deposit of apostolic letters, designed to be read in churches and even to circulate among them (though possibly conceived by the writer as having immediate rather than long-term significance).

From the earliest days of the Christian movement, therefore, the 'searching of the scripture' in the context of 'the apostles' teaching and fellowship' was a creative movement which led to a definitive understanding of the scriptures in Christo-centric perspective. Like the Ethiopian in Acts 8:26–40, Christians and enquirers need guidance in order to 'understand'; and like Philip, apostles and community leaders ('prophets and teachers') had to begin with the scripture and relate the good news of Jesus (cf. Acts 8:35). Hence, the logic of the situation suggests that the Old Testament scriptures were accompanied

[7] J. H. Charlesworth, *The Odes of Solomon*, Oxford 1973, p. vii (Preface).
[8] *Early Christian Worship*, E.T., London 1953, p. 23.
[9] Cf. 1 Corinthians 12:3; and see in particular James Moffatt's comments *in loc*, in his volume on *1 Corinthians* in the Moffatt New Testament Commentaries.

in Christian worship by Christian commentary; that this commentary would comprise 'the things concerning Jesus'; and that the commentator would attempt to bring scriptures and Christian tradition alike into dynamic relationship with the contemporary situation of the hearers. It is therefore not surprising that impressive evidence has been put forward to suggest that Matthew, for example, 'wrote his Gospel to be read in church round the year; he took the Jewish Festal Year, and the pattern of lections prescribed therefor, as his base; and it is possible for us to descry from MS evidence for which feast, and for which Sabbath/Sunday, and even on occasion for which service, any particular verses were intended'.[10] Whatever may be the final verdict of scholarship on this detailed case, it certainly fits the general pattern that has emerged in our discussion. It was inevitable that in course of time, the traditions concerning Jesus, 'handed down to us by the original eyewitnesses and servants of the Gospel' (Luke 1:2), would cease to be simply 'the utterances of a living and abiding voice'[11] and acquire written form. In the case of Paul's (and other) letters, written to specific churches as part of his care of the churches, the question was one of collection and perhaps even editing. Certainly, 1 Clement (96–97 AD) is familiar with Pauline writings as well as being 'saturated' in the Old Testament.[12] Justin (*c.* AD 155) completes the picture:

> ... on the day called Sunday there is a meeting in one place of those who live in cities or the country, and the memoirs of the apostles or the writings of the prophets are read as long as time permits. When the reader has finished, the president in a discourse urges and invites (us) to the imitation of these noble things. Then we all stand up together and offer prayers ... .[13]

The prayers are followed by the Eucharist. It is noteworthy that the service *begins* with scripture lessons; then comes the homiletic application; then the sacrament. There is no specific suggestion of lectionary here: the readings seem 'open ended'; but there is a decided move towards a Christian canon of scripture. Although this matter would not be finally settled until much later, it is interesting that Eusebius conducted his

[10] M. D. Goulder, *Midrash and Lection in Matthew*, London 1974, p. 172.
[11] Papias (early second century), cited in Eusebius H.E. III.39.
[12] Cf. C. C. Richardson, *Early Christian Fathers*, London 1953, p. 37.
[13] Justin, *Apology* 1,67; see Richardson, *op. cit.*, p. 287.

research into the issue by noting which books were actually in use in the churches.

(iii) Scripture and worship

How may we express briefly the relations between scripture and worship?

(a) *Scripture permeates worship.* Old and New Testaments proceed from living communities of faith. They include compelling examples of these communities at worship. In the Old Testament we have the prayers of Solomon at the dedication of the Temple, the Book of Psalms with its wide range of spirituality and worship, and the worship practices of Israel in festival. In the New Testament we have the instructions given by Jesus to the disciples on the matter of prayer, and in the apostolic letters a variety of prayers is exemplified: thanksgiving, supplication, intercession, and at least by implication confession. The same sources give abundant evidence of the praises that are inherent in all worship. An interesting aspect of all this is the extent to which the Old Testament prayers and praise were taken over and 'christianized' in the churches. The hymns which we find in the Gospels (cf. first two chapters of Luke) are directly derived from the worship of Israel, yet they refer specifically to the coming of Christ. The early Christians apparently made the transposition without difficulty. For them, Jesus was Lord. It is not without significance that the first outside view we have of Christian worship speaks of them 'singing hymns to Christ as to a god'.[14] The language needed for such hymns was readily available through the scriptures and worship of Israel and Judaism. The intensity of Christian devotion, fired by prophet and charismatic, sparked the gap and made the transposition possible.

By its very nature, worship is offered by worshippers in their particular situation in life. In the Christian tradition above all worship must not become so formalized as to be thought-less and automatic. The teaching of Jesus expressly forbids it. There must always be a *contemporary* aspect to worship, otherwise it is not truly the offering of the worshipper. That is not to say that Christians cannot use the words of others in

---

[14] Pliny, Epistles X (to Trajan), xcvi.

the worship they offer. As we have seen they have traditionally done so in using scriptural language, and not least the Lord's Prayer itself. But they must identify with the scriptural meaning so that it speaks for them.

The most famous example of scriptural worship is the use of the Psalms, prose and metrical, in Christian worship. *Literally*, their points of reference are outwith the Christian tradition: the place of Zion is a case in point. However, Christian worship itself provided the context which informed and reinterpreted the psalmist's imagery. Thus, Zion became the symbol for the Church or the New Jerusalem, while the spiritual life of the psalmist was reinterpreted in Christian terms. Christian worship supplies its own hermeneutic, which is similar to that applied from the beginning to the Old Testament. Sometimes this is made explicit by appending to a psalm, for example, an ascription of praise in Christian terms. While we can make no objection to this practice, it would be unfortunate if this appendage were regarded as legitimizing or 'christianizing' the Old Testament material for use in Christian worship.

Generally speaking, the scriptures have immensely enriched Christian worship throughout the ages. They have given a wealth of symbolism which has helped the worshipper to understand his or her own position in relation to God and the *koinonia*, and also to express this in prayer. In short, Christian prayer must be contemporary, but not *merely* contemporary, with the worshippers. In their devotions, they are united with the devotions of the faithful of all the ages; and nothing is better equipped to give expression to this facet of their experience than the language and symbolism of scripture, their common heritage.

(*b*) *Scripture is itself a major element in worship.* The church service that Justin describes began with an unspecified number of scripture readings. Probably a certain informality characterized the proceedings: possibly interpretations and discussions of meaning interspersed the readings. Certainly, exposition followed. One thing is clear: scripture itself was the first major element in the service. It represents and conveys the revelation of God to man, supremely in Jesus Christ. Without this, there can be no Christian worship. In time, it was thought fitting to begin worship on a note of praise and prayer, before introducing the Word. The focus

has not changed. One simply approaches it in a wider
liturgical context than Justin's order provides.

Thus, worshippers today approach the place of revelation
through praise and prayer. The reading of the scriptures
takes them beyond the vestibule, so to speak, into the holy
place where God reveals himself through the scriptures.
Hence there is an obligation on the part of those leading
the worship to ensure that the lessons are as appropriate
and meaningful as possible. There is, however, no automatic relationship between reading the scriptures and
hearing the Word of God. To identify the Word with the
words of scripture in a literal and positive way is a major
error which obscures the moving of the Spirit in the hearts
and minds of the worshipping community. Hence one
might say that the words of the Bible are heard as the Word
of God only in the context of worship and devotion where
the human spirit is made open to God's Spirit. A pre-
condition is the attentive hearing of the words; participation by the congregation in reading – orally or silently –
helps towards this end. A full appreciation of the
liturgical movement of the service – hearing the Word,
responding to the Word, exposition of the Word, response
to the exposition – alerts worshippers to the demand which
the service is placing upon them. There is therefore an
element of mystery at the heart of the liturgy here: a mystery
which consists of nothing short of the encounter of God
and his people. Truly, when this encounter takes place, it is
as the gift of God and as an act of his grace. Yet the liturgy
itself also helps worshippers in their search for God and
for the divine revelation through the scriptures. 'Seek and
ye shall find . . .' is appropriate to them, 'for it is in seeking
that we are found . . .'

Finally, the impression may have been given that Christian
worship as described here is rather academic and cognitive.
This has not been the intention, although one would wish
to suggest that in the position in which the Churches find
themselves today it is important that all worshippers who
have the capacity should understand what is involved in
Christian worship and interpretation, and be able to 'give a
reason for the faith that is in them'. But the Christian
response to the divine approach is a response of 'the whole
person': it involves both the cognitive and affective domains,

and is concerned with knowledge, feeling, relationships and action.

(*c*) *Scripture gives specific warrant for certain practices in worship*

> Go therefore and make disciples of all nations, baptizing them in the name of the Father and of the Son and of the Holy Spirit . . .

> For I received from the Lord what I also delivered to you, that the Lord Jesus on the night when he was betrayed took bread, and when he had given thanks, he broke it, and said, 'This is my body which is for you. Do this in remembrance of me' . . .

Whatever else may be said about these passages, two liturgical acts are expressly warranted by them: baptism and the Lord's Supper.

This is not the place to follow out the baptismal controversies of many centuries. The dominical warrant sanctions baptism in the context of evangelism and teaching. Matthew sees 'all nations' (i.e. the Gentiles) as potential catechumens, to be baptized by water and so received into the true Israel. It must be admitted that the Evangelist's concern is far removed from later controversies. He does not specify whether adults alone should be baptized and children excluded, any more than he specifies at what age one becomes adult! He does not specify *how* the rite of baptism is to be carried out, although some hints may perhaps be derived from other New Testament writings. The basic point is that baptism, in Christian understanding, is carried out by Christ's warrant. When the rite is administered, appropriate scriptural passages are read, both as warrant for and interpretation of the meaning of baptism. Thus, in the case of infant baptism, the reading of the 'child pericopae' interprets what the church is doing in terms of Jesus' attitude to children while instructing the adults present on important aspects of discipleship. As always, the church's teaching function is important. The whole rite, being Christo-centric, is properly interpreted further in terms of Christian doctrine: but care should be taken not to overload the liturgy with too much didactic material, for this will lessen the impact of the liturgical action rather than enhance it.

The Lord's Supper is the climax of Christian worship. Its place in the liturgy is discussed below. One notes, however, that when Paul was writing to the Corinthians, a eucharistic tradition – whether as 'the breaking of bread' or the *Agape* or fellowship meal – was already in existence: Paul was not introducing the sacrament for the first time. Equally, Paul had to assert his apostolic authority in order to correct the excesses which Church tradition by itself was unable to handle. Hence the significance of incorporating the narrative of 1 Corinthians 11:23ff. in the communion service as warrant and model for the liturgical practice. One notes also the kerygmatic emphasis in Paul: 'for as often as you eat this bread and drink this cup, you proclaim the Lord's death until he comes'. The Lord's Supper is a powerful proclamation of the Cross and Resurrection, and this proclamation must be made and heard. The ministry of Word and Sacrament is a unity. Indeed, in the full service of Christian worship, the people of God are helped by the liturgy to approach God through the vestibule of praise and prayer to the holy place where the Word is heard and understood and response made; and finally to the most holy place where the bread of life is offered in word and action: a holy mystery interpreted by scripture and therefore properly the object of study in the continuing teaching ministry of the Church.

Sacrament

The term 'sacrament' is not found in the Bible, and was not used in the earliest Church, although what we now know as sacramental worship was a central focus of the encounter with God. The equivalent term to sacrament in the New Testament is *mysterion*, 'mystery'. In the synoptic Gospels we read of the 'mystery of the Kingdom of God'. In Paul the mystery is God's plan for the salvation of all which has been realized in history as well as revealed in Christ's death and resurrection – the 'paschal mystery' which is implanted again and again in history through the proclamation of the Word. The 'mystery of God' (1 Corinthians 2:1 in some MSS) is identical with the mystery of the crucified Jesus (1 Corinthians 1:23; 2:2), and with the proclamation of the Gospel. The good news, God's secret plan, is now revealed and realized in the events of passion and resurrection. The mystery which had been hidden in God is now revealed through the Spirit (1 Corinthians 2:7–16). In Colossians and Ephesians it is explained that the mystery once secret and now made manifest is that in Christ, God was reconciling the whole cosmos to himself, and all things are involved in a process which might be called 'christification' (Colossians 1:15–29, 2:8–12; Ephesians 1:8–10, 2:4–10, 3:1–13). To sum up the New Testament understanding of the term *mysterion*: it is used in three related senses: (*a*) God's secret purpose for the salvation of all, now revealed in Christ (e.g. Romans 2:25, 8:19–21); (*b*) An earthly reality expressing in a hidden way a meaning related to God's secret plan (e.g. Ephesians 5:32; Revelation 1:20, 17:5–7); (*c*) An historical happening with a special significance related to God's plan (e.g. 1 Corinthians 15:51; 2 Thessalonians 2:7).

In secular usage *mysterion* meant, in a general way, a secret, while the plural form, *mysteria* referred to the cults of the pagan 'mystery religions'. The question of the relation of early Christianity to these mystery religions is a very complex matter into which we cannot go here, except to say that most modern scholarship rejects the view, enthusiastically propounded in a former generation, that early Christianity (and particularly its cult) was shaped very largely on the model of a mystery religion. The Fathers are on the whole very cautious about any use of the term mystery to refer specifically to Christian worship, presumably because they fear confusion with the pagan rites of the mystery religions. But Clement of Alexandria – notable among the Fathers for his eagerness to relate the Faith to its cultural context – speaks of three Christian mysteries, or categories of mysteries: first, the 'lesser mysteries' which were received as preparation or preliminary to greater ones, for example, initiation by baptism; secondly, the 'greater mysteries', the central truths of the Faith, which were to be lived and contemplated so that gradually more of their meaning became plain and could be appropriated by believers; and thirdly, the 'great mystery' which the other mysteries reflect or point towards, Jesus Christ himself. The Latin Fathers seem to have had a certain suspicion of the Greek term *mysterion* and tended to borrow a current term *sacramentum* as an alternative. *Sacramentum* had a plurality of meanings, but the one which made it most suitable for Christian usage was the *sacramentum militiae*, the ritual of entry of recruits into the Roman army, which included the taking of a solemn oath of loyalty and was often accompanied by the 'brand of fidelity' (*fidei signaculum*). Tertullian was the first to use *sacramentum* in a Christian context.

In the case of baptism, he understood it on the model of the military recruit's *sacramentum*, as indicating a binding faith and commitment of one's self and the start of a new life. His talk of marriage as a sacrament suggests that he saw *sacramentum* as a direct translation of the *mysterion* of Ephesians 5, where the analogy between the love of Christ for his church and a husband and wife is declared 'a great mystery'. Cyprian interprets *sacramentum* in a less legal (or military) way than Tertullian; a sacrament is a matter of symbols, figures, and signs representing spiritual realities. Accordingly he speaks of the Eucharist as a sacrament in addition to baptism and marriage. Hilary of Poitiers knows of three *sacramenta*: initiation, Eucharist and the incarnation. But the three are clearly not 'on a level', as it were: the Incarnation is the foundation and basis for the other two; they draw their meaning and significance from the Word made flesh.

Augustine, the first great systematizer of Latin theology, understood a sacrament as the 'sign' of a sacred reality, the visible form of an invisible grace. He distinguished four components: (*a*) the *signum*, the outward visible and material element, such as bread, wine, or water; (*b*) the *virtus sacramenti*, the 'virtue' or inward, invisible grace conveyed in the sacrament; (*c*) the *verbum*, the spoken formula pronounced by the minister which provided the link between the sign and its 'virtue'. The *verbum* is, in fact, the Word of God, not a magic spell, and the sacrament must never be separated from the Word or it ceases to be a sacrament. As Augustine wrote in relation to baptism: 'Take away the Word and the water is nothing but water. But when the Word is joined to the element the result is a sacrament . . . Where does the water get its lofty power to bathe the body and cleanse the soul if it is not through the action of the Word? And not because it is spoken, but because it is believed.'[15] (*d*) *The 'agent' of the sacrament is Christ himself, who is the Word.* One cannot but notice that in the transition from the New Testament understanding of *mysterion* to the developed theology of *sacramentum* in Augustine something has been lost and the concept has been significantly narrowed. What had originally denoted God's secret plan for all creation revealed and realized in Christ, and only derivatively the cult in which the Church re-presents the mystery of Christ,

[15] *On the Gospel of John* 80.3, cited in J. Martos, *Doors to the Sacred*, London 1981, pp. 191f.

now suggests mere rites rather than on-going realities. The primordial 'sacramentality' of Christ is all but forgotten, and the understanding of the cult consequently impoverished and opened to all sorts of distortions. Sacraments considered as rites are viewed in isolation from their proper context and accorded a significance on their own which differs substantially from the primitive view. Now new questions of a quite different order arise, such as the number of sacraments that exist (Peter Lombard taught that there were seven; the Reformation recognized only two) or whether explicit institution by Christ is required to make a sacrament (Hugo of St. Victor – twelfth century – emphasized the need for dominical institution, as did the Reformers, but there was disagreement as to how explicit such institution need be). Consequently, Thomas Aquinas taught that the sacraments work *ex opere operato*, which came to be interpreted as a way of affirming the objectivity of the sacraments and their independence of the spiritual, moral or emotional state of the minister or of the recipients. Sacraments, he taught, are the work of God and not of man, and the minister (representing the Church) and the Church itself (in whose name the rite is administered) are only instrumental causes of Christ's own saving activity. A sacrament is an objectively valid offer of grace made by God himself. Sacraments confer the grace they signify, not for any superstitious reason or in a magical way, but because in them Christ the High Priest is acting through his Body, represented by the minister, whose worthiness, while desirable, is not essential to the efficacy of the sacrament. After Thomas the prevalent legal and juridical thinking resulted in the validity of the sacrament being seen as depending upon the correct performance of the rite in the prescribed form, with the proper words, by the legally authorized minister. This legalistic understanding of the sacraments became very widespread in the later Middle Ages so that sometimes a juridical view almost totally obscured a theological understanding of their meaning and significance.

The Reformation attempted to recover a biblical under-standing of the sacraments but was only partially successful in escaping from the legacy of the later Middle Ages. The Reformers' views covered a wide spectrum, from the Zwinglian extreme where they were understood as little more than visual aids for the commemoration of past events, to strong affirmations of the Real Presence of Christ with his people in their celebration. For an act of worship to be a sacrament it had to have been specifically instituted by the Lord, with a promise of divine grace attached; accordingly only two sacraments, rather than the mediaeval seven, were recognized. This narrowing of the category of sacrament was not really a recovery of the New Testament view – as we have seen the early Church was perfectly familiar with baptism and the Lord's Supper but understood them as elements in the vast *mysterion* of God's dealings with mankind in Christ rather than the two members of a particular class of rites. The strong affirmation that Word and Sacrament belonged together protected the two sacraments from an unhealthy isolation, but fell short of a rediscovery of the primitive comprehensiveness. Because sacramental quality was believed to inhere only in baptism and the Eucharist, the theological understanding of other forms of worship was inhibited and the Reformed Churches were even reluctant to speak of preaching as sacramental although their practice seemed to suggest such an interpretation. In principle the assertion of the complementarity of Word and Sacrament and the understanding of a sacrament as a *verbum visibile*, or as a seal and confirmation of God's Word of promise, should have opened up the recovery of the proper integration of Christian worship into the economy of salvation; in practice mediaeval problems about the number and validity of the sacraments and opposition to late mediaeval sacramentalism ensured that a narrow view of sacramentality was maintained while baptism and the Eucharist were separated sharply from all other forms of worship (which were thereby deprived of any sacramental significance) and theologically relegated to little more than an appendix rather than relating to the heart of the Christian mystery.

The Eastern Churches followed a very different path. They continued to use the term 'mystery' in their liturgies in the biblical sense: for them the Incarnation, the Eucharist, Marriage, Baptism, the Veiling of a Virgin, the setting apart of oil for liturgical use and numerous other events, acts, rites, and doctrines are all 'mysteries', in the sense that they are earthly realities fundamentally related to Christ, the mystery of our salvation. There was no question of identifying two, three, seven, or more *rites* as sacraments or mysteries to the exclusion of all else. Rather, they were concerned with identifying the whole of revelation and salvation with a series of historical, temporal focuses of encounter fundamentally related to the primordial mystery of Christ. These views were partially abandoned only where the influence of Latin thought led to the adopting of Western post-Aquinas sacramental theology.

At the heart of the modern movement for liturgical renewal is a recovery of the understanding of sacrament as mystery, never totally lost in the East. Going back to scripture and the Fathers, pioneers such as Odo Casel in Germany understood sacraments as rites in which participants encountered the living Christ, and his saving activity was re-presented to them. Worship was seen as participation in the mysteries of the Christian Faith, and the rite itself had a significance which was simply instrumental. Building on such foundations a number of recent theologians, most notably Edward Schillebeeckx, have developed a sacramental theology which faithfully reflects neglected emphases in Scripture and the Fathers and transcends many ancient controversies, suggesting possibilities of ecumenical consensus in this field so long devastated by warring armies. Sacraments are understood as loving encounters between the believer and God which, like loving encounters between two human beings, reveal truths which are not apparent on the surface or accessible to the detached, 'objective' observer.

Disciples of today, just as the disciples of long ago, in encountering Jesus come into touch with a mystery which they know to be the mystery of God's being and acts, the secret of the universe and the meaning of life. In the primary sense, then, we should speak of Jesus Christ as being the Sacrament.[16] In Christ, the Incarnate Son, through his physical, historical and material humanity we encounter the mystery, and the reality of God himself. In a secondary sense, the Church which is the Body of Christ should be regarded as a sacrament. It is the community in time and space, the visible fellowship, in which the God and Father of our Lord Jesus Christ is encountered, and as his Body, it represents Christ sacramentally to the world. Thus, the Church is also to be understood as the sacrament of the unity of all mankind: it shows in sacramental form the saving purpose of God for all humanity, it is a sign of hope for all, a working model (to use a rather crude image) of what God wills

[16] Cf. the title of Schillebeeckx's book, *Christ the Sacrament of the Encounter with God*, London 1963.

for everyone: loving fellowship with God and with one another. And the Church is a sacrament because the visible, empirical reality of the fellowship points beyond itself to its Lord, to Christ the sacrament of the encounter with God. Thirdly, there are sacraments of the Church which are sacraments, Schillebeeckx argues, precisely because they are also acts of Christ himself. 'A sacrament', he writes, 'is primarily and fundamentally a personal act of Christ himself which reaches and involves us in the form of an institutional act performed by a person in the Church who . . . is empowered to do so by Christ himself.'[17] And since the sacraments are acts of Christ, Schillebeeckx insists that 'he must in some way have instituted them himself'.[18] Indeed, without conceding the extreme Protestant position that there are two and only two sacraments, baptism and the Eucharist, an emerging ecumenical consensus concurs in according a very real primacy to these two rites while affirming that they cannot be properly understood except as special focuses of a more broadly conceived sacramentality. God is not confined to encountering his people only in baptism and the Eucharist, but he has trysted to meet them there, and these two meeting places encourage and help believers to discern the presence of God elsewhere and encounter him in Christ in all sorts of times and places, which thereby become sacramental. For wherever God is encountered believers may say, with Jacob, 'This is none other than the house of God, and this is the gate of heaven' (Genesis 28:17.)

Finally, to understand sacraments as ways of introducing and intensifying the experience of encounter with God in Christ involves the necessity of holding together the Word and the Sacrament. Apart from the Word, the symbols and actions of a sacrament would mystify rather than reveal the mystery of God's purpose in Christ; the Word integrates these acts and symbols into the mystery of salvation; Word, symbol and action mutually clarify one another and cannot be held apart without danger of radical distortion.[19]

---

[17] *Op. cit.*, p. 62.

[18] *Op. cit.*, p. 137.

[19] Thus, D. Coggan advocates a bi-focal understanding of the means of grace: '. . . the Living God comes to us both in the Sacrament of the Body and Blood of Christ and in the sacrament of the Word . . .': *The Sacrament of the Word*, London 1989, p. 24.

FURTHER READING

J. Barr, *Old and New in Interpretation* (2nd edn.), London 1982.

—, *Holy Scripture: canon, authority, criticism*, Oxford 1983.

—, *The Scope and Authority of the Bible* (Explorations in Theology 7), London 1980.

D. Coggan, *The Sacrament of the Word*, London 1989.

A. Lewis, 'Ecclesia ex Auditu: A Reformed View of the Church as the Community of the Word', *The Scottish Journal of Theology*, vol. 35, 1982, pp. 13–31.

C. F. D. Moule, *Worship in the New Testament*, London 1961.

H. H. Rowley, *Worship in Ancient Israel*, London 1967.

E. Schillebeeckx, *The Sacrament of the Encounter with God*, London 1971.

D. N. Power, *The Eucharistic Mystery: Revitalizing the Tradition*, London & Dublin 1993.

FOR DISCUSSION

1. 'The liturgy is scripture's home rather than its stepchild, and the Hebrew and Christian Bibles were the Church's first liturgical books.' (A. Kavanagh.) What then is the importance of the worshipping community for the interpretation of the Bible?

2. How far is scripture itself dependent on the tradition of the faith community, and how far is Church tradition guided and corrected by scripture?

3. What do you consider to be the most creative way of viewing the relationship of Word and Sacrament?

4. Is a 'non-sacramental' service of worship a defective or incomplete form of Christian worship?

CHAPTER 5

━━━▶◉◀━━━

THE WORD AND THE WORDS IN
WORSHIP – PREACHING

Introduction

Preaching is in crisis. This awareness has been with us for some time now, reducing pastoral morale and congregational fervour. But the way out, toward new effectiveness in preaching, is not yet clear. What is quite evident, though, is that the old topical/conceptual approach to preaching is critically, if not terminally, ill.[1]

Talk of crisis can be dramatic and alarmist. A crisis can be 'talked up'. Yet there can be little doubt that in many societies today, and in many Christian communities, preaching does not emerge as an outstandingly effective mode of communication. Doubtless the reasons are complex, and raise many questions about the secularization of society (and its impact upon church communities) and the relationship between preaching and culture. Some preaching *has* been enormously effective in the modern world. Here one thinks not so much of the American media evangelists, with their huge following, nor even of Billy Graham, with his remarkable preaching crusades, but at an arguably deeper level of Martin Luther King in the Civil Rights campaign, and Desmond Tutu in the struggle against *Apartheid*. In the last two cases, one can discern a total coalescing of the concerns of people and preacher for a changed world, and a readiness to hear language and imagery as immediately relevant to their situation. People, preacher and biblical text were all part of the contemporary momentum for change and transformation.[2]

[1] R. L. Eslinger, *A New Hearing*, Nashville 1987, p. 11.
[2] For a discussion of hermeneutics, cf. J. I. H. McDonald, *Biblical Interpretation and Christian Ethics*, Cambridge 1993, pp. 200–46.

Situations which give rise to crisis talk could hardly be more different. The sermon is no more than a conventional element in a conventional act of worship. There is an apparently determined passivity on the part of the congregation, combined with a lack of expectation that anything will change. Such preaching is a non-event. It *may* result from basic errors or misconceptions on the preacher's part, whether about the nature of communication or what is to be communicated. But it is too easy to blame it all on the preacher. Preacher and congregation together may bear a share of the blame. Together they have failed to generate the kind of situation in which the Spirit of God can move. But possibly both are victims of a kind of cultural captivity in which it is very difficult to sing or respond to the Lord's song.[3]

To begin to address this situation is a daunting task, well beyond the scope of this chapter. Its complexity demonstrates the fact that preaching cannot properly be viewed in isolation from the worship and community life of which it is part. If the sermon is a non-event, perhaps much the same is true of the worship. If the sermon is emotional froth, perhaps the worship is like that too. Preaching presupposes a degree of expectation: not of being entertained, nor having one's prejudices or opinions reinforced, but of having the horizons of one's understanding widened and one's commitment to Christian discipleship challenged and strengthened. Yet, while accepting the importance of this lively community context, it is still legitimate to separate out for special treatment some of the presuppositions of effective preaching. Let it be said that preaching is never easy, and that the preacher is ultimately in the hand of God and delivers the message he or she believes to be given from above. Nevertheless, that does not spare the preacher the struggle not only to prepare a sermon that will be effective but also to understand, like any professional, the nature and implications of the task entrusted to him or her. This is what is addressed in this chapter.

This task itself is wide ranging and cannot be discussed exhaustively. However, several important dimensions may be indicated briefly here. One involves biblical interpretation. The New Testament message, as is well known, comes to us from the alien cultural setting of the Graeco-Roman world, two thousand years ago (or the equally strange world of ancient Israel).

---

[3] Cf. chapter 11 below.

Rudolf Bultmann had little need to exaggerate its alien nature
(which perhaps he did); nor Dennis Nineham the difficulty of
communicating across cultures.[4] The horizons of the ancient
world were very different from those of today. Yet the New
Testament writings not only move in the thought world of
demons, 'principalities and powers' and angelic appearances;
they also deal with explosive issues such as 'eating meat offered
to idols', 'Korban' and the table-fellowship at Antioch.[5] In all
such issues there is an attempt to apply, in the relevant cultural
setting, the Christian message or 'good news' as the basic
principle and motive of Christian existence. This is what is
translatable into other cultures and ages. And its translatability
is enhanced in that there is, down the ages, a chain of Christian
worship and witness, each link of which denotes the attempt, in
a different cultural milieu, to express the gospel in contemporary terms. To stand in this tradition and recognize
oneself to be part of this chain is to acknowledge that the gospel
can be translated meaningfully into the language and culture
of today. It does no more, however, than provide an initial
impetus to the process. The actual translation has to be under-
taken afresh in each generation, if not in every sermon or act of
worship.

The second dimension is that of communication. Communication theory can teach us the rudiments of the science, but
preaching has to come to terms with the fact that communication itself has been revolutionized in modern society. In times
past, the preacher was the communicator *par excellence*, the
fountainhead of wisdom and inspiration. As Derek Weber has
emphasized, the media age has changed the situation radically.

> In a media age (filled with messages of all shapes and colours,
> wrapped up in 3-hour films and 10-second sound bites, surrounded
> by computer technology and psychological research into sound
> and image response) the preacher feels like an amateur in a world
> of professional communicators.[6]

The problem must be addressed; it cannot be bypassed. The
effect of television in particular may be to shorten the attention

---

[4] Cf. R. Bultmann, 'The New Testament and Mythology', in *Kerygma and Myth*
(ed. H. W. Bartsch), London 1954, pp. 1–44; D. E. Nineham, *The Use and Abuse of
the Bible*, London 1976, *passim*. For a review of Nineham, cf. R. H. Preston, 'Need
Dr Nineham be so Negative?', *Expository Times* XC 9, 1979, pp. 275–80.

[5] For meat offered to idols, see 1 Corinthians 8; 'Korban' occurs in Mark 7:11;
on Antioch, see Galatians 2.

[6] D. C. Weber, *Discerning Images*, Edinburgh 1991, p. 91.

span, to crave visual images, to seek participation, and to demand straightforward language. Traditional preaching does not accord with these emphases but they may point the way to effective modern preaching. Such questions are addressed below.

Yet the most important dimension of all remains. The 'source' of the message is two-fold: in the immediate perspective the source is the encoder (i.e. the preacher, teacher, liturgist or communicator) but ultimately, it transcends the human dimension. The words of the encoder are designed to convey the Word from Beyond, the address of the wholly Other. Liturgist and preacher as part of the Church, bear witness to the Word from Beyond made manifest in the human dimension in the person of Jesus the Christ. Through him, preacher and liturgist are given a Word to speak; indeed a Word to embody. Underlying our attempts to grapple with homiletics and liturgics is a confidence that the work on which we are engaged is part of a much larger scene, not only in this-wordly terms but in terms of the *communio sanctorum*. Ultimately, it is God's work that we do, and the issues are in his hand.

> All this has been the work of God. He has reconciled us to himself through Christ, and has enlisted us in the ministry of recon- ciliation. God was in Christ, reconciling the world to himself, no longer holding people's misdeeds against them, and has entrusted us with the ministry of reconciliation. We are therefore Christ's ambassadors. It is as if God were appealing to you through us: we implore you in Christ's name, be reconciled to God.[7]

Origins

Preaching is sometimes assumed to be a peculiarly Christian phenomenon and to characterize particularly the Reformed Christian tradition. In fact, it characterizes many religious traditions. After his enlightenment, Siddhartha Gautama, the Buddha, committed himself to a preaching ministry. The Benares sermon, with its kernel of *dhamma*, translated his spiritual experience into intelligible doctrine; the 'sermon on burning' sets forth the Buddhist view of human existence as fevered by passions and thus enslaved to the world.[8] In

---

[7] 2 Corinthians 5:18–20, REB.
[8] Cf. *Man's Religious Quest*, Whitfield Foy (ed.), London 1978, pp. 176–82.

Christianity, the catholic tradition of East and West enshrined a great preaching tradition: Origen, John Chrysostom, Gregory of Nazianzus, Augustine, Ambrose and Savonarola are names to conjure with in this regard.

The prophets of Israel were essentially messengers of Yahweh. The formula 'Thus says the Lord . . .' appears to be derived from the sending of royal messages: 'Thus says my Lord the King . . .' It is a proclamation, to be delivered with sovereign authority. The apprehension of the message falls within the realm of religious mystery and is not fully open to our scrutiny. Often, we deduce, it occurred in the course of intense religious experience; it was accompanied by a commission to convey the message, whatever the consequences, sometimes with more than a sense of urgency, almost a compulsion to utter the divine communication.

Amos at Bethel and Jeremiah at the gate of the Temple are examples of prophecy which assumes the form of a proc- lamatory sermon. Deuteronomy provides further examples of sermons as the instruments of prophetic leadership. A char- acteristic of true prophecy is that it uses intelligible language (cf. Paul in 1 Corinthians 14) and that it reinforces and applies the tradition of Moses, the *magnalia* or mighty works of salvation which God wrought in Israel in the event of the Exodus and at Sinai. Preaching in the prophetic tradition consists primarily of two related forms: the message of salvation and the message of judgement. In addition, it can convey eschatological urgency ('the day of the Lord is near . . .'). These characteristics are carried over into early Christianity. Here, the message of salvation (*euangelion*: good news) predominates; but its obverse is the warning against rejecting God's grace and incurring his judgement, and the eschatological emphasis, though modified by the fact that the Christ has already come in the midst of history, nevertheless remains strong in New Testament proc- lamation.

One of the distinguishing marks of post-exilic Judaism is the emergence of written scripture, the Torah, as focal in the life and worship of the faith-community. With it there came the synagogue, the scribes, rabbinic exegesis – and synagogue preaching. At what point the homily or sermon became a regular part of synagogue worship is unclear, but Luke 4 implies it was not uncommon in Jesus' time, while in Alexandria, Philo was a philosophical preacher with apologetic objectives. However, the rabbinic tradition of preaching was fundamentally exegetical. There were two forms of homily which merit particular note. One was the *proem* homily, in which the preacher selected a text which would enable him to bring the second lesson (from 'the Prophets') into new life and relevance for the hearers and move on from there to elucidate the primary lesson (from the Torah). As with the Pharisaic tradition generally, the emphasis was on the claim of divine obligation on the lives of the hearers. Hence parable, analogy and illustration formed a prominent part of the homily. The second major form was known as the *yelammedenu* homily. Here the starting point was a question put by the leaders of the congregation: 'Let our teacher instruct us . . .' In the ministry of Jesus, the address in the synagogue at Nazareth and the discourse on the bread of life in the Fourth Gospel appear to be of the former type, while questions such as 'Is it lawful to heal on the sabbath?' (Matthew 12:10) appear to be of the latter variety.[9]

That the synagogue homily was at least influenced in its development by external models, especially hellenistic preaching, is very likely, for Greek rhetoric and education had a lasting impact on Jewish practice, even when Greek culture as a whole was rejected as inimical to the Jewish faith.[10] Popular preaching emerged in the Greek worlds with the diatribe, which deliberately adapted philosophy to the popular market. The homily was therefore a homely, conversational presentation of a philosophical position: the word implies 'familiar dialogue'. Vivid illustrations and analogies abounded. Questions – sometimes rhetorical, sometimes direct – brought the hearers into active engagement with the subject-matter. Humour, repartee, stories and a variety of rhetorical devices heightened the effect. In a later phase, however, the homily became much more of a formal discourse or lecture. There can be little doubt that early Christian preaching was considerably influenced by the Graeco-Roman homiletic tradition and that the synagogue homily also mediated rhetorical form and art.

Examples of early Christian preaching in the New Testament suggest that the various strands were well represented in it. The prophetic strand is reflected in the kerygmatic sermons of Peter and Paul in Acts: they proclaim the Christian *magnalia*

[9] Cf. J. I. H. McDonald, *Kerygma and Didache*, Cambridge 1980, pp. 48ff.
[10] Cf. M. Hengel, *Judaism and Hellenism* I, London 1974, pp. 65–83.

or 'mighty acts of God'; they call for repentance, with urgency born of an eschatological faith. Indeed, such prophetic models pinpoint the basic Christian stance from which the scriptures of the Old Testament are 'peshered' or given their distinctive Christian interpretation. However, Paul's address to the synagogue congregation at Antioch in Pisidia (Acts 13:15–41) bears some resemblance to a *proem* homily, though it has been thoroughly Christianized. Another good example of a Christianized synagogue sermon is the speech of Stephen (Acts 7:2–53), while a more hellenistic example is the Areopagus speech in Acts 17:22–31. Paul's preaching is echoed in many of his letters, and homiletic influence is strong in letters such as Hebrews and 1 Clement. The words *dialegesthai* (Acts 20:7, 9) and *homilein* (20:11) both suggest that Paul's preaching invited participation in dialogue and argument.

The main factor which separates Justin's description of early Christian worship from that of the New Testament is that Christian writings have taken their place alongside the Old Testament scriptures, and Christian preaching is basically exegetical. In Origen, the homily expounds a pericope or selected passage verse by verse. Even such unpromising material as the Song of Songs is expounded in this way in two homilies. In Origen, careful commentary or textual study lays the foundations of homiletics, though of course he had his own assumptions about how scripture should be interpreted.[11]

The homily, however, was not the only preaching from Origen knew. He used *logos* to describe a more systematic discourse on a selected theme. Augustine, too, distinguished between homily and sermon, the former being relatively informal and the latter (the *sermo*) referring to a discourse in a great basilica. The *sermo* had a more systematic structure, building up an argument by logical steps and reaching a conclusion which combined the completed argument with an appeal to the hearers. Increasingly, it reproduced the procedures and devices of classical rhetoric, and was a form

---

[11] Origen had a three-fold exegetical method: the literal or direct sense (e.g. Song of Songs is a love poem or lyric); the deeper or indirect sense (the Song is an allegory of Christ and the Church); and the spiritual (the Song offers an image of heaven: the marriage of the Logos and the human soul). Cf. R. P. Lawson, *Origen: the Song of Songs, Commentary and Homilies*, London 1957, pp. 8ff.; R. A. Greer, *Origen*, London 1979, pp. 23f.

that was to have much influence on the Christian tradition of preaching.

Theology

The notion that the Gospels, and much other material in the Bible, are essentially kerygmatic, that is, designed to proclaim God's message of salvation, was given proper prominence by Martin Kahler in 1892. He wrote, 'The real Christ is the preached Christ, and the preached Christ is the Christ of faith.'[12] Thereafter, for the best part of a century, Reformed theology has been 'dialectical', 'kerygmatic', 'the theology of the Word'. Hence it is integrally related to the preaching ministry. Through the work of Karl Rahner and others, this emphasis has also come to the fore in Roman Catholic thinking.

Karl Barth was one of the most outstanding proponents of kerygmatic theology. Particularly in his earlier writings – for example, in *the Word of God and the Word of man* – he gave prominence to the perspective of the preacher, concerned to relate simultaneously to the word of scripture and the world of his hearers. Even in the *Church Dogmatics*, the emphasis he placed on preaching is evident in the way he pinpointed the three forms of the Word of God: (i) the proclaimed Word; (ii) the written Word; (iii) the revealed Word.[13] The proclamation which the preacher makes Sunday by Sunday nourishes the faith of the Church. It is not *simply* a human process; for where the Word is truly proclaimed, the Holy Spirit is at work in the proclamation leading the hearers into truth (cf. John 16:13). Indeed, it has been suggested that we can apply the full Trinitarian analogy and develop – but with suitable caution – the relation between the written Word and God the Son, and the relation between the revealed Word and God the Father.

> The New Testament seems to require these analogies. They are not artificial dogmatic constructions, but reflect truly the fact that it is the Father who creates and commands with his Word, that it is the Son who is the expectation of the Old and the witness of the New Testament, and that it is the Holy Spirit who leads us into the full truth after the Ascension.[14]

[12] *Der sogennante historische Jesus und der geschichtliche biblische Christus*, Leipzig 1892, p. 63 (E.T., Philadelphia 1966).
[13] Cf. *Church Dogmatics* I.I; E.T., Edinburgh 1936, pp. 98–140.
[14] D. Ritschl, *A Theology of Proclamation*, Richmond, Va. 1963, p. 29.

On the other hand, one could claim that all three 'persons' or 'modes of being' are present at each stage, and that the christological dimension is particularly relevant to the understanding of preaching.

Rudolf Bultmann combined three main elements in his kerygmatic mode. (*a*) It is dialectical: God is proclaimed through the Word he utters, particularly on the Cross. Bultmann has a strong affinity with Pauline theology: 'We preach Christ crucified . . .'. (*b*) It draws freely from Heidegger's existential analysis of human existence. How does the Word of preaching relate to those who hear it? It summons them to decision. It calls upon them to adopt a new understanding of their own existence: to effect the transition, by the grace of God through his Word, from the 'inauthentic' life of unbelief to the 'authentic' life of faith. Hence, according to Bultmann, biblical language and imagery ('myth'), which derived from an ancient world-view wholly alien to modern man, has to be interpreted existentially. Heidegger's descriptive analysis of human existence, Bultmann believed, was of great assistance in setting out the meaning of the 'new life in Christ' for his hearers. (*c*) It makes full use of biblical criticism to enable us to understand the purport of the text in its ancient context and so identify its essential message for today. Thus, when the biblical text is preached and heard as the Word of God, *something happens*: in Bultmann's terms, preaching is an event that effects change or transformation in the life of the hearer. In some sense, he or she becomes a new being.[17]

This relational aspect of preaching is beautifully developed by Paul Tillich in a justly celebrated sermon:

> Sometimes at that moment a wave of light breaks into our darkness, and it is as though a voice were saying: 'You are accepted. *You are accepted*, accepted by that which is greater than you, and the name of which you do not know. Do not ask for the name now; perhaps you will find it later. Do not try to do anything now; perhaps later you will do much. Do not seek for anything; do not perform anything; do not intend anything. *Simply accept the fact that you are accepted!*' If that happens to us, we experience grace. After such an experience we may not be better than before, and we may not believe more than before. But everything is transformed . . .[18]

---

[17] For an introduction to Bultmann's thinking and its relationship to Heidegger, cf. J. Macquarrie, *An Existentialist Theology*, London 1954.

[18] *The Shaking of the Foundations*, London 1949, pp. 161ff.

Preaching is therefore a *personal* transaction in the fullest sense: a person-to-person encounter, permeated by grace. The proclamation must be made lovingly, for it is an expression of and a vehicle for the love of God. It is – now and forever – *good news* (gospel), even though it carries the pain of revelation of the truth about oneself, or the sting of judgement or rebuke (and the preacher can never exclude himself or herself; he or she, too, is a receptor). It is gospel because, if it is authentic Word, it conveys with the judgement the assurance that God accepts us *now*: that this gracious moment of truth is the effecting of the transformation, the *now* of salvation.

Nevertheless, we do well to heed the protest of J. B. Metz and others against the 'privatizing' of the gospel, which occurs when preaching is related too exclusively to the individual.[19] Preaching, like worship, is a community action; and, like worship, it sends us out into the world in Christ's name. 'God so loved *the world* . . .' The ministry of Jesus was a public event, as political as it was spiritual. It is all too easy for preacher and congregation to retreat into the comfortable shelter of some form of neo-orthodoxy. The essential complement of 'orthodoxy' (right belief) is 'orthopraxis': right expression of faith in action. Love to God is inseparable from love to neighbour, and the latter involves action in the world. If Christians are to share in Christ's ministry of reconciliation, then preaching must provide some of the training for this front-line engagement.

Exegesis

Important as it is for the preacher to have a theological understanding of preaching, the acid test comes when he or she sits down at the desk to prepare the sermon for next Sunday. If the preacher is to be faithful to the ministry of the Word, a central concern must be with a sound exegesis. Allied to this is the necessity to communicate with the hearers. The preacher must steer a course, as Karl Barth put it, 'between the problem of human life on the one hand and the content of the Bible on the other'. There are no easy answers to this predicament, nor should anything offered below be interpreted in that way. At most, certain guidelines can be indicated.

(*a*) The preacher owes it to the hearers, to have a knowledge and appreciation of the full range of the Biblical literature

[19] Cf. *Theology of the World*, London 1969, pp. 107–15.

that comprises the canon of scripture, to be aware of the findings of Biblical scholarship and to be able to apply its insights to the interpretation of scripture. All this represents, as it were, the primary elements of his or her science.

The preacher will only reach a defensible and productive resolution of the problem of scripture through an intelligent study of all the evidence. That there is considerable danger in divorcing the academic and the practical (*theoria* and *praxis*) is illustrated from time to time by solecisms perpetrated by churchmen: e.g. the appeal in time of war or conflict to the warlike Yahweh, leader of Israel's hosts in the destruction of her enemies; the appeal to the Mosaic Law to justify capital punishment or opposition to (say) blood transfusion or spiritualism, or the appeal of the first-century codes cited in the New Testament to justify opposition to all forms of abortion or to the relaxing of the law on homosexuality; or the pathetic spectacle of the 'creationist' *versus* 'evolutionist' debate in some circles today. Such 'direct transference' or 'instant exegesis' takes no account of the importance of the context or the difficulty of extrapolating texts in this way.

(*b*) The use of a lectionary assists exegesis. It is helpful to have a carefully arranged selection of passages – usually Old Testament, Epistle and Gospel – related to the Christian Year; for the liturgical season itself is a help to interpretation, and the lectionary provides a discipline for the preacher. One cannot simply repeat one's favourite passages or themes; and the discipline imposed by the lectionary affords greater objectivity to the use of scripture and makes for better coverage of the whole range of biblical texts. Above all, it requires the preacher to clarify his or her understanding of the relationship of Old Testament, Epistle and Gospel.

Whatever part of the Bible it comes from, a biblical passage attempts some kind of crystallization; of faith, tradition, message, understanding of life, or gospel. It is a crystallization that includes the original receptors in the faith-perspective in question. Later generations (including ourselves) are partly excluded from immediate appreciation of this perspective because the original communication presupposed a wholly different cultural setting from our own. Hence the need, in the Church as in Judaism, for interpretation, midrash, exposition –

in short, for the work of exegesis that 'gives the sense', translates and applies the meaning in modern terms. Christian exegesis is Christo-centric, since Jesus the Christ represents the full expression of God's saving work; hence the interplay of Old and New Testaments, and the Christian *pesher* standpoint. Every exegetical sermon, therefore, is a new crystallization of the Gospel of Christ; a new statement of God's acceptance of us in Christ. And this new statement involves the receptors, the congregation. Preaching is an event which changes and reshapes their lives, their community and their world. E. Best concludes his study of exegetical preaching in this way:

> The purpose of all understanding of Scripture is to make Christ appear in his church so that he shapes that church to be like himself. The purpose of the preaching is the formation of the church to be the true body of Christ. The purpose of the devotional study of Scripture is the harmonizing of the individual into the whole which is the church. But the preacher needs to remember that there are more factors at work than his preaching in the shaping of the church to be the true body of Christ. Certainly this takes place through worship and in the sacraments, but it also takes place as the individual members come to their own understanding, form in themselves a new crystallization, and so contribute to the upbuilding of the whole body. The movement is then from Christ through the crystallizations which are Scripture and the history of the church into the crystallization of the sermon and out again to be the life of the Church, which is the life of the risen Lord, and the only crystallization that really counts.[20]

The methods of exegesis are governed by our overall understanding of exegetical interpretation. Careful study of the text, with commentaries, is a prerequisite; but the material from the commentary is not the substance of the sermon. If it were so, the sermon would, almost certainly, be academically over-charged and conceptually inappropriate to the congregation, and it would in consequence lose impact. Commentaries enrich our understanding of the passage and enable us to bring about a more worthy crystallization of the Gospel for the congregation.

'Every sermon should be ruthlessly unitary in its theme,' writes Ian Pitt-Watson, with perhaps some exaggeration.[21] 'This is the first and great commandment!' It is important to

[20] Cf. E. Best, *From Text to Sermon*, Edinburgh 1978, p. 113.
[21] Cf. *A Kind of Folly*, Edinburgh 1976, p. 65.

determine what the central thrust or theme of the passage is. Provided the selected theme is inherent in the passage and not extraneously imposed, it is of much help in establishing a consistent line of approach in the interpretation and exposition, for it establishes the kerygmatic unity – the crystallization of truth – that brings the hearers into active exploration of the meaning for themselves. H. Thielicke commends this textual-thematic kind of approach.

> First, in this way one remains within the text and allows it to be an end in itself. One discovers in it a centre and periphery and one illuminates it on the basis of its main ideas.

> Second, this way of determining the theme not only helps to keep the sermon true to the text but also helps the preacher to achieve order and clarity . . .

> Third, the method is also helpful to the hearer. He retains it better and can more readily pass it on to the others . . .

> But the thematic sermon is helpful most of all to hearers who are interested in a question and perhaps have no desire to listen to any biblical exposition whatsoever.

> This will be true especially of those who are on the fringes or outside the church. They may sit up and take notice when they find that the theme announced is 'The Meaning of Life' and perhaps they will be much surprised to hear a sermon on the Rich Young Ruler subsumed under this theme. They may also recognize that some unexpected problems are dealt with in the Bible.[22]

Forms

Thielicke's exegetical procedure aptly illustrates the relationship between the substance of the sermon (i.e. exegetical concern) and the form which the sermon assumes. Biblical material, in fact, prompts more than one form, as we shall see. Thielicke seems most at home with the thematic (or textual thematic) discourse, but it has its drawbacks.

(*a*) *Thematic preaching.* A descendant or heir of the tradition of classical rhetoric, thematic preaching represents the systematic development of a selected theme, which may be based on a verse, a passage or even a book of scripture. Sometimes parodied as 'three points and a poem', it has an introduction, designed to capture the attention of the

---

[22] *The Trouble with the Church*, London 1966, pp. 63ff.

listeners and to lead them to interested engagement with the substance of the discourse. It develops its argument by means of a series of reasoned steps; not only systematically expounding and commending the theme or thesis, but also refuting objections or counter-theses, as the whole armoury of rhetorical devices – questions, illustrations, anecdotes, quotations, repetitions, similes and other figures – is at the disposal of the speaker. The impact which the preacher hopes to achieve does not operate at the intellectual level alone (even if the argumentative nature of the procedure might suggest otherwise): it is concerned with the emotions and the will, the affective and volitional as well as the cognitive. It seeks a response from the hearers as whole beings. The conclusion, therefore, is not only the goal of the argument: it is the crowning appeal to the listeners, summoning them to respond in faith and obedience to the Word which has been mediated to them through the exploration of the theme.

There is virtually a consensus among homileticians that traditional conceptual preaching simply does not communicate in today's world. One of its ancestors is the *sermo* delivered in the large basilica, with an overtone, perhaps, of the lecture hall or large auditorium. But many of the liturgical settings in which the thematic discourse is used today are not of this type. One thinks of the sparsely attended evening service, or the morning service in a rural area or depopulated city centre; and one reflects also on the TV age, the effect of the mass media on communication, and a whole range of social changes which mark off our age from its predecessors. Is the declamatory form of oration really suitable, when the setting might suggest a more informal, perhaps conversational, type of talk? It highlights the authority of the preacher, but may also suggest that he or she stands 'six feet above contradiction', beyond challenge or questioning, despite the fact that some sermon content may be open to question or positively invite discussion. In considering the most appropriate form of sermon, the preacher must reflect on its relation to the congregation and the liturgical setting. Again, does the thematic discourse lend itself to the exposition of *every* type of scripture, whether prose or verse, narrative or parable, epistle or apocalyptic book? One might take 'race relations' or 'prejudice' as the theme of the parable of the Good Samaritan, but this hardly does justice to the parabolic *story* which Jesus told, which seems to require a different form of discourse, namely one much more directly related to narrative or story-telling. There is therefore a direct relation between sermon form and the nature of the scriptural material.

(*b*) *Popular exposition.* In its early Christian setting, the homily is essentially the exposition and discussion of a passage of scripture (or 'pericope'). The application of the passage to the lives of the participants is kept in view throughout and is sometimes made explicit at the end. As H. J. C. Pieterse has put it, 'We can say . . . that a homily is linked to a pericope, which it expounds verse by verse in a largely analytical way; that it is characterized by an intimate atmosphere and is geared to dialogue with listeners.'[23] Pieterse points out that it is particularly suited to 'factual' texts: by which we take him to mean texts which only come to life for readers or hearers when they are made aware of the background or setting-in-life. For example, to understand what Paul was saying about 'meat sacrificed to idols', one has to learn something of the social and historical situation of the early Christians at Corinth and also of groups and tendencies already forming in their community. It is the preacher's task to elucidate this 'background', so that the whole congregation can read and explore the passage and come to an understanding of Paul's meaning and aim in writing. Thus, preacher and congregation are brought into dialogue not only with each other but with the biblical writer. Their minds meet with his or her mind, and their lives are open to the challenge of the message.

The advantages of this method are considerable. It invests authority not in the preacher (who is seen as a facilitator of interpretation) but in the text. It can be applied to a variety of types of texts: to poems and psalms as well as letters or other prose passages. Taken to its logical conclusion, it would provide opportunity for putting questions to the expositor, and for sharing ideas and insights, and it would thus obviate the inherent weakness of the monologue as a mode of communication.

[23] 'Sermon Forms', in *Journal of Theology for Southern Africa* 36, 1981, p. 12; *Communicative Preaching*, Pretoria 1987, pp. 158–63.

The method as described above lends itself to the smaller, more intimate group: the evening or mid-week service, or the bible study group. The discussion or 'feed-back' may be relatively informal or it may be structured (e.g. dividing into smaller groups). Many may feel that the lack of such opportunities in many churches is an evident weakness, but that preachers and congregations need time to adjust to a new situation which puts the preacher in a more vulnerable position and the congregation in a more active role, which may not be to everyone's liking. But if we genuinely believe that preaching has to do with communicating meaning, both adjustments are essential. One reflects on the need for much more effective adult education in our churches. It is a gap which the expository homily can go some way to fill.

(*c*) *The story sermon.* The Gospels consist largely of stories. The story-teller clearly had an important place in the communication of the early Christian message, and especially the tradition about Jesus. The Old Testament relates the story of Israel, Jesus himself was a skilled story-teller and early Christian preaching focused on the story of salvation. It is surprising, therefore, that many modern preachers tend to make relatively little use of the art of story-telling, except when talking to children or for the purpose of illustrating a thematic discourse. In other words, the modern preacher seems to be much less *dependent* on the story than his biblical predecessors. Yet it is doubtful if narrative texts can be properly expounded without making substantial use of narrative. The story is more than the means of conveying the message. It is not dispensable. In a real sense, it *is* the message. In the interaction of the characters in a given situation and in the drama that is generated in the telling, the hearers are drawn into dialogue with the picture of reality that is created in the narrative. In this way, they are brought to question their own understanding of life in a new and radical way.

To make proper use of the narrative form, preachers must do their homework on the biblical narrative. They must observe carefully how the biblical story-teller structured his narrative, what his aims were and what devices he used to effect them. They must also consider how modern interpreters (preacher and hearer) might engage with the theme of the story as something that matters vitally in their lives. The following is a brief example, using the story of Jonah:

Introduction. How difficult it is to forgive one's enemies! Focus on a telling image of the struggle to forgive: for example, the struggle many former POWs have to forgive their enemies of half a century ago, especially if they received bad treatment at their hands. Or present a picture of individuals who surprised themselves by finding reconciliation possible – though never easy. The story of Jonah is about this very issue.

I. Focus briefly on the power and glory of ancient Assyria, whose capital was Nineveh: on its wars of imperial conquest: on its conquest and subjugation of Northern Israel (Jonah's country), when

> The Assyrian came down like the wolf on the fold,
> And his cohorts were gleaming in purple and gold;
> And the sheen of their spears was like stars on the sea,
> When the blue wave rolls nightly on deep Galilee. (Byron)

The result: the destruction of the country, the ruin of a culture and religion, the dismembering of Israel, the imposition of alien ways. How dreadful, when everything that is precious to you collapses before your very eyes. Such is the legacy of wars, ancient and modern.

II. Jonah, as the prophet of the Lord, is told to go and preach God's message of salvation to the people of Nineveh, the Assyrians whom he hated. Picture the struggle in Jonah's heart and mind. He does not want his enemies to be saved. He prays for their destruction. Focus on Jonah's attempt to frustrate God's purpose by sailing off in the opposite direction. Forgiveness is never an easy matter – even for a prophet of the Lord! Nor was it easy for his people.

III. The story tells of God's determination that human hardness of heart will not triumph. The harder Jonah tries to escape from God, the more God pursues him and returns him to his vocation. The episode of the great fish highlights the struggle between God and Jonah in a most dramatic way. But it is impossible to escape from God. His purpose demands fulfilment, even when we try to frustrate it.

IV. Jonah returns to his mission with a heavy heart, hoping that he will die before he sees the salvation of his enemies. But even that hope is shattered, as God frustrates his tactics time and time again. Finally, the prophet has to face up to the reality he tried so hard to conceal from himself. While he felt such bitterness towards the enemies of his people, God was concerned for all the people of Nineveh – to say nothing of their cattle (which also matter).

Conclusion. Bitterness, resentment, even hatred characterize the human condition, especially when people have suffered terribly. That was Jonah's experience. And one can easily justify to oneself one's implacable hostility. Yet Jonah, who thought he was opposing the enemies of God, learned to his chagrin that God was concerned for these very people. We don't know how Jonah felt after he was compelled to realize how God saw things. Probably a current of resentment would last a long time within him. Maybe he tried to tell himself that God might forgive, but he himself was only human. But, like us, he could not shut out the Voice which says:

> Love your enemies and pray for your persecutors; only so can you be children of your heavenly Father, who causes the sun to rise on good and bad alike, and sends the rain on the innocent and the wicked. (Matthew 5:44–45, REB)

New Developments in Homiletics

'How can preachers work within an increasingly visual culture?' This is one of the most pressing questions faced by homileticians today. This issue, combined with the problems outlined earlier in this chapter, have led some commentators to argue that the sermon is 'under attack'[24] and that 'preaching is in crisis'.[25] Such pressure has led to a number of new approaches to the art of preaching.[26] A central assumption of this section is that 'television and motion pictures have shaped a visually orientated generation'.[27] Our visual culture is like a bank of TV monitors showing many different scenes – it has

---

[24] Klaas Runia, *The Sermon Under Attack, Exeter 1983.*.
[25] Richard L. Eslinger, *A New Hearing*, Nashville 1987, p. 11.
[26] See *A New Hearing* for a clear exposition of new movements within homiletics.
[27] Patricia Wilson-Kastner, *Imagery for Preaching*, Minneapolis 1989, p. 21.

many faces. This section will identify four aspects of this visual culture, and explore what the recent developments within homiletics can contribute to those attempting to communicate in such a rapidly evolving context.

(i) From static points to imaginative moves

One significant shift in our perspective of reality could be highlighted by contrasting the Lumière brothers' earliest film shots in 1895 with recent action movies such as *Rob Roy*, *Braveheart* and the *Batman* triology. This first film, *Sortie d'usine*, was made by a stationary camera as workers left the Lumières' factory.[28] The result resembles a picture with moving figures on it. The current movie industry, represented by the action adventure genre, relies on very different techniques. Tight-editing and rapid cuts combine with movements of camera angles to allow viewers to see and hear far more than they ever could without the camera's aid. David Buttrick recognizes the significance of this shift:

> Times have changed, and so, apparently, has human consciousness. We look at movies from early in our century and laugh at their stilted, fixed-camera unreality. Nowadays a single scene in a television drama may involve hundreds of different camera angles from cameras mounted on moving booms. We view the product and remark its realism. The electronic media are a product of a changed, highly complex human consciousness and, in turn, act on the consciousness of the age.[29]

On the basis of this change in perception Buttrick argues for a similar development in approaches to making moves within preaching. A single, fixed, point of view adopted by a preacher, may seem slow and turgid to an audience more used to rapid shifts in viewing angles.

The parables, for example, provide many opportunities for preachers to invite their listeners to join them in making imaginative leaps. Consider the classic tale of the Good Samaritan (Luke 10:29–37), where the story could be retold from a variety of angles. Persuading the listener to stand by the

---

[28] Lumière film *Sortie d'usine* (1895), in *Early Cinema, Primitive and Pioneers*, a British Film Institute video.

[29] David G. Buttrick, 'Preaching to the "Faith" of America', in Leonard I. Sweet (ed.), *Communication and Change in American Religious History*, Grand Rapids 1993, p. 316. See especially Part 1 on 'Moves' in his *Homiletics: Moves and Structures*, London 1987.

listening lawyer, walk with the religious professionals and lie in the ditch with the mugged traveller could all provide provocative insights into this story.[30] Even a view from the inn might elicit a new response to this familiar parable.

On the one hand, what could be described as a *single-fixed camera approach*, which merely allows the characters to pass across the screen of the imagination, may limit the story's potential power. On the other hand, a *multi-camera approach*, if sensitively handled, could lead listeners into and through a story and so allow them to experience its movement. The power lies not in discovering and making a single point in three different ways, but rather through enabling listeners to step into the story itself and so encounter its original force afresh.

(ii) From monologue to dialogue

A second aspect of our visual culture is an increased suspicion of monologues. Television thrives on conflict, on disagreement, and on discussion. Producers are expected to represent opposing views and so create dialogue and debate. Preachers who ignore this phenomenon are in danger of alienating or at least distancing their listeners. Fred Craddock argues that:

> ... sermons which begin with conclusions and general truths arrived at by the minister in the privacy of a study tend to oppress and treat as less than fully faithful and capable a listening congregation. Today, this is often called the banking method of communicating; that is, the speaker simply makes deposits of information in the mind of the listener.[31]

Craddock is not arguing here for a balanced, tame, or objective style of preaching which lacks passion or vision. He is rather explaining how he came to prefer an inductive approach over a deductive approach for preaching. He suggests *inductive* movement is from the 'particulars to the general', and *deductive* is from 'the general to particulars'.[32] The inductive approach attempts to turn the sermon into a conversation between 'the congregation and the biblical text'.[33]

[30] See McDonald, 'View from the Ditch', forthcoming in *Scottish Journal of Theology*.

[31] Fred Craddock, 'Inductive Preaching' – unpublished paper for the Societas Homiletica – Stetson University, 20–23 August 1990, p. 8.

[32] *Ibid.*, p. 10.

[33] *Ibid.*, p. 12.

In the parable of the Pharisee and the Tax Collector (Luke 18:9–14), for example, a deductive approach might be to begin with the general statement: 'every one who exalts himself will be humbled, but he who humbles himself will be exalted' (v. 14). The parable would be used as a tool to demonstrate and illustrate this truth. An inductive approach, might invite the listeners to reflect on the characters portrayed in this story. How do they act? What do they say? How is it relevant today? These could be questions raised to consider. In short, Craddock's approach to inductive preaching is an attempt to move the authority from the preacher to the text. The congregation is invited to explore it with the help of the speaker, rather than have the answers thrust upon them.

(iii) From single images to visual stories

A third aspect of our visual culture is the multiplicity and plurality of images. Some pictures are static, whilst many others are rapidly moving. In television news, for example, it is not uncommon for disaster images to be placed side by side with sporting images. This constant visual juxtaposition can anaesthetize audiences to the messages conveyed.

In radio programmes, for instance, the location of a 'little picture' within the structure of the overall programme or report can add significantly to the texture of the broadcast. An image, however, may be so powerful that it can interrupt the flow of the programme. The same is true in the context of a sermon. While a picture adds depth and colour, it can so provoke or evoke the listeners' imagination that the preacher loses their attention, or the image is remembered and the message is forgotten. The 'unforgettable' verbal image and visual story is a potentially dangerous weapon.

Preachers who are operating within a visual culture need to develop a sensitivity to using images effectively in sermons. One of the central factors here is to consider the structures made use of by the preacher. In a private interview, David Buttrick argued:

People tend now to think through image systems. Your problem, however, is that a lot of young preachers are trying to preach solely in images; and again, without a logical structure in which these images can form, occur, and mean, they aren't going to do much for you. They are simply going to be images which don't necessarily provoke contemplation.[34]

For Buttrick, images can provoke thought so long as they function structurally. Image piled upon image, without obvious meaning, is one of the confusing characteristics of Post-modernity. Many of the parables are rich in verbal imagery. Take a selection of Lukan parables. They graphically portray, for example, a man who builds his house on rock (Luke 6:48–49), a sower who broadcasts his seed (Luke 8:5–8), and a father who runs, embraces and kisses his profligate son (Luke 15:20). These active images are often woven together imaginatively to create unforgettable stories.

(iv) From dry words to visual plots

Stories built around pictures are another significant aspect of our visual culture. Advertising parables with a materialistic twist often rely on short stories being told through pictures.[35] This contrasts sharply with early advertising in the seventeenth and eighteenth centuries, which relied almost entirely on words to promote its wares.[36] The current primacy of the visual is also to be found in many other longer television programmes and films. Popular hospital dramas, such as *ER*, *Casualty* and *Cardiac Arrest*, increasingly draw on traumas made visually explicit. The sight of stab wounds, grief-stricken relatives, and violent fights in the hospital upsets the equilibrium and adds to the crafted narrative suspense. The tension inherent within cycles of conflict and resolution, as well as multiple plotlines, is often heightened through an image of a traumatized patient or an exhausted doctor. In this context, the well-chosen image speaks many words and adds to the plot development.

[34] David Buttrick, recorded private interview, Vanderbelt Divinity School, USA, 29 March 1994.

[35] See the Wrigley's Spearmint Gum Advert: An attractive man and woman sit apart on a Greyhound bus, they share a piece of chewing gum, they meet, talk and laugh, but the man gets off the bus, in the bar he is pictured alone, he stares sadly at his half of the chewing gum stick, and suddenly the second half appears. She had got off to join him after all! This simple thirty-second story has no words, lively music and over three dozen shots.

[36] Gillian Dyer, *Advertising as Communication*, London 1982. An advert for toothpaste in 1658 from the *Mercuris Politicus* provides a flavour of the beginnings of the verbal craft of advertising: 'Most excellent and approved Dentifrice to scour and cleanse the Teeth, making them as white as ivory, preserves them from toothache ... it fastens the teeth, sweetens the breath, and preserves the Gums and Mouths from cankers.'

'Plot' is the significant word here. Both metaphors and pictorial language contribute to the 'plot' of a sermon. Eugene Lowry's work on *The Homiletical Plot*,[37] is useful in this context. He argues that 'plot' is 'the key term for a reshaped image of the sermon. Preaching is story-telling'.[38] This theme, especially the importance of story-telling, recurs in much recent homiletical literature.[39]

Interestingly, Lowry goes beyond the simple cycle of conflict and resolution found in much contemporary television drama. His approach has been associated with the 'Copernican Revolution' within homiletics.[40] This is the move from a spatial building block approach to sermon preparation, towards a sermon as an '*event-in-time*, a narrative art form'.[41] In Lowry's eyes there are a number of parallels between, on the one hand the preacher, and on the other hand the playwright, the novelist and the television writer. Significantly, however, he does not attempt to mimic the multiple plot development common to most 'soap operas'.

Instead, Lowry identifies a number of stages within the sermonic plot. They could be stated imperatively as: (1) Upset the equilibrium, (2) Analyse the discrepancy, (3) Disclose the clue to resolution, (4) Experience the gospel, (5) Anticipate the consequences. Underlying Lowry's argument is the belief that listeners are more likely to encounter a story for themselves, if they also move through these stages. Assuming a visual culture, one way of making these stages more accessible would be for the preacher to create an image or a scene for each of these stages.

The parable of the Good Samaritan, for example, provides ample opportunity for a number of vivid scenes. Portrayals rich in contemporary imagery might also aid the listeners' movement through this parable. In the mid-1990s a Balkan re-telling might make this tale more accessible. First, upset the equilibrium: a Bosnian Serb soldier lies in a pool of blood on a

[37] Eugene L. Lowry, *The Homiletical Plot – The Sermon as Narrative Art Form*, Atlanta 1980. See also his *Doing Time in the Pulpit: The Relationship between Narrative and Preaching*, Nashville 1985.

[38] *Ibid.*, p. 15.

[39] See Wayne Bradley Robinson (ed.), *Journeys Toward Narrative Preaching*, New York 1990.

[40] Richard L. Eslinger, *A New Hearing*, Nashville 1987, p. 65.

[41] Eugene L. Lowry, *The Homiletical Plot - The Sermon as Narrative Art Form*, Atlanta 1980, p. 6.

road to Sarajevo; he has been hit. Second, analyse the discrepancy: a Catholic and a Protestant soldier, both wearing blue
berets of the UN walk over and ignore him. A bearded, black-
robed Orthodox priest trips over him by mistake, and then darts
to the other side of the track. Third, disclose the clue to
resolution: an elderly Croatian Muslim woman in a tatty brown
shawl kneels beside the soldier. She thinks of her own sons
killed in the war. Fourth, experience the gospel: she wipes the
blood off his face, pulls him on to her wooden cart, and takes
him back to her village. Finally, and perhaps most problematical
in this interpretation, anticipate the consequences: A Bosnian
Serb journalist writes the story up. His headline is: 'The Road
to Peace.' Such an approach relies upon well-chosen pictorial
language to develop the plot.

Many homileticians underline the importance of using vivid
pictorial language, 'words which you can see, smell, touch, hear
and feel'.[42] For others, 'imagery' in preaching means more than
pictures; it includes the whole physical and sensory dimension
for the world portrayed in a sermon.[43] One of the strengths of
verbal imagery is that it can work on many different levels,
feeding different parts of the listeners' imagination. It is
potentially multi-dimensional.[44] If David Buttrick is correct
when he asserts 'pulpit language must relate to a new twentieth
century consciousness that is simultaneous, perspectival and
complex',[45] then the use of verbal imagery partially answers that
need.

The writer and preacher, Fred Buechener, speaks evocatively
of 'preaching the King who looks like a tramp, the prince of
peace who looks like a prince of fools, the lamb of God who
looks like something hung up at the butcher's.[46] Such visual
language in preaching has the potential to act like a 'magnet'
drawing 'a cluster of reflections and emotions'.[47] This imagery
is drawn from a scholar already cited, who has been described
as one of the fathers of homiletics, Fred Craddock. A recurring
theme in his work is the importance of a well-selected verbal

[42] Edward F. Markquart, *Quest for Better Preaching*, Minneapolis 1984.
[43] Patricia Wilson-Kastner, *Imagery for Preaching*, Minneapolis 1989, p. 20.
[44] Wilson-Kastner highlights the 'rich ability of images to sustain many meanings'.
She describes this as 'multidimensionality', *ibid.*, p. 54.
[45] David Buttrick, *Homiletic – Moves and Structures*, London 1987, p. 56.
[46] Fred Buechner, *Telling the Truth, The Gospel as Tragedy, Comedy and Fairy Tale*,
San Francisco 1977, p. 60.
[47] Fred Craddock, *Preaching*, Nashville 1985, p. 197.

image.[48] A preacher who imaginatively experiences the world of the scriptural text will also be more open to the visual opportunities it provides. Homiletician Charles Rice argues that 'if we have an experience of the text, allow ourselves to be led deeply into its images – in our mind's eye to see its people, places, and things – to experience its language as a new dawning, there is every likelihood that the resulting sermon will in form and content, rely upon and awaken the imagination'.[49] One of the great strengths of pictorial language is its ability to create images on the screens of the listeners' imagination.

Another relevant strand of scholarship within homiletics, partly prompted by our increasingly visual culture, explores the relationship between the imagination and preaching. Paul Scott Wilson's *Imagination of the Heart* and Thomas Troeger's *Imaging a Sermon* represent two key texts in this field.[50] Both writers recognize the power of words to create images and stories which could aid the listeners' encounter with God.

Conclusion

There are signs that preaching is bravely facing its critics and enjoying a renaissance in some areas. As a face-to-face medium, relying primarily on verbal communication, preaching stands out as a rare species in a media-saturated society of mass communication. Preachers cannot afford, however, to ignore our increasingly visual context, nor should they acquiesce entirely in its more seductive images. Both the theory and practice of homiletics need to continue to adapt to an environment where many listeners will become more used to interactive and visually based communication.

Many homileticians are now attempting to come to terms with this rapidly evolving visual culture. The attention given to imaginative moves, dialogue, visual stories and pictorial language is a vital part in this process. There is much to learn

[48] Fred Craddock, *As One without Authority*, Nashville 1979, p. 78.
[49] Charles Rice, 'Shaping Sermons by the interplay of Text and Metaphor', in *Preaching Biblically*, Don M. Wardlaw (ed.), Philadelphia 1983, p. 104. Also cited by Richard Eslinger in *A New Hearing*, p. 22.
[50] Paul Scott Wilson, *Imagination of the Heart – New Understandings in Preaching*, Nashville 1988, and Thomas Troeger, *Imagining a Sermon*, Nashville 1990. See also Derek Weber, *Preaching to be Heard in a Televised Age*, Edinburgh; unpublished thesis, 1993.

from the varied faces of our visual culture. Preaching, however, in both method and content, should always maintain a counter-cultural edge. There is a time to be iconoclastic and a time to be iconofiers.[51] There is also a time to speak, and a time to be silent.

FURTHER READING

E. Best, *From Text to Sermon*, Edinburgh 1978.
D. Buttrick, *Homiletic – Moves and Structures*, London 1987.
F. Craddock, *Preaching*, Nashville 1987.
R. L. Eslinger, *A New Hearing*, Nashville 1987.
I. Pitt-Wilson, *A Kind of Folly*, Edinburgh 1976.
T. Troeger, *Imagining a Sermon*, Nashville 1990.
P. S. Wilson, *Imagination of the Heart – New Understandings in Preaching*, Nashville 1988.

FOR DISCUSSION

1. Is there a difference between preaching and teaching? If so, what is it?
2. In what ways may the use of commentaries be helpful or unhelpful to preachers?
3. How would you distinguish an 'inductive' from a 'deductive' approach to preaching?
4. How can the preacher set about creating images on the screens of the listeners' imagination?
5. Do you agree that TV has transformed the whole business of communication in the modern age? If so, how can preachers learn from it, and what should they avoid?

---

[51] Gregor T. Goethals, *The Electronic Golden Calf*, Cambridge, Mass. 1990, p. 153. Goethals also uses the word 'iconofiers', in the parallel context of creating symbols of faith.

CHAPTER 6

THE WORD AND THE WORDS IN WORSHIP – PRAYER

Prayer as Dialogue

Prayer is like a dialogue between God and his people; a kind of conversation which sustains and deepens a relationship and is indeed virtually indispensable to that relationship. The relationship is continuous. Prayer in the sense of time set aside for this particular dialogue is not continuous, although prayerfulness, a prayerful attitude, should inform the whole of life.

In suggesting that prayer is to be understood on the analogy of dialogue or conversation – an image which must not be pushed too far – we are explicitly excluding the idea of prayer as magic, a matter of spells and incantations. Christian prayer has indeed been understood as magic – witness the English term for jugglery or deceit, 'hocus pocus', very possibly derived in the seventeenth century from the Latin of the Mass, *hoc est corpus meum*. Malinowski and other anthropologists make a clear (perhaps too clear) distinction between magical and social language in prayer. Magic is concerned with the control and manipulation of supernatural forces, it is an impersonal and rather mechanical way of achieving one's ends. Social use of language (in prayer or otherwise) is concerned with the establishing and nurture of relationships, with 'bonding', with the establishment of fellowship through communication. The distinction between the social and the magical use of language is helpful, but should not be pressed too far; many actual instances of prayer language have an intrusive magical element. But Christian theology has a well-grounded tendency to be suspicious of magical language in worship, and prefers to understand prayer socially, or as a dialogue. It also follows from this that Christians do not understand prayer as primarily self-exploration. It is rather an encounter with God which inevitably issues in self-examination and a deepening of self-understanding. Similarly, prayer should not be understood simply as a form of psychological hygiene, although prayer may well be cathartic or result in an improved sense of well-being and peace.

The shape, tone and content of any dialogue are always determined by the participants. The Boston newspaper which in reporting the visit of a famous preacher said, 'Never before had so eloquent a prayer been addressed to a Boston congregation', was confused about the parties to the prayer-dialogue; but perhaps pardonably since some public prayer does give the appearance of being addressed to the congregation rather than to God. But if we assume that Christian prayer is addressed to God, that God is a participant in the prayer-dialogue, particular understandings of God must deeply affect the understanding and practice of prayer.

Jesus shocked the people of his time by teaching that we should approach God confidently, joyfully, simply as children coming to Daddy, *Abba* in Aramaic. The use of the term *Abba* was so striking that it survives in its Aramaic form in the New Testament (Mark 14:36; Galatians 4:6; Romans 8:15) and lies behind the slightly more formal 'Our Father' with which the Lord's Prayer begins. The use of this term in prayer, as James Mackey writes, 'at once gives expression to the lived conviction and appeals for its continuance, the lived conviction, namely, that God cherishes all things great and small, and all people, good bad and indifferent, as a father cherishes his children. Like so much taught by Jesus, it is disappointingly simple to say, and all but impossible to live.' The Church down the ages has spent much energy trying to escape from the simplicity and directness of Jesus' teaching on prayer. His 'model prayer', The Lord's Prayer (Matthew 6:9–13; Luke 11:2–4), his own practice of prayer and the things he taught all suggest the availability of God to listen to the prayers of his people, his readiness to respond, and the similarity of prayer to conversation within a loving family. It is this basic conviction about the nature of God, his approachability and loving responsiveness, which gives Christian prayer its distinctive shape and mood and content and calls for language, words, appropriate to the encounter with this loving *Abba*, Father, Daddy, who draws his people to participate in the outworking of his purposes and the life of his Kingdom.

The Place of Formulae

In everyday language we constantly use formulae – forms of words which sometimes do not have a very easily specifiable meaning, or are used with scant regard to the meaning of the words (which may not even be known) because it is the social function of the formulae which is important. We say 'hello', or 'hi', 'goodbye', or 'cheerio' simply as formulae of greeting or farewell. We send letters with 'yours sincerely', or 'yours faithfully', and it certainly does not guarantee the honesty or integrity of the writer. 'How do you do?', seems well on the way to ceasing to be a question expecting any answer. And in Britain at least, many conversations start with a highly formularized little exchange of comments about the weather.

Such formulae are a necessary part of social interaction. We teach our children to say 'please' and 'thank you' even when the words bear little relation to what they are, in fact, feeling. These are not only signs of good manners, but tutors of feeling and not an unimportant part of the socializing process, the induction into a particular community and set of relationships. Much conversation never gets beyond the level of formulae – polite, cocktail-party chit-chat, what is often labelled 'small talk'. Indeed, formulae may be used as a way of avoiding real conversation, real dialogue, real encounter. We may even convert them into magical spells, or allow over-familiarity to deprive them of meaning. But there is also a sense in which formulae may be the preliminary to real conversation, the prelude to frank and fresh interaction. We can use formulae as a way of defending ourselves against real meeting, or as a kind of testing the water before we plunge into significant conversation.

Prayer, and particularly public prayer, is full of such formulae and set forms. Most of them are familiar and much loved, with all sorts of associations gathered around them. But if you asked the members of an average congregation what 'Kyrie eleison', 'Amen' and 'Halleluia' mean, you would get a bewildering diversity of replies and, if people were honest, a large proportion of 'don't knows'. It would be interesting to know what worshippers today make of the phrase 'world without end' with which so many prayers are concluded. A long obsolete translation of the Latin *in saecula saeculorum*, meaning 'For ever and ever', or 'throughout all ages', the old phrase continues vigorously in use although it conveys either no meaning at all, or a misleading one.

Much of the language of public prayer is constantly repeated. This is as characteristic of most extempore prayer as it is of more formal liturgical prayer. Phrases, sentences, and whole prayers such as the Magnificat, Nunc Dimittis, and the Lord's Prayer are used so frequently in worship that reformers of a puritan inclination dismiss them as 'vain repetitions'. It is, however, a mistake based on a wrong translation of Matthew 6:7 to suggest that Jesus rejected the repetition of familiar forms in prayer. The Greek term *battalogein* translated in the Authorized Version as 'use in vain repetitions', is better rendered as 'to heap up empty phrases' (RSV) or 'to go babbling on' (NEB). The clear intent of the verse as a whole is to discourage pointless verbosity in prayer rather than repetition. It would appear that Jesus himself used repetition in prayer (Matthew 26:44), as any pious Jew would be accustomed to doing, and did not see the new intimacy in prayer into which he introduced his disciples as excluding the use of set forms or in any way incompatible with participation in the formal prayers of the temple and synagogue.

Like the formulae of everyday conversation, prayer formulae can be the preliminary to, and a training for, a more profound, spontaneous, and direct dialogue. And the movement from the formalities to more authentic and revealing communication is often a penetration into the depths of meaning and imagery contained in the formulae rather than a passing beyond the formulae in such a way that they are made dispensable.

The Shape of Prayer

All dialogue has a shape, a flow, a movement, a structure. Otherwise it would be nothing but meaningless jumbles of words, phrases and sounds, very much the 'babbling on' that Jesus warned his disciples against in their prayers. All public prayer must have shape; but some prayers in shape and sequence are more spiritually and aesthetically satisfactory than others.

The various kinds of prayer may be classified in terms of their purpose and content. Not all are indispensable in every act of worship, but an awareness of the various types of prayer helps us to maintain a proper balance in worship. There is also a sequence, a development from one kind of prayer to another, which has been found in the experience of the Church to be psychologically and spiritually helpful and to fit naturally into the movement of Christian worship. The various forms are not wholly distinct from one another and tend to flow together. Perhaps we should regard them as ways of focusing the content of prayer. A list of the main types is as follows: the order in which they occur is variable. Here we follow roughly the sequence of an act of worship which reflects the shape of the Eucharist:

(*a*) *Adoration.* Here, at the start of worship, the worshippers remind themselves of the presence of God, turn their attention to him, and enjoy his company, giving him the glory and the love that is his due. It thus sets the tone for the whole of worship: the focus is on God and not on ourselves, on God's wonderful love and power and faithfulness, rather than on our own feelings.

(*b*) *Invocation.* This is a prayer asking for God's presence and help in our worship, so that it may be worship 'in Spirit and in truth', acceptable to God and enlightening to his people.

(*c*) *Penitence or Confession.* Briefly, and early in the service, we think of ourselves in the light of the glory of God. Shame, penitence, sorrow are expressed for all the ways in which we have fallen short of God's glory and failed in his service. We have broken our relationship with him; now we seek his forgiveness to restore that relationship, a forgiveness which is declared at the end of the prayer.

(*d*) *Supplication.* Still focusing on ourselves, and before we turn back to God and the needs of the world, the prayers of penitence and confession are naturally followed by a prayer for some special graces and for God's help in living as disciples.

(*e*) *Illumination.* In the context of the Ministry of the Word, and usually before the sermon, or sometimes before the scripture readings, comes a prayer that our minds may be illuminated so that we can hear and understand what God is saying to us, and respond with alacrity and joy.

(*f*) *Intercession.* At the beginning of the response to the Word of God, in the prayers of intercession the needs of the Church and the world are offered to God, often in very specific terms, with people in need being prayed for by name and the issues of the day and the concerns of the congregation being remembered in some orderly sequence.

(*g*) *Commemoration* of the Blessed Departed. In churches of the Roman Catholic and Orthodox traditions it is customary to pray for the dead, and to ask the saints and the Virgin Mary to pray for us. The Reformation rejected prayers for the dead as superstitious and too closely tied to the belief in Purgatory, and prayers for the intercession of the saints as impugning the sole mediatorship of Christ. Most Protestant churches now encourage a prayer which is a kind of extension of the prayer of thanksgiving (and may come at the end of that prayer rather than after the intercessions), giving thanks for the life of all the faithfully departed, and asking that we may be strengthened to follow their example. It is desirable, however, that even those who feel continuing theological difficulties involved in prayers for the dead should be reminded that their prayers are joined with the prayers of all the saints in earth and heaven, and in that sense we pray with the saints in heaven and they presumably pray for us even if we feel it inappropriate to pray for them!

(*h*) *Thanksgiving.* This is, of course, the heart of the Great Prayer of the Lord's Supper, and in a very real sense thanksgiving, the praise and glorification of God, is the heart of all prayer. Thanksgiving is accordingly most properly one of the climaxes of a service, whether or not that service be a celebration of the Lord's Supper. It is placed at this point in the service because thanksgiving is the dominant note in the response to the declaration of God's truth and love in the Ministry of the Word. We give thanks for what God has done and will do – leading naturally to a commitment to his service.

(*i*) *Oblation.* In this prayer the whole Church, each individual Christian in fellowship with one another, with the Body of Christ in every land and every age, and with the Risen Lord, offers herself to the Father to be used for the work of the Kingdom. In the Lord's Supper this prayer commonly comes at the end of the Great Thanksgiving; in other services it may appropriately be allied to the dedication of the offerings of the people.[1]

Prayers may also be classified in terms of their structure, or form.

1. *Collect.* This highly developed and much loved form of prayer has a simple and clear structure, encourages succinctness, and is often of great beauty. Collects usually consist of five parts: (*a*) an address to God; (*b*) a relative clause indicating the activity or attribute of God on the basis of which we approach him; (*c*) the petition; (*d*) the purpose of the petition; (*e*) a doxology, and (*f*) the conclusion declaring the sole mediatorship of Christ. For example:

(*a*) Almighty and everlasting God,
(*b*) by whose Spirit the whole body of the Church is governed and sanctified;
(*c*) hear our prayer which we offer for all your faithful people;
(*d*) that each in his vocation and ministry may serve you in holiness and truth
(*e*) to the glory of your name;
(*f*) through our Lord and Saviour Jesus Christ.

(Alternative Service Book collect for Good Friday)

Some of the parts may be omitted, but a collect is always terse and follows strict rules of rhythm and development. But all the short prayers are not collects, and the collect is only one of the forms of prayer available. Collects have a significant place in worship, particularly at the start of worship (when people are collected), or as a summing up of prayers or of the theme of the Ministry of the Word. But the public prayer should never be allowed to become great strings of collects, and nothing else.

2. *General Prayer.* This is a prayer the contents of which is general rather than specific. It is usually longer and more loosely constructed than a collect, but classic prayers of this sort such as the General Confession and General Thanksgiving of the Book of Common Prayer, the Prayer for the Whole Estate of Christ's Church in the Church of Scotland *Book of Common Order*, 1940 (itself derived from a similar prayer in the *Book of Common Order* of 1564) and indeed the Lord's Prayer itself are

[1] This list is somewhat indebted to that in Raymond Abba, *Principles of Christian Worship*, London 1957, pp. 87–96. Cf. the *Book of Common Order of the Church of Scotland*, Edinburgh 1994.

splendid instances of English prose, dignified, lucid and musical. The danger with general prayers is that they tend to become verbose and lacking in unity unless very skilfully composed. And by definition their content is general rather than specific to the time, place and congregation.

3. *Bidding Prayer.* In this form of prayer a list of subjects for prayers of thanksgiving or intercession is given out, either interspersed with versicles and responses or followed by a period of silence and a brief prayer summing up the prayers offered. Most modern liturgies suggest this form for the prayers of intercession. It has the virtues of being highly adaptable and combining extempore elements – or even spontaneous prayer from members of the congregation – and set forms within a clear and simple structure.

4. *Litany.* This is a responsive prayer, rather like a bidding prayer, but usually excluding any extempore or spontaneous elements. Many of the older litanies, such as that in the English *Book of Common Prayer* or those in the *Scottish Book of Common Prayer* (1929) are comprehensive and lengthy prayers, really amounting to a special office in their own right. Modern litanies, such as the two litanies of intercession in the Church of South India *Book of Common Worship*, are far shorter and almost indistinguishable from bidding prayers. The traditional Western litany was a long chain of very short phrases, going through Invocations, Depreciations, Observations and Suffrages, with a concluding collect and often Kyries, the Lord's Prayer and other elements added. Many of the traditional litanies can still appropriately be used in whole or part on special occasions, but are too long and often too archaic to be used frequently.

5. *Acclamations.* Many modern liturgies have restored this ancient form of prayer said, sung or shouted out, by the people. In the eucharistic prayer of the Roman Mass the people say immediately after the words of institution:

Christ has died,
Christ is risen,
Christ will come again.

or another brief acclamation.

Most other modern forms of worship also have acclamations for the people. In addition, the *Sanctus* and *Benedictus* are more properly classified as acclamations than as responses.

6. *Versicles and Responses.* These are short responsive prayers, sometimes used as an introduction to a prayer, sometimes forming a shorter litany in an office such as the *Book of Common Prayer* Matins, or the Office of Compline.

7. *Free Prayer.* For long, charismatic sects were the main groups that allowed members of the congregation to have a 'speaking role' in public prayer, apart from set responses and prayers said together. It has recently, however, become common in most of the mainline denominations for opportunities to be given to members of the congregation to pray aloud, particularly in the prayers of intercession, confession and thanksgiving. The re-introduction of this primitive practice is often met with some initial but short-lived embarrassment, yet quickly it is accepted as a privilege which adds reality to prayer and greatly improves the sense of participation as well as blending surprisingly well with the more formal prayers.

All prayer has a shape, which may be more or less adequate. 'If in transacting business', wrote Calvin, 'some form must always be observed, which public decency and therefore humanity itself require us not to disregard, this ought specially to be observed in churches.'[2] This applies whether the prayers in question are an ancient or modern set form, composed for the occasion (or 'conceived' prayers, to use Isaac Watt's phrase) extempore (not prepared word for word before the service), or free, when members of the congregation may lead in prayer as they wish and the Spirit moves. The single most important reason why shape or form is important in public worship is that it is far easier for the members of the congregation to appropriate and make their own clear, well-structured prayer than to enter into a disjointed and loosely structured prayer. This may be perfectly appropriate in private or small group prayers, but does not 'work well' in the necessarily rather more formal setting of public worship.

There is an emerging ecumenical consensus that there is a proper place in public worship for all these kinds of prayer, that they blend well together, and that this provides a more balanced experience of prayer for the congregation than the use of one kind alone. The great classical prayers, together with the best modern prayers, remind worshippers of the great heritage of Christian devotion, broaden and deepen their

---

[2] Cited in R. Abba, *op. cit.*, p. 107.

spiritual horizons, remind them that they pray in solidarity with the whole Church, and are so rich that they can be used again and again without exhausting their meaning. Extempore, composed or free prayer allows for the freedom of the Spirit, and recognizes that it is a particular congregation in a particular place at a particular time which is praying, and has specific matters to bring before the Lord. A sensible combination of these kinds of prayer in public worship shows that they complement and fertilize one another, and together enrich and enliven the congregation's experience.

The Word beyond Words

In ordinary conversation we often find it hard to pass beyond polite formalities to a real encounter with other people and significant conversation. Most people have the experience of coming away from a party feeling that everything has been at a superficial level; people have kept one another at a distance and never got beyond small-talk to matters of importance. We have already argued that conversational small-talk and polite formalities have important functions in social relations, as do their equivalents in prayer. Polite but superficial exchanges come alive if we suddenly realize that the person who is asking 'How do you do?' is really interested in us, really cares for us, and wants an answer which is honest and detailed, not just a verbal push-off. And besides, such conversational formulae can be the preliminaries to a real encounter even when they themselves are not invested with much significance.

Set forms of prayer are not prayer-wheels or magic, earning merit by their repeated incantation. Rather, they prepare us for, and open us to, the possibility of a more profound, authentic, and disturbing encounter with God. This encounter, like all encounters, involves communication. But no language can be really adequate for communication with God and his people. Nevertheless, real communication in prayer can take place through set formulae, now 'come alive' and used with a fuller awareness of the richness of meaning, in coherent, balanced and rhythmic sentences, or in the 'inarticulate groans' in which the Spirit himself pleads for us, because we do not know how to pray as we ought (Romans 8:25, NEB). True prayer is spontaneous, honest, personal, and from the heart; it is a kind of lovers' discourse. And lovers' conversation is not always very polished or grammatical or coherent. What matters is that it comes from the heart.

Lovers often communicate in silence, gazing into one another's eyes, or sitting quietly side by side, holding hands and simply enjoying each other's company with a quiet confidence and joy. In worship, too, there is an important place for silence, the quiet in which the congregation together can enjoy the company of God. Most people need some training in the use of silence in prayer, and some preparation for it, or the time of silence has an atmosphere of tenseness, the uneasy quiet of those who expect every moment to be filled with words, the children of a culture that is saturated with words, tired of words, and distrusts words. The silence in prayer should be the silence of lovers, enjoying one another; the silence in which one appropriates and adds to the spoken prayers; and above all, the silence in which the worshipper stops chattering and listens to the Word, to the other party in the dialogue of prayer.

The Language of Prayer

Christian prayer is properly in the common tongue, in ordinary speech. In this Christianity differs from many other religions which make an emphatic distinction between the sacred language used in worship, and often not understood by the people, and the profane language of everyday discourse. For Muslims, nothing can take the place of the Arabic Qu'ran. The tendency to use a special language for worship is widespread, and it is often felt that it is proper if the language of prayer is not understood. The obscurity and specialness of the language safeguards and emphasizes the mystery. At the time of Jesus a large number of Jews did not understand the Hebrew of the scriptures and the synagogue prayers. The Scriptures were read, first in Hebrew, and then a *Targum*, or paraphrase in Aramaic, the *lingua franca* of the Levant, so that the people got the gist of what had been read in the unknown sacred tongue.

It would appear that from the beginning Christians believed that prayer should not be in a strange and sacred language; ordinary language was the appropriate vehicle for the new and intimate kind of communication between God and people which had been made possible by Jesus. Early Christian prayer may have been commonly in Aramaic – so the survival of words such as *Abba* and *Maranatha* in the New Testament would suggest. And from early times it is clear that Christians used the Septuagint, the Greek translation of the Jewish scriptures, in preference to the Hebrew. The earliest Christian documents to have survived, including many prayers, are in *koine* Greek, the common, ordinary language of most of the Mediterranean basin. Time and again in the early centuries of the Church there is evidence to suggest that there were no doubts or hesitations about the need to translate the Bible and the liturgy into the language actually spoken by the people.

But there appears to be an inherent tendency towards archaism and contrived mystery in the language of prayer, and gradually this infected the Christian Church. By the ninth century some theologians were arguing that only the three languages of the superscription on the cross – Hebrew, Latin, and Greek – were legitimate for Christian worship. These three were recognized as 'sacred tongues'; the emerging vernaculars were profane and undignified. This argument was used against Cyril and Methodius, who translated the liturgy into Slavonic. Ironically their translation continued in use unchanged for many centuries after it, in its turn, had ceased any longer to be intelligible to the ordinary people; such is the conservatism of worship that the ordinary language of many centuries before becomes in course of time a sacred tongue, shrouding rather than communicating the mysteries of the faith.

The most obvious example of the perpetuation in worship and church usage of an archaic language which only a small and declining minority understand is the use of Latin in the West. Originally adopted as the language of the people (rather than Greek, which had become the language only of the scholarly elite), Latin spread throughout the Western Church, eclipsing almost all vernacular forms of worship, eventually becoming for most worshippers a mysterious and unintelligible sacred tongue. This, of course, drastically affected the quality of participation possible for the laity in worship. A strange tongue excluded the people from meaningful participation in worship, as this letter from Bishop Stephen Gardiner to Cranmer in 1547 makes clear:

> For in times past ... the people in the church took small heed what the priests and the clerks did in the chancel, but only to stand up at the Gospel and kneel at the Sacring, or else every man was

occupied himself severally in several prayer . . . It was never meant
that the people should indeed hear the Matins or hear the Mass,
but be present there and pray themselves in silence.[3]

In 1661 Pope Alexander VII denounced those who 'in con-
tempt of the regulations and practices of the Church have
reached such pitch of madness as to have translated into French
the Roman Missal'. Such an 'attempt to degrade the most
sacred of rites by both debasing the majesty which the Latin
tongue gives to the sacred rites and by exposing them to the
eyes of the common people' was condemned in the strongest
terms.[4]

As late as 1947 Pius XII argued for the retention of Latin:
'The use of the Latin language prevailing in a great part of the
Church affords at once an imposing sign of unity and an
effective safeguard against the corruption of true doctrine.'[5]
But there are other, and better, ways in which worship may
express the unity of the Church; and even if the Latin liturgy
expresses orthodox doctrine verbally it certainly does not
effectively communicate this doctrine, and opens the way to
all sorts of strange distortions and eccentric misunderstandings of the faith on the part of ordinary people. In addition
the use of a special 'church language' such as Latin emphasizes
the difference between clergy and laity, the elite who know
and use the cultic language, and the majority who are mystified
by it.

The Reformers, with rare unanimity, affirmed that the
vernacular, the language of the people, should be the language
of prayer, just as they stressed the central importance of putting
the Bible, carefully translated, into the hands of the people. 'In
the church', said Luther, 'we ought to speak as we used to do at
home, the plain mother tongue, which every one is acquainted
with.' In this as in so much else, the Reformation strove to
recover the emphases and practices of the early Church: the
whole People of God should participate fully in worship and
this is impossible without understanding. The unnecessary and
artificial mystery of an unknown tongue must be removed if the
true mystery of faith is to become accessible. The use of a dead
language in worship is far more questionable than the ecstatic

---

[3] Cited in R. Abba, *op. cit.*, pp. 23–24.
[4] *Bulla of Alexander VII*, 1661, in P. Guéranger, *Institutions Liturgiques*, Paris 1880,
vol. 2, p. 118.
[5] Pius XII, Encyclical *Mediator Dei*, 1947, London 1954, § 64.

'tongues' that St. Paul sought to control by insisting upon interpretation or translation. Cranmer was typical of the Reformers
in believing that the move to vernacular in worship was clearly
in accordance with the will of God:

> ... God's will and commandment is, that when the people be
> gathered together ministers should use such language as the
> people may understand and take profit thereby, or else hold their
> peace. For as a harp or lute, if it give no certain sound, that men
> may know what is stricken, who can dance after it? For all the sound
> is in vain: so it is vain and profiteth nothing, saith Almighty God by
> St. Paul, if the priest speak to the people in a language which they
> know not ... For (St. Paul) speaketh by name expressly of praying,
> singing, lauding, and thanking of God, and of all other things
> which the priests say in the churches ... ; that whether the priests
> rehearse the wonderful works of God, or the great benefits of God
> unto mankind above all other creatures, or give thanks to God or
> make open confession of their faith, or humble confession of their
> sins, with earnest request of mercy and forgiveness, or make suit
> unto God for anything: then all the people, understanding what
> the priests say, might give their minds and voices with them, and
> say, *Amen* ...[6]

The move to the 'plain mother tongue' did not, of course, mean
that the languages of liturgy and of Bible translation became
conversational or marketplace vernacular. The Reformers
believed in the use of clear, simple and dignified language,
and their most notable productions such as the Anglican *Book
of Common Prayer*, Luther's Bible, and the Authorized Version
did much to shape and encourage the development of the
vernacular.

But the norms of liturgical English laid down between 1550
and 1662 tended to ossify, while the 'plain mother tongue'
developed vastly. This is as true of extempore prayer as of the
authorized forms, for the language of the former was
dominated by the Authorized Version and increasingly
demonstrated the inbuilt conservatism of liturgical language.
As a consequence a good deal of the language of prayer has
become opaque and obscure to many worshippers, and
sometimes conveys a very different message from that originally
intended. Not many worshippers today realize that 'Prevent us,
O Lord' in the familiar collect means 'Go before us, O Lord, to
enable us' rather than 'Stop us from doing'. The schoolboy

[6] Martin Luther, *Table Talk*, E.T., W. Hazlitt, London, p. 185.

who, being asked what 'divers temptations' might be, thought for a moment and then replied, 'Might have been mermaids', was simply demonstrating an extreme case of the misunderstandings generated by the continued use of a cultic language which is now so different from the 'plain mother tongue' of everyday usage. Another complication is that some archaic English has acquired in the passage of time sexist overtones which are understood as excluding a goodly part of the congregation. Even some recent liturgies are replete with gratuitous sexism – 'fellow men' instead of 'fellows', 'all men' instead of 'everyone', and 'men' where 'people' is really meant.

The importance of not using exclusive language in worship can hardly be too strongly emphasized. A faith which has at its heart reconciliation and the overcoming of division and hostility should never in its worship use language which makes whole categories of people feel excluded from the community and from the loving purposes of God. It is not always easy or appropriate to modify or change exclusive language in older material, but modern worship language should be constantly sensitive to this issue. Controversy rages in most of the Churches about whether it is allowable to address God as Mother, but it is now widely agreed that there must in worship be an explicit recognition of the feminine qualities in the Godhead, and that in worship and theology down the ages there has been an unbalanced stress on the masculinity of God and indeed of Jesus, sometimes even suggesting subtly that it was maleness rather than humanity that God assumed in Christ.

A rather different, but no less serious, problem arises from the continued use of the pronouns 'thee' and 'thou' in addressing God. In the sixteenth and seventeenth centuries these were in English, as their equivalents are still in French and German, the intimate terms used in family life or between close friends. 'You' was the more deferential form, used in addressing someone of great status and power. As late as the reign of Charles II a Quaker woman caused a public outcry by addressing the king as 'thou' – it was considered an impertinence. The Reformers' choice of 'thou' language for the address to God was indeed a daring affirmation of what one might call the '*Abba* principle' – that God is above all our Father, and we approach him as children coming to their Daddy. But since the seventeenth century 'thou' language, with all its complicated impediments of verbal inflections, has fallen out of common usage. Except in prayer, no one addresses anyone else as 'thou' and all the associated forms – thy and thine, and wilt and shalt and didst and so forth – have so fallen into disuse that those who lead in prayer frequently land themselves in comic and unnecessary confusions. But the real problem is this: the development of the English language and the entropy of liturgical English have led to an exact reversal of the original theologically well-grounded reason for choosing to address God as 'Thou'. Today some people argue that this preserves a sense of the glory and the otherness of God, of his transcendence, and discourages too easy familiarity with him. But it was precisely intimacy and familiarity which Jesus offered in teaching us to come to God as Abba, and the Reformers tried to safeguard by addressing God as 'thou'. Today sound theology and the Reformation insistence on the use in worship of the 'plain mother tongue' both demand that 'thou' with all its quaint linguistic accompaniments be set aside in Christian prayer.

It has to be admitted, however, that there is still a vast, intractable problem in finding an appropriate and satisfactory English style and idiom for public worship – always remembering that no language can possibly be adequate for speaking with God, or for speaking of God. Cranmer, the translators of the Authorized Version and the others who established the norms of 'church English' which were to last for centuries, were primarily translators who put faithfulness to the text, accuracy and clarity above all other considerations. But, like all educated people of the time, they had been immensely carefully trained in language and the art of writing. Their studies in classical literature and in rhetoric gave them a remarkable sense of rhythm, emphasis and style. They did not use the language of the market place, or conversational English or even slang, but a dignified, slightly formal, but above all clear language. They realized that there is a difference between the language of private prayer and that of public prayer; and that the language of prayer and the language of Bible translation are not the same. Nonetheless, the language of Christian prayer must be soaked in the language of the Bible so that the Bible provides a kind of grid on which worshippers locate the images, concepts, symbols and allusions in prayer.[7]

---

[7] C. S. Meyer (ed.), *Cranmer's Selected Writings*, London 1961, pp. 90–91, cited in D. L. Frost, *The Language of Series Three*, Bramcote 1973, pp. 5–6.

The language of prayer is the language of a community, the Church which cannot be understood without reference to the community's book, the Bible. The philosopher Wittgenstein is certainly right in saying that meaning depends on the context in which words are embedded, and in the case of the words of prayer, this means the household of faith and its book above all else.[8] The language is not esoteric to the community; it 'is not a special sort of language, but just ordinary language put to a particular use'.[9]

Prayer is not a self-contained language-game without imping-ment on ordinary language or the ability to communicate beyond the bounds of the church, although it can degenerate to this. But the language of prayer should help people to break out of the banal literalism of so much modern language and demonstrate the ability of language to penetrate to the depths and lift to the heights, to show the riches and the possibilities so often neglected in the modern world.

The language of prayer is replete with images, metaphors, symbols, and narrative, much, but not all of it, borrowed from Scripture. Some of this material is vibrant and living. Other images, metaphors and symbols seem dormant, or dead and incapable of resuscitation. It would seem that one of the functions of liturgy is to preserve a treasury of images and symbols from which each generation finds some that are meaningful. Sometimes an image that had seemed long dead is suddenly reborn and discovered to be relevant to a new situation. Other symbols seem inaccessible and un-recoverable, embedded totally in ancient contexts alien to the modern experience. And to find fresh imagery which can act as a vehicle for Christian prayer and communicate at the depth of the old is no easy task. A good deal of modern liturgical work has been stripped of so much imagery, symbol and allusiveness that it seems bald, reflecting the banal literalism of so much modern language. Other attempts at a modern imagery do not wear well (for instance, the hymn 'God of concrete, God of steel, God of piston and of wheel', with its rather crude sanctification of modern industry) or are just plain ludicrous:

[8] See A. C. Thiselton, *Language, Liturgy and Meaning*, Bramcote 1976, p. 21.
[9] W. D. Hudson, 'Some Remarks on Wittgenstein's Account of Religious Belief' in *Royal Institute of Philosophy Lectures*, vol. 2, London 1969, p. 40, cited in Thiselton, *op. cit.*, p. 5.

Oh ye thirsty of every tribe
Get your ticket for an aeroplane ride,
Jesus our Saviour is a-coming to reign
And take you up to glory in His aeroplane.[10]

For really fine modern imagery we should turn, as D. L. Frost suggests, to the poets. He instances T. S. Eliot's fine section on the suffering, healing love of God, the wounded surgeon in *Four Quartets*. To that one might add R. S. Thomas's very different, but equally evocative and moving poem, 'The Musician'; the poems of Edwin Muir, and many others.

'What language shall I borrow, to praise thee, heavenly friend?' No language, ancient or modern, is really adequate for prayer, for converse with God. The finest of words 'the tongues of men and angels', we are reminded by St. Paul, are merely noisy gongs and clanging cymbals if separated from love, for the language of prayer is the language of love, which is often simple and fragmentary, but comes from the heart and speaks to the heart. And because prayer language is words offered to God, we should strive to ensure that they are as fresh and authentic and lively and beautiful as may be.

FURTHER READING

D. Z. Phillips, *The Concept of Prayer*, London 1965.
A. C. Thiselton, *Language, Liturgy and Meaning*, Bramcote, Notts 1975.
A. J. Gossip, *In the Secret Place of the Most High*, London (4th) 1957.
J. Dalrymple, *Simple Prayer*, London 1984.

FOR DISCUSSION

1. 'Prayer is like a dialogue between God and his People; a kind of conversation . . .' But how does the dialogue or conversation or communication work? In what way is prayer different from an inner dialogue in which one talks with oneself? How does *God* converse with us?
2. What factors should influence the language of prayer?
3. How important is it that congregations should develop a theological understanding of worship?

[10] Anon, *c.* 1935, in Donald Davie (ed.), *The New Oxford Book of Christian Verse*, Oxford 1981, p. 292.

4. How important is it to insist that the language of prayer in worship should expressly include 'recognition of the feminine qualities of the Godhead'? Why should this be required today rather than in the past? If this demand is resisted, what does that say about the Church today?

CHAPTER 7

BECOMING A CHRISTIAN

Becoming a Christian is the work of a lifetime. It is a long process that begins before the first awakening of our faith and can end only at the moment of death.

According to Christian theology, in the matter of our salvation we are dependent on God's grace. The initiative is always God's. It cannot be ours. Without what is technically known as God's '*prevenient grace*', we would remain unaware of his call to faith. Furthermore, hearing God's call and being able to answer it are completely different matters. To be made able to answer God's call, and to go on doing so, we need what is technically known as '*concomitant grace*'.

A good analogy to this initial phase of the process of becoming a Christian can be found in the operation of the now largely superseded *off-set* printing machines. To make it possible for the printing plates to be properly inked, a priming solution had to be spread over them. A different kind of solution, known as *fountain* solution would then have to be continually spread over the printing plates to make sure that they remained properly inked and continued to work the way they were meant to. Having been 'primed' by God's *prevenient* grace, for as long as we go on being bathed in the fountain solution of God's *concomitant* grace, we will be able to remain in the faith, put on the new self which progresses towards true knowledge the more it is renewed in the image of its Creator[1] and, finally, attain to that maturity which is measured by nothing less than the full stature of Christ.[2]

The relation of God to his People, the world and the *eschaton* is fundamental to the understanding of the revelation of the

[1] See Colossians 3:10.
[2] See Ephesians 4:13.

Old and the New Testament. It is an integral part of God's design that his Name (i.e. his power) should be imprinted in the heart of the hearers of the Word and imposed on the whole of their existence. The Word of God always makes a reality of what it says. Therefore, when God's Word is spoken and heard, its hearers are made to identify with God's final purpose and become consecrated to it as efficacious signs of God's coming universal reign. As Scripture says, in the richness of his grace God has lavished on his people all wisdom and insight. He has made known to them, his Church, his secret purpose to be put into effect when the time was ripe: namely, that the universe, everything in heaven and on earth, might be brought into unity in Christ, for it was his will that those who were the first to set their hope on Christ should cause his glory to be praised.[3] The mystery of God's final purpose, fully accomplished in the person of Jesus, the first-born of the new creation,[4] was unknown to humanity in previous generations, but is now revealed in the Spirit to us, his holy apostles and prophets. The Church is now to show to the principalities and ruling forces of this world how many-sided God's wisdom is, according to the plan which he had formed from all eternity in Christ Jesus our Lord.[5]

God's call to faith, therefore, is not only a call and an enablement to begin to grow into the perfect humanity of Christ, the second Adam,[6] but also a call and an enablement to become a visible instrument of God for the coming of his kingdom within the Body of Christ that is his Church. The primary object of the Church is to live and work to God's praise and glory. God's call to *faith* and *salvation* is indivisible from God's call to *mission*. Therefore, no one could be said to have faith who was not prepared to become a *visible* member of the missionary Body that is the Church. Hence the necessity to have rites in which candidates are publicly initiated into the Church.

In most Christian churches, the rites of initiation have traditionally been three: baptism, confirmation and admission to Communion. These rites are closely bound with one another, with the gospel of Christ and with individual Christian identity. Yet, important as they are, they have been variously interpreted, combined and administered through the history of the

---

[3] See Ephesians 1:8–12.
[4] See Ephesians 1:15.
[5] See Ephesians 3:10.
[6] See Corinthians 15:45–50.

universal Church.[7] The various Initiation theologies we have inherited from the past were little more than rationalizations of current liturgical practices seen in isolation both from the original motive forces that brought them into existence and from the subsequent historical factors that made them what they are. They were *ex post facto* theologies. For this reason, our inherited patterns of Christian Initiation are now being questioned on theological as well as pastoral grounds.

Though the possibility of making proselytes from among the Gentiles was not excluded, in the Old Covenant effective belonging to the People of the Covenant was a matter of physical birthright and correct genealogy. Judaism was, and still is, fundamentally an *ethnic* religion. As Scripture says, in the New Covenant, though former Gentiles, we are no longer aliens or foreign visitors, but fellow-citizens with the holy people of God and part of God's household. We are built upon the foundations of the apostles and prophets, and Christ Jesus himself is the cornerstone. Belonging to the people of God is now the physical birthright of *any* human being who is prepared to respond to God's grace. Through Jesus, then, we all in the one Spirit have free access to the Father, those who were far as well as those who were near.[8] What matters is not the mere performance of a rite of initiation or the imparting of new knowledge, as Pagans and Gnostics believed, but the final result of the process of initiation: a Spirit-filled life in a Spirit-filled community that is totally consecrated to God's purpose.

We are talking here, therefore, of *two* distinct processes: the liturgical/sacramental process of Christian *Initiation* and the wider process of *becoming* of which the liturgical/sacramental process of Christian Initiation is only a part. Though intimately connected, these two processes should never be confused the one with the other.

The Liturgical–Sacramental Process

In the New Testament, the individual's response to the apostolic preaching of the Word is followed by a water-bath and the outpouring of the Spirit, but not necessarily in that order.[9]

---

[7] See e.g. Daniel Stevick, *Holy Baptism*, Supplement to Prayer Book Studies 26, New York 1973, p. 9.

[8] See Ephesians 2:17–22.

[9] See Acts 8:26–39.

By means of the water-bath, the believer did not receive a personal and unconditional guarantee of salvation, but a token, earnest and foretaste of it within a community of believers. The final salvation of the individual baptized depended still on his or her continued obedience to God's will. It was clearly understood that for a Christian there could be no salvation if he or she refused to belong visibly to Christ's Church, or, having done so, to work for the coming of God's kingdom in and through the Church.

We cannot regard the New Testament data on Christian Initiation as the foundation of immutable policies and practices. History teaches us a different lesson. In post-apostolic times, two different patterns of Christian Initiation were already in existence, with theological emphases and nuances of their own that had been obtained through a deliberate policy of adaptation of the original New Testament data to suit different cultural *milieux*.

The first of these patterns of Initiation originated in East Syria and Armenia, two regions of the ancient world that were outwith the borders of the Roman Empire. The *Acts of Thomas*, the *Didascalia Apostolorum* and the Armenian *Order of Baptism* (third to sixth century AD) testify to the following structure:

1. A *messianic anointing* on the head, known as 'marking' or 'signing'.

2. A *water-bath* with triple total immersion in the Name of the Trinity.

3. *Admission to the eucharistic community* and *reception of Communion*.

At a later date, an *anointing* of the *whole body* with consecrated oil for the purposes of *healing* was added to the ceremonies and placed *before* the water-bath. Later on still, a third anointing, this time with a specially consecrated *chrism* (a mixture of oil and balsam) was placed *after* the water-bath. Anointing was known as *hatma*, or '*seal*'. It is not difficult to work out where the inspiration for both of these added anointings came from: in the days in which soap had not yet been invented, one used oil to rub the dirt off one's skin *before* plunging into the bath and, again, a mixture of oil and perfume to restore the proper tone to the skin *after* coming out of the bath itself. These two extra anointings were very probably added to this pattern of Initiation in imitation of what was happening already within the Roman Empire. Their symbolism is not difficult to work out and is amply testified by the Church Fathers and writers of that part of the world: only God can cleanse us from sin and make us as 'new' as one feels after a relaxing bath. The meaning of the original ceremonies is equally clear. In the Old Covenant, God's anointed were his kings, priests and prophets. In the New Covenant, through the ceremonies of Christian Initiation the believer is visibly made a member of the visible royal and priestly body whose purpose it is to speak for God and so be his prophets.

The second of two ancient patterns of Christian Initiation originated instead within the confines of the Empire, in the Greek-speaking world of Carthage and Rome. It contained six distinct moments:

1. *Formal instruction in the faith* before any liturgical action.
2. *Formal renunciation* of Satan and *anointing with the oil of exorcism.*
3. *Water-bath* with triple immersion in the Name of the Trinity.
4. A second *anointing*, originating in North Africa and explicitly associated by Tertullian with the reception of the fruits of the Spirit.
5. A *laying-on of hands* with a further *anointing*, originating in Rome, that – according to Hippolytus – 'sealed' the baptized as members of Christ's Body.
6. First *Kiss of Peace* and *admission to the eucharistic community* (i.e. participation in the Prayer of the Church and reception of Communion.

A discrepancy exists therefore between Tertullian (*c.*160–225) and Hippolytus (*c.*170–236). Tertullian knows of only *one* anointing after the water-bath, whilst Hippolytus mentions *two.* The Hippolytan pattern was characteristic of Rome and Milan. The pattern known to Tertullian continued instead to be characteristic of the rest of the Latin world until the enforced Romanization of its practices in early mediaeval times.

The parallels between the East Syrian/Armenian pattern of Christian Initiation and that of the Western, Graeco-Roman world are self-evident. With the multiple anointings, their final, more developed pattern was based on the common experience of taking a bath. However, the East Syrian/Armenian pattern was more *consecratory* than *initiatory.* Its primary, ostensible purpose was not just the *admission* of the believer into the Church, but his or her *consecration* to the royal, priestly and prophetic messianic Body of the Church. The more immediate

Scriptural sources of this pattern of initiation are to be found in the baptismal imagery of the third chapter of the Gospel of John and in the eschatological/messianic themes of the Gospels of Mark and Matthew. The Graeco-Roman pattern of Christian Initiation is 'later' in feel, more elaborate and more finely articulated. It is more *initiatory* than *consecratory*. Its primary ostensible purpose was *initiation* into the Church, and not *consecration* to its purpose. Moreover, from the fourth century onwards its more immediate Scriptural sources became more and more the baptismal imagery of *death and resurrection* of the sixth chapter of Paul's Letter to the Romans.[10]

By the end of the fourth century, both of these patterns of initiation were fully established. By then, a new problem confronted the Church, namely that of making, the accepted pattern of Initiation meaningful to the newly converted masses. Once again, the problem was solved in different ways in different parts of the Christian world. Taking advantage of his privileged geographical situation on the very scene where the death and resurrection of Christ had taken place, Cyril of Jerusalem (AD 386) strove to show the vividness of the self-offering of Christ through the accepted liturgical signs. More than a little embarrassed by the tendency of a half-converted Empire to think of itself as the kingdom of God, John Chrysostom (AD 354–407) attempted to show through those same liturgical signs the radical challenges of the secular city and stressed the necessity for the believer to re-live in the present the Lord's life, death and resurrection. Living at the edge of a rapidly declining Western Empire, Ambrose of Milan (AD 339–397) pointed instead to the symbols of the transformation of the world brought about by God in Christ. For Ambrose, the cleansing water, the perfumed oil and the white robes of the newly baptized into the family of God were the visible and tangible beginning of an incorruptible world to come. As a member of a small and still persecuted minority outside the Roman Empire, Theodore of Mopsuestia († AD 428) interpreted the baptismal liturgy as a message of hope and as the token of an eschatological reality that had already begun and yet was still to be revealed. Coming from an East Syrian background, Theodore insisted on the role of the Christian community in the coming about of the promised future and,

[10] See Aidan Kavanagh, *The Shape of Baptism,* New York 1978, pp. 3–78.

consequently, on the necessity of the total commitment of the individual to God's plan for the world.[11]

Many, perhaps the majority, of the half-converted masses had become Christian for no more than appearance sake. Because of their pagan background, the greater number of those who had come to believe was more concerned with their own personal salvation than with God's universal plan or their own role in it. In the view of many, the Church (or better, the Church's hierarchy) existed for no other purpose than to procure the salvation of its adherents by means of appropriate ceremonies and the preaching of the Word. In this context, baptism was seen as the principal means to obtain the remission of one's sins. It made sense therefore, in their view, to delay the celebration of baptism for as late in life as possible, lest one should sin after baptism had been conferred. The fact that many, including the Emperor Valentinian, miscalculated and died unbaptized, did not serve much to stop this practice, especially since on the death of Valentinian Ambrose himself solemnly proclaimed from his pulpit in Milan that, although unbaptized by either the baptism of *water* or by the baptism of *blood* (i.e. martyrdom), Valentinian had died baptized by the baptism of *desire*.

Starting from where Ambrose had left, Augustine of Hippo (AD 354–430) added to all this a theory of his own. Since baptism was the only known means of regeneration, when an infant – who by definition was as yet incapable of being baptized by either martyrdom or desire – died unbaptized by baptism of water, it could not possibly be admitted to the life of heaven. No baptism: no regeneration. No regeneration: no salvation. Thanks to Ambrose and Augustine, who did no more than reflect what was being felt at the time, the theology of Initiation of the Western Churches lost sight of the wider *process* of becoming a Christian and turned into the theology of the *rite* of Initiation. Once more, what happened to Rome after its conquest of Greece happened also to the Church after its victory over paganism, as in the well-known Latin tag '*Graecia capta ferum victorem coepit*'![12]

---

[11] See Hugh M. Riley, *Christian Initiation: A Comparative Study of the Interpretation of the Baptismal Liturgy in the Mystagogical Writings of Cyril of Jerusalem, John Chrysostom, Theodore of Mopsuestia and Ambrose of Milan*, Washington DC 1974, pp. 452–55.

[12] In English, 'Having been made a captive, Greece captured its fierce victor'.

In apostolic time, infants may or may not have been baptized, though they probably were – as an exception – on the basis of the '*household*' principle. By the beginning of the third century AD, infants were certainly being baptized in the Rome of Hippolytus, but still in such a small number for it to be still considered as the exception rather than the rule. By the end of the fifth century, however, the Church had already begun to run out of available adult baptizable material. The change of circumstances had been so gradual, that no one actually noticed and so the Church, in a triumph of liturgical conservatism, went happily on baptizing unresponding infants with a rite that had originally been devised for the baptism of fully responsible adults. Baptism was seen as the God-appointed way to take care of both original sin and any other sin the candidate might have committed (as Augustine had taught following in the steps of his mentor Ambrose), there could hardly be a cause for undergoing the upsetting experience of change. As we learn from the *Ordo Romanus XVIII*, the only change to take place was that that baptismal liturgy of the Church eventually gave up the pretence of asking infants to renounce Satan and profess their belief in God and commanded that the infants' *parents* should be asked to do so on their behalf.

To cope with the new situation in which the baptism of a large number of infants had become the rule, the Eastern and Western Churches resorted to different solutions. In the East, the burden of the complete Initiation of infants was left to the local presbyter, who performed the liturgical ceremonies in their entirety. As a consequence, having been fully initiated into the Church, the infant was straightaway admitted to Communion. In the West, the rites of Initiation were split into two temporally separated liturgical units. In Rome and most of the rest of Italy, the local presbyter was allowed to carry out the ceremonies of Initiation up to, but not including, the '*seal*' of the laying-on of hands and the final anointing that were to be performed by the Bishop at some later date. It would appear that, in the beginning, the rest of Europe followed the practice of the Eastern Churches and opted for a complete rite of Initiation to be conferred on infants, but this custom may not have lasted for long. Later on, at the time of the enforced Romanization of their liturgical practices, the Northern nations – who knew only of *one* anointing after the water-bath after the manner of Tertullian – were compelled to administer *two* separate anointings after the water-bath, in the Roman manner of Hippolytus. As a protest against this unwanted change of custom, the Northern nations made a point of administering this compulsory second anointing with laying-on of hands a full week after the celebration of their customary initiatory rites (which they, of course, considered to be already a *complete* form of Initiation). Gradually, the interval between the celebration of the two sections of the rite increased to an interval of months and then years. However, not all the Bishops could or would be bothered to go around their vast Northern dioceses to '*confirm*' the liturgical actions of the local priests. Even when the Bishop did so, unwilling to depart from their ancient customs, not all the candidates would turn up for such a new-fangled ceremony. The result of it all was, of course, utter chaos, until Archbishop Peckham of Canterbury decreed in 1281 that no one was to be admitted to Communion if he or she had not been first episcopally confirmed. This regulation seemed to make pastoral sense and as a consequence the local law concerning '*confirmation*' and the admission to Communion became eventually the law of the, as yet undivided, Western Church. The initiatory pattern was clear:

1. Baptism was to be administered as soon as possible by the local parish priest.
2. Confirmation was to be administered by the bishop after the infant had reached the age of discretion.
3. Admission to Communion was to be allowed only *after* one had been episcopally confirmed.

In this way, some appearance of order was established in the Western Church, in theory if not always in practice, but a heavy price had to be paid. From that moment on, in the minds of many the reception of Communion (that was now to take place only after one had reached the age of discretion) was made conditional to the intellectual ability to understand what it was that was being received. The fact the Communion was supposed to be a mystery (and that consequently only God and his Incarnate Son were likely to be capable of a full intellectual understanding of it) was never taken into account. No one had as yet worked out that there are many ways of learning and that the mere imparting of information has never been among the most successful ones. In point of fact, there are many people today who have no idea of the difference between education, nurture and formation.

Peter Lombard (*c.* AD 1100–1160) identified and the IV Lateran Council (AD 1215) proclaimed the existence of *seven* sacraments that were instituted by Christ for the purpose of containing and causing what they signified. On the whole, these sacraments had come to be administered at crucial moments in the life of the individual. Baptism was therefore seen as the sacrament of birth and confirmation as the sacrament of coming to maturity. Marriage and orders marked the beginning of a new kind of life-role within society. Penance was seen as the repeatable means of obtaining the remission of one's sins and therefore also as the repeated beginning of a new life of grace after sin. The anointing of the sick was seen as the sacrament of the dying. The only exception was the Eucharist. It was not to be received only at crucial moments in one's life, but regularly, since – as from the formula of its administration – the believer was by it *'preserved unto everlasting life'*. Apart from the Eucharist, the sacraments of the Church had become the rites of passage of the Christian society.

At the Reformation, the notion of Hugh of St. Victor (AD 1096–1141) that only those signs that were specifically instituted by Christ could properly be called '*sacraments*' was accepted without question. Since the Scriptures could hardly provide a specific moment in which Christ instituted the rite of confirmation, its sacramental status was irredeemably compromised in the eyes of the Reformers, along with the sacramental status of every other 'sacrament' except baptism and the Lord's Supper. Unwilling to grant to confirmation the status of a sacrament, John Calvin saw nevertheless the pastoral advantages of the practice and recommended that all young people who had been baptized as infants should continue to be given the opportunity to respond publicly to God's Word by making a personal decision for Christ.[13]

The Initiation practice of the sixteenth-century Western Churches remained practically unchanged until modern times. The first major change took place in the Roman Catholic Church when Pius X allowed children who had reached the age of discretion to receive Communion before they were

[13] See J. C. D. Fisher, *Baptism in the Medieval West,* London 1965; and *Christian Initiation: The Reformation Period,* London 1970.

episcopally confirmed. The American Episcopal Church was the first major Church to opt for a pattern of complete Initiation of infants, to which they added an optional and fully repeatable service of '*Affirmation*' to be celebrated after the baptized infants had reached the age of discretion. Another notable change took place when the Church of South India and, later on, the Roman Catholic Church established that, in theory, if not always in practice, from then on the Initiation of adults should be seen as the norm.

The Legacy of the Past

The legacy of such a confused past is a number of difficult questions most of which are still not fully answered. Is confirmation a sacrament distinct from the sacrament of baptism and, if it is, what does it do? What is its theological rationale? At which point does one receive the Spirit: at baptism, at confirmation, or at some other time? What are the requirements for admission to baptism? Must the infants' parents be practising members of the Church? Is there any difference between the baptism of infants and that of adults, and if so, what is it? Should one baptize infants in the first place? How much sense does it make to say that the baptism of adults should be considered to be the norm, when what we actually baptize is mostly infants? Is baptism the sacrament of *complete* Initiation, or not? Should complete sacramental Initiation be administered at one and the same time, or is it better to do it in stages? Are baptism and confirmation rites of passage or is their primary nature something totally different? Can baptism be repeated, and if so, under what circumstances? Given that more and more adults are still unbaptized in Western society, should one re-institute the discipline of the catechumenate? Should a kind of catechumenate be instituted also for lapsed Christians, involving the entire congregation? If one is justified by faith, what is the point of *sacramental* Initiation? When should people – be they infants, children or adults – be admitted to Communion: after Baptism, after confirmation, or at any time at all?

All these questions could well be turned into a single, disheartening one: can we still speak of a Christian theology of Initiation after so many centuries of tentativeness and confusion? We can, but not without a thoroughgoing attempt at reconstruction. We have more data about it now than at any other time: the existing confusion must be bravely sorted out in the light of what we now know.[14] This we will be unable to do unless we are prepared to keep an open and objective mind. We must question what we are accustomed to take for granted because of our denominational allegiance and give up our cherished habit of fighting again and again the denominational battles of the past.

In the first place, we should get away from the mediaeval notion that the most important thing about the sacraments is that in the performance of the correct ritual by the minister of the sacrament as the lawful representative of the Church we can identify a '*moment*' in which God effects 'change'. As Antoine Vergote argued a quarter of a century ago, doing so would reduce the '*expressive*' actions that are characteristic of the sacraments to the mere level of '*performative*' actions: in that there can be in them no manipulation of objects (water, for instance, or bread and wine), to obtain a pre-determined aim. To see sacraments in this light would be nothing short of magic, or even idolatry.[15]

Let us make a number of hypothetical cases. Titius and Caius, two friends in ancient Rome, hear about Christianity and decide to enrol as cathechumens. Having successfully passed the necessary scrutinies, the two are admitted to a course of formal instruction. On the way to one of the lessons of this course, Titius is run over by a mad chariot driver and dies in the arms of his friend. Is Titius saved? Will he go to heaven? The traditional answer is that Titius, having been baptized by baptism of desire is, all things being equal, assured of eternal salvation. One should wish to know why. Surely the only possible answer is that Titius is assured of eternal salvation because, although not yet baptized by water, he had already come to *faith* and was therefore justified by it. The same would apply also to those who, though not yet baptized by water, had witnessed to their faith by undergoing martyrdom (or 'baptism of blood'). We are saved by faith, not by baptism, though this is not to say that baptism is therefore an option: the call to faith involves a call to become visibly a member of Christ's Body the Church.

---

[14] See e.g. G. Kretschmar, *Recent Research on Christian Initiation*, in *Studia Liturgica* 12:2/3 (1977), pp. 87–103.

[15] See Antoine Vergote, *Symbolic Gestures and Actions in the Liturgy*, in *Concilium*, vol. 2, no. 7, February 1971, pp. 40–52.

On Easter Eve, Caius, the surviving friend, is baptized together with the other successful cathechumens who had proved their knowledge and understanding of the baptismal Creed. It would be reasonable to assume that, like his dead friend Titius, Caius had come to faith and was therefore already justified by it. In traditional theology baptism is said to be the sacramental sign of entry '*into Christ*'? Does it follow from this that it is possible to be justified without being '*in Christ*'? Is not being '*in Christ*' what justification also is about? In the case of Caius, the '*moment*' of baptism would have coincided with the '*moment*' of justification only in the unlikely event that he was accidentally to have come to faith in the very instant in which the water was poured and the formula pronounced by the lawfully appointed minister: even then justification, and therefore entry '*into Christ*', would have come to Caius by faith and not by baptism as such.

So, why baptism? Does it achieve anything at all? Of course. One should remember that baptism is not just about one's first entry '*into Christ*' as about *visible* entry into Christ through initiation into Christ's visible Body, the Church. Until the '*moment*' of baptism, the candidate, however justified and '*in Christ*', is not yet visibly a member of Christ's visible Body: water baptism is still necessary, because no one can be saved who is prepared to obey only one half of God's call and refuses to become a visible member of Christ's spiritual army. The moment the candidate is visibly incorporated into the visible Body of the Church through baptism, the grace that is necessary to fulfil his or her new role of '*soldier of Christ*' becomes available to the neophyte by means of the one and same sacramental sign. It was not just for the sake of it that, before being baptized, the candidate had been made to make a public renunciation of evil and a solemn profession of faith!

Being baptized takes only a few minutes, but we should never forget that the transitory moment of baptism has a vital *pre-*history (the initiative of God in bestowing his prevenient grace on the future believer, the bestowal of God's concomitant grace and, finally, the individual's coming to faith and there-fore to justification) as well as an equally vital *follow-up* (the coming to baptism in due course and the living-up to its promises throughout one's life). In other words, the time-line of liturgical/sacramental process should be seen so to speak to '*float*' over the time-line of the much more comprehensive process of becoming a Christian.

The fundamental principle of the Church as a community of faith is that, revealing himself of his own initiative, God addresses us in many and various fragmentary ways throughout the course of our lives. His *call* enables and demands a *response* that is to become visible in every aspect of our existence as members of the community of faith. God's call is twofold:

1. We are called to identify with his eternal design for all creation and become consecrated to it.
2. This we must do by becoming visible members of his Body the Church which is the creation of the Spirit and, after Christ's ascension into heaven, the primordial instrument of God's visible presence on earth.

The entire process of becoming a Christian consists, in fact, of a series of repeated encounters with God that contain a *call*, an *enabling* and the demand of a specific kind of *response* that will lead to the growth of both the Church and the individual member of it to a new kind of humanity to be measured only by the full stature of Christ, the first-born of the new creation.

Since God himself has chosen to address us, enable us and demand our response not only in our private lives but also by means of the liturgical signs of the sacraments of the Church (the *ecclesial* sacraments of which Schillebeeckx speaks),[16] these sacraments also derive their meaning and efficacy from the life, death and resurrection of Jesus Christ, as does our eternal salvation. The sacramental signs are not arbitrary signs, words and actions. They are filled with the mystery which is Christ himself. They are efficacious because, being acts of the Church *qua* Church, they are not just the acts of the Church but the acts of God *through* the Church.

In all ecclesial sacraments, we can therefore discern the very same three-fold pattern of call, enabling and demanded response that is characteristic of any however less formalized types of encounter with God. As we would in any other *one-to-one* kind of personal encounter, we can distinguish in all ecclesial sacraments between the activity of the two partners. We can distinguish between the action of God addressing,

---

[16] See Edward Schillebeeckx, *Christ the Sacrament of Encounter with God*, London, 1971.

enabling us, and demanding a response and the desired responding action, or absence of it, of us the addressees. The difference between a sacramental encounter and any other encounter with God is not in the sequence of call, enabling and demanded response that is common to all encounters with God, but in the specific nature of the eccclesial sacraments.

According to Schillebeeckx,[17] an ecclesial sacrament is a visible action proceeding from the Church as redemptive institution; it is an official ecclesial act performed in virtue of either the character of ordination or of the characters of baptism and confirmation. An ecclesial sacrament is the visible act of the visible Body entrusted by God to demand a visible and public response to a visible and public call and enabling that, through the Church, is the visible and public act of God himself. Once this simple fact is taken into consideration, the answer to the many questions that vex us today may not prove as difficult as we may have thought them to be.

The Shape of Things to Come

Daniel Stevick so sums up the historical development of Christian Initiation:

> It is striking how often in this process of adaptation the forms of Christian Initiation were shaped by extrinsic forces. Augustine derived his theology from current Church custom and defended it by a critical misreading of St. Paul. St. Thomas's doctrine of confirmation reflected the practice of confirming at a moment in life subsequent to baptism. The Roman view that the Bishop should retain the right to confirm prevailed in the West by a process that had little to do with the merit of the issue. . . . The rites of the sixteenth-century Reformation and Counter-Reformation were shaped without the historical data as to how initiatory practice had developed. Pragmatic, disciplinary and polemic considerations have dominated the history of Christian Initiation. Few new departures have stemmed from a fresh insight into the meaning of becoming a Christian.[18]

Perhaps the way to come out of the impasse is to distinguish carefully between the liturgical/sacramental process and the intimately connected but far from identical process of becoming a Christian.

---

[17] Edward Schillebeeckx, *op. cit.*, p. 62.
[18] Daniel Stevick, *op. cit.*, pp. 34–35.

Salvation has two aspects: what we are saved from and what we are saved *for*. We are saved *from* all kinds of sin, and therefore also from the very limitations of the '*old nature*' we inherited from the first Adam. What we are saved *for*, and *by*, is the *new nature* of Christ the second Adam, so that, by being made able to want to follow God's law, we might be for ever free from its extrinsic demands. It is not possible to make a distinction *in re* between these two aspects of salvation, because it is simply not possible to be saved *from* sin and not be saved *for* God at one and the same time. The symbolical immersion in the water that drowns, cleanses and gives life points to what we are saved *from*: alienation from God. The anointing and laying-on of hands point to what we are saved *for*. If the water-bath is seen as baptism and the anointing and/or the laying-on of hands is seen as confirmation, we should not be able to distinguish between the two any more than we can distinguish between the two different and yet totally inseparable aspects of salvation: baptism and confirmation cannot possibly be seen as *two* distinct sacraments, but as two distinct stages, separated for pastoral and not theological reasons, of the celebration of the one sacrament of Initiation. As it was in the beginning, and ever should be.

At what point does one receive the Spirit? Those who first asked this question did not even try to take into consideration the accepted doctrine of the Trinity. The trinitarian doctrine of the '*operations ad extra*' clearly states that when God acts on something other than itself within the inner life of the Trinity, the *act* is the act of *one* of the divine persons, but the *operation* is the operation of the *undivided* Godhead. By virtue of the doctrine of the divine *processions* and *relations* (the doctrine of the so-called '*operations ad intra*'), any operation of the undivided Godhead by means of which the new life we receive in Christ is bestowed is said to be the act of the Holy Spirit by virtue of its being the Love of God the Father and that of God the Son. Therefore, the bestowal of God's grace is not just the operation of the undivided Trinity, but also the specific act of the Holy Spirit. In other words, receiving God's grace and being acted upon by the Holy Spirit are one and the same thing. We are acted upon by the Holy Spirit the very moment we receive God's prevenient grace even *before* we come to faith. Once – in the process of becoming a Christian – we come to faith through the act of the same Spirit and are justified, we are born anew into the new creation. Is this not the same as *'receiving the Spirit'*? We do so every time we receive God's grace, so, far from receiving the Spirit *for the first time* when we are confirmed, we are likely to have received him umpteen times before. If this is so, what could confirmation do? It could only mark us *publicly* as the new creature we should already have become. The Greek formula of what we call confirmation is very eloquent on this point: '*Σφραγίζεται ὁ δουλος του θεου* ...': '*The Servant of God N.N. is <u>marked</u> in the name of the Father, the Son and the Holy Spirit. Amen.*' Did not Tertullian say the baptism was a '*sacramentum*', the oath of allegiance of the soldier of Christ, and the anointing was the '*fidei signaculum*', or the equivalent of the indelible mark that was burnt into the members of a Roman legion on joining it?

What are the requirements of baptism? That would surely depend on whether we would be baptizing an infant or an adult. When we baptize an adult, God makes public his demands through the Church as redemptive institution, and the adult candidate, who is capable of a personal response, is expected to respond to God's call in the *here-and-now*. When we baptize an infant, God makes equally public his call to the infant through the Church as redemptive institution, but the infant's personal response will of necessity have to come at a later stage. God's action is valid and, as far as God is concerned it is also fully *effective*. God's grace is effectually bestowed on the infant, but it will still be up to the infant, once grown up, to accept or reject it at will. So, in the case of *adults*, the one requirement of baptism is *faith* and the renunciation of evil that goes inseparably with it. In the case of infants, the one requirement would be the fact that there was indeed a chance that the child would be brought up *within* the Church and was likely to undergo in it a process of Christian formation. If this should not likely be the case, there would be little point, either pastoral or theological, why one should proceed to baptize. The local church would have to start discriminating between its fringe and its inner core, the drivers and the passengers. Some kind of discrimination would become necessary. Children of parents who were prepared to allow their children to grow up in the Church (whether or not the parents were prepared to make themselves part of the life of the Church) would have to be disentangled from those parents who were merely asking of some kind of half-understood rite of passage vaguely connected with Christianity without being connected with the Christian life, or for some quasi-magical form of spiritual insurance against the eventuality that there might be something in Christianity after all.

Should we baptize infants in the first place? Surely the answer is 'why not', if pastoral rather than theological reasons should suggest that it was advisable in the circumstances? As we all know, the young learn by suggestion and imitation much more than they could ever learn later on through a process of Christian education alone. No one will ever learn who is not made to feel to belong, and one can be said to belong in the Church only when one has been baptized.

Should the baptism of adults be considered as the norm and the baptism of infants the exception? The answer would surely depend on the actual proportion of adults and infants that were available to be baptized. What is the point of a norm when in fact all we may have is a number of exceptions? Different pastoral situations will determine what is best in the circumstances.

Is baptism the sacrament of *complete* Initiation? That would depend. Of course it is, and that whether or not we want the water-bath to be followed, immediately or after a period of time, by a ceremony of anointing and/or laying-on of hands. If we thought differently, we would imply that it was possible to be saved *from* sin without being saved *for* God in the new life in Christ, and as we know only too well, this is not possible. The confusion arises only when we insist in seeing in confirmation, whatever we may mean by it (and the opinions about it are legion), as a rite of passage into maturity. We may well wish to make it so for *pastoral* reasons, but, theologically, confirmation is not it. The justification for administering the one sacrament of Christian initiation in two distinct sacramental stages can only be a pastoral and not a theological one.

Can baptism be repeated, or not? That would also depend. If one thought that just because one was not aware of God's action, God's action was therefore invalid, most certainly not. The Word of God makes a reality of what it says. In an ecclesial sacrament, God's call, his enabling and his demand of our response are made once and for all whether we like it or not and whether or not we are aware of it at the time. It is the action of God, and not our own action that matters in this respect. But what of other cases?

Let us assume for the sake of the argument that someone should be admitted to baptism when he or she had no faith and had no intention whatever to live as a true soldier of Christ. Through the Church as redemptive institution, the call of God, his enabling, and his demand of a positive response would validly make that, because God is God, once and for all. All that remained to be done by the once insincere baptismal candidate was to elicit the correct kind of response at any later time in life, without any further liturgical or sacramental action. Is not this what the doctrine of sacramental *character* is actually about? But does this necessarily mean to say that, having eventually come to faith through his or her acceptance of God's prevenient and concomitant grace, that very same baptized person should be denied in all circumstances the chance to respond publicly to God's sacramental call, providing it was made clear to all that this second water-bath was most definitely *not* a re-celebration of the sacrament of Initiation? The same could possibly apply to those who, having been baptized as infants, wished to make their own formal response to the *past* action of God on them (when the sacrament of Initiation had been celebrated). In either case, the service would be no more than a service of '*affirmation*' and the nature of the *baptismal character* would still be preserved, arguably, both inwardly and outwardly. It would be then a matter of pastoral discretion, and not a question of theology. But one would have serious reservations about this practice in the case of someone who, having been baptized as a sincere adult, having subsequently lapsed from the faith, wished to do everything all over again. For this case, the re-institution of the Order of Penitents, rather than re-submission to some kind of catechumenate, may not be after all such a bad pastoral idea. Should the catechumenate be re-instituted? Why not, where there should be valid pastoral reasons for doing so!

At what point should people be admitted to Communion? By turning the question around, we may well ask at what point one should be admitted to be present at the Eucharist. Should children be excluded from it until they reach the age of discretion? Doing so has often been proved to do untold pastoral harm. If it makes the children feel excluded and causes them only too often to come to the conclusion that Communion is nothing to do with them and a game adults like to play among themselves. The children lose interest in the whole thing. They become bored with the entire service and are denied the possibility of Christian formation. One learns by living the Eucharist, and not by being given the correct intellectual information about it at a later stage. Here, too, imitation and suggestion could do the trick. The objection that intellectual understanding is a necessary pre-condition to the reception of Communion is pure nonsense. Is anyone truly capable of it at any stage of his or her development? It would be like saying that in order to be invited to a banquet and satisfy one's hunger one had first to pass an examination on *cordon bleu* cookery.

With regard to admission to Communion of the unbaptized, the answer would depend on what we thought the Eucharist to be about. If we thought of it, as many do, as merely sitting and being fed at the Lord's Table, then the answers would surely be '*why not?*'. But is this all that the Eucharist is really about? If we thought that the Eucharist was the ecclesial sacrament in which the individual and the Church are asked once more to become with Christ a single, holy and living self-offering to God for the coming of his Kingdom and to renew once again our total commitment to God's eternal purpose, by admitting the unbaptized to Communion would we not run the risk of making liars of them, whether they knew it or not?

What is needed today is not just the creation of '*up-to-date*' services of Christian Initiation. Doing just that would be little more that a waste of time. What is needed today in all the Churches is a clear *policy* of Initiation that is capable of reflecting the pastoral exigencies of the time. It has always been so. Should it be different now? In some pastoral circumstances it may be advisable to administer Christian Initiation only to responsible adults, providing it was made crystal clear that children of Christian parents already truly belonged to Christ's Church. In other pastoral circumstances, it may be advisable to split the liturgical/sacramental process into two distinct stages, provided is was made crystal clear that when an infant is *baptized,* as far as God is concerned he or she is a full member of the Church and has already been given the necessary grace to grow into the new creation that is God's will for humankind. In other cases, it may be pastorally advisable to choose a policy of *complete* liturgical/sacramental initiation of infants. In this case, baptized children could be re-accepted into any Christian congregation and admitted to Communion without further ado at any subsequent stage of their life should they have become estranged from the life of the Church. In all three cases, pastoral necessity should reign supreme and theology be kept where it belongs. In all three cases, theological necessity would be respected and there would be no need to quarrel about it.

Any policy of Christian Initiation we may be led to choose would of necessity have to be accompanied by a concomitant policy of Christian nurture, education and formation. In the absence of such a policy, we would run the risk of introducing (or should one say *'perpetuating'*?) a certain element of magic and superstition in our understanding of the sacraments. Whichever way we may wish to turn, the way ahead will be fraught with dangers. Living with danger should not be foreign to those who profess to follow the One who promised to send to us the Spirit that will lead us into all the truth. Whatever else will happen, painful change will await us. Let this be a true process of the kind of conversion the Gospels call *'metanoia'*. We must renew our very understanding of what the Church is about and then reorganize its structures accordingly from their very roots. After that, we could do worse than following the conclusion of Aidan Kavanagh that it would then be for the local church to put itself into the hands of the Gospel and Christ's Spirit rather than under the safer and more manageable tutelage of conventions and programmes.[19]

FURTHER READING

J. D. C. Fisher, *Christian Initiation: Baptism in the Medieval West*, London, 1965.

—, *Christian Initiation: The Reformation Period*, London 1970.

R. Burnish, *The Meaning of Baptism*, London 1985.

D. S. M. Hamilton, *Through the Waters: Baptism and the Christian Life*, Edinburgh 1990.

F. C. Quinn, 'Confirmation: Does it Make Sense?', *Ecclesia Orans* 5/3 1988.

D. G. Hamilton and F. A. J. Macdonald (eds), *Children at the Table*, Edinburgh 1982.

---

[19] Aidan Kavanagh, *op. cit.*, p. 169.

FOR DISCUSSION

1. 'Baptism once received is unrepeatable, and any rites of renewal must avoid being misconstrued as baptism.' Do you agree, or not? Why?

2. 'Baptism is complete sacramental initiation and leads to participation in the Eucharist/Lord's Supper. Confirmation and other rites of affirmation have a continuing pastoral role in the renewal of faith among the baptized but are in no way to be seen as the completion of baptism or as necessary for admission to communion.' Discuss.

3. 'The renewal of baptismal practice is an integral part of mission and evangelism. Liturgical texts must point beyond the life of the Church to God's mission in the world.' What significance do you see in this statement for the understanding of baptism?

CHAPTER 8

―――

CHRISTIAN FORMATION

Christian formation is one of the most important aspects of practical theology. It is concerned with encountering God through the worshipping Christian community, and with the shaping of Christian character. It thus involves basic orientation in life and the appropriation of Christian story and vision. It relates to the provision church communities make for Christian nurture and education, and for the development of Christian attitudes and discernment. It is also concerned, inseparably, with the Christian's life in the world, as well as with ultimate horizons. It has to embrace the diversity of Christian experience, as well as the paradoxes of the faith itself. Therefore, while it has much in common with 'human growth and development', it is also markedly different in important respects. Secular thinking tends to focus on individual happiness, fulfilment and autonomy. Christian thinking emphasizes the interdependence of humankind under God and recognizes that it is in giving that one receives, and that it is in losing one's life that one finds life. Life is a joyous gift, to be 'realized' in serving others. Christian understanding is irrevocably relational: it is lived with and for others – God and neighbour. Christian formation and Christian worship are therefore closely interrelated.

New Testament Perspectives

Encounter with God

The decisive feature, both in Jesus' preaching and that of the early Christians, is the new orientation of life brought about through turning to God. In the Gospels, John the Baptist and Jesus are credited with the summons, 'Repent, for the kingdom

of God is at hand'.[1] Repentance here is not primarily sorrow for
sin. It means 'turning back' – *teshuvah* in Hebrew – and marks
the point in one's life at which one turns back 'decisively and
irrevocably' to God.[2] The early Christians spoke of their 'conversion' or 'turning around' (Latin *conversio*, Greek *epistrophe*). The
Thessalonian Christians, who had 'turned to God from idols'
(1 Thessalonians 1:9), must now 'live lives worthy of the God
who calls you into his kingdom and glory' (1 Thessalonians
2:12). Wayne Meeks emphasizes the social implications of
Christian conversion.[3] Encounter with God – the reforming and
transforming event that is God's gracious gift – provides a new
context, a new story, a new goal, and a new identity for the
convert, and leads on to growth in the faith. To reflect Pauline
terminology and later theology, justification goes hand in hand
with sanctification. It is not our purpose here to reflect on the
exaggerated emphasis which converts typically impart to their
conversion accounts. It is part of their concern with their
identity and standing in the new community. Nor do we take
the stereotype of their conversion as applicable to everyone.
But some points should be underlined: particularly the process
of *decentring* and *recentring* that is involved, and the *resocialization*
associated with it. The dynamics of Christian formation presuppose the centring of life in Christ and the solidarity of the
member with the Christian community in its worship, witness,
fellowship and spirituality. This centring on Christ is given ritual
expression in baptism and constantly reinforced in worship.

Baptism into the community of faith

Even in the New Testament, not all converts came from outside
the faith. Some were members of Christian households to
whom faith was mediated by parents or masters already committed to the faith. The believer has a sanctifying influence on
other members of the household: 'otherwise your children
would be unclean, but as it is they are holy' (1 Corinthians 7:14).
They were already socialized or in process of socialization in
the Christian household. They were brought to baptism as the
sign and seal of their belonging to the Christian community.[4]

---

[1] Ed Sanders has questioned the place of repentance in Jesus' message, but this
need not detain us here.
[2] G. Vermes, *The Gospel of Jesus the Jew*, Newcastle 1981, pp. 24–25.
[3] *The Origins of Christian Morality*, Yale 1993, pp. 18–36.
[4] Cf. chapter 7.

> Christ is like a single body with its many limbs and organs, which, many as they are, together make up one body; for in the one Spirit we were all brought into one body by baptism ... ; and we were all given that one Spirit to drink. (1 Corinthians 12:12–13; cf. Galatians 3:27–28)

Baptism, as we have seen, has many aspects. It is a rite of initiation, cleansing, new beginnings, and much more. It marks the boundary between the community cleansed by the Spirit of God and the outside world as the sphere in which the writ of the devil obtains. It is, particularly in Pauline thinking, incorporation into the community that bears Christ's name, 'the body of Christ'. However decisive baptism may be for individuals, the blessings it bestows are *realized through the community of faith*. Indeed, while we read of individual conversion and baptism, as in the encounter of Philip the evangelist with the Ethiopian eunuch, the rite of baptism always involves the community (even if in the isolation of the encounter in question the community is represented by Philip alone). In Acts the whole Christian community was devoted 'to the apostles' teaching and fellowship, to the breaking of bread and the prayers' (Acts 2:42). Hence, whether one thinks of adult or child baptism, one has always to relate the action of baptism to continued growth within the fellowship of the faithful, and to the active assistance which the worshipping community gives to the process.[5]

Growth and development in Christian life and community

The perspective of growth is prominent in the New Testament.

> Like the new-born infants you are, you should be craving for unadulterated spiritual milk so that by it you may grow towards salvation; for surely you have tasted that the Lord is good. (1 Peter 2:2–3)

There are several points here. Perhaps the writer has recently converted Christians in mind here, but what he writes applies to all. Infants are utterly dependent on their mothers' milk for the sustaining of life itself. The spiritual life of the faithful is dependent on wholesome teaching – 'the pure milk of the word' (*logikos*) – so that their growth and development 'into salvation' may be sustained. Here, salvation is an eschatological

---

[5] On baptism, see chapter 7 above.

goal. It is not something given in its entirety on conversion or entry to the Christian community, but is rather the completion and wholeness to which one aspires. The final sentiment reflects Psalm 34:8: Christians have indeed tasted and seen that the Lord is good or kind. Spiritual growth is possible only through an encounter, however mediated, with the divine goodness. The worshipping community is central to this process. The second letter attributed to Peter ends with the exhortation to 'grow in the grace and knowledge of our Lord and Saviour Jesus Christ' (2 Peter 3:18). Christ embodies the grace of God for us. Response to the grace of God in Christ thus represents the primary condition of Christian formation. The Christian's life is modelled (*mimesis*) on Christ and the apostle (1 Thessalonians 1:6). A necessary corollary is that we must already have begun to learn and to internalize the Church's definitive story. Again, the worshipping community is a catalyst.

In his care of his churches, Paul presupposed a perspective of moral and spiritual growth.

> Friends, we are always bound to thank God for you . . . because your faith keeps on increasing and the love you all have for each other grows ever greater. (2 Thessalonians 1:3)

Sometimes with Paul – or writers acting in his name – there is a preference for the metaphor of building: the building up of the faith community, to which all who exercise the gifts they have been given contribute materially.

> And it is he who has given some to be apostles, some prophets, some evangelists, some pastors and teachers, to equip God's people for work in his service, for the building up of the body of Christ, until we all attain to the unity inherent in our faith and in our knowledge of the Son of God – to mature manhood, measured by nothing less than the full stature of Christ. (Ephesians 4:11–13, REB)

This many-sided ministry has an immediate goal. It is 'to equip God's people for work in his service'. Christian learning is learning for service. This service, as well as the 'learning' on which it is based, contributes to a further goal, which is the realization of the oneness of the faith community as 'the body of Christ'. The ultimate or eschatological goal – the vision that is part of the story – is the complete personal formation manifested in 'the fullness of Christ'. Christian formation looks beyond what is achievable in the present scenario, but it represents a kind of 'impossible possibility' towards which Christians move.

Sometimes, in the struggle to articulate perceptions of Christian formation, the writer mixes his metaphors:

> You are built on the foundation of the apostles and prophets, with Christ Jesus himself as the cornerstone. In him the whole building is bonded together and grows into a holy temple in the Lord. In him you are also being built with all the others into a spiritual dwelling for God. (Ephesians 2:20–22)

The mixing of the metaphors of building and growth is readily comprehended. It enables the writer to bring together the notion of essential foundations and structures (Christ and the apostolic message) with that of the holy temple which is thus rising through Christ (cf. 'the body of Christ') from these foundations, and finally the idea of the incorporation of the addressees and other faithful people in this 'spiritual dwelling for God'.

The goal of Christian growth and development can be conceived in a variety of ways.

- It can be conceived in terms of the growth of the community as 'the household of God', comprising Jew and Gentile, bond and free, male and female. As always, true growth comes from God and is inspired by the Spirit of Christ. It means identification with him who is our peace, who 'has broken down the dividing wall of hostility' (Ephesians 2:14; cf. Galatians 3:28). All this must be expressed in worship.

- It can be conceived as an eschatological goal: 'the measure of the stature of the fullness of Christ' (Ephesians 4:13). But growth *towards* such an eschatological growth is *also a process of personal growth here and now.* 'Personal maturity' is the result of a process of growth and development, not a sudden acquisition. Such dimensions are built into Christian worship.

- It can be conceived in moral terms. Speaking the truth in love (Ephesians 4:15) is the by-product, if not the condition, of growth 'into Christ' and growth in community. Indeed, maturity of faith and moral action go hand in hand. It is 'renewal in mind and spirit' (Ephesians 4:23),

involving truthfulness and the upright devout life which
goes with it.

> Have done with all spite and bad temper, with rage,
> insults and slander, with evil of any kind. Be generous to
> one another, tender-hearted, forgiving one another as
> God in Christ forgave you. (Ephesians 4:32, REB)

It involves growing away from worldy conformity as one is
'transformed by the renewal of your minds'(Romans 12:2),
which brings discernment of the will of God.

- It can be conceived in terms of using the gifts God has
  given us (Romans 12:6); or of letting ourselves be channels
  of the Spirit for some useful purpose in the community
  (1 Corinthians 12:7).

- It can be conceived in terms of training for discipleship.
  The disciples' commission was to preach, teach and heal.
  But the disciples had to be with Jesus for some time before
  they could undertake such a mission. The word 'disciple'
  means 'learner': itself a clue to the process of growth
  through interaction with their teacher.

In the culture of the Lord

Christian formation has often been conceived in terms of a
process of sanctification. The Christian community, whether
thought of as a congregation or a family or, in extreme cases,
represented by a single parent or sponsor, can bring others
within the embrace of its holiness (1 Corinthians 7:14). It is
not surprising, therefore, that from apostolic times the
Christians emphasized the importance of the family. Families,
however, are always deeply affected by their cultural setting.
Socio-historical factors are evident in the household structures
presupposed in the New Testament epistles. Their ethos of
Hellenistic urban households was paternalistic; domestic slavery
was accepted as a normal part of life, and socially conditioned
assumptions about discipline and upbringing, as well as the role
of women and children, are not hard to detect. Paul and other
teachers did not attack such structures but rather allowed
Christian faith and culture to influence and modify the
ethos of the family so that it could serve as an instrument of
Christian nurture. Thus, while the leadership role of the father
and husband remained, the mutuality of the relationship of

husband and wife was emphasized. While slaves remained part of the household, they could become full members of the church communities. Current notions of upbringing and discipline inevitably affected the Christian view of the up-bringing of children, but the worst features of heavy-handed paternal chastisement were expressly forbidden. In this connection, the most famous phrase occurs in Ephesians 6:4: '. . . bring them up in the discipline and instruction of the Lord.' Two key words are *nouthesia* ('discipline') and *paideia* ('upbringing'). The former undoubtedly carries overtones of 'warning' but it also contains the notion of 'reminding'. It suggests Christian *paraenesis*: the kind of instruction which reminds the catechumen of his or her identity as a Christian and warns against the corruption of the world as well as commending Christian virtue. It is illustrated in the fourth century by John Chrysostom's sermon on *Vainglory and the Right Way for Parents to bring up their Children*. The word *paideia* has a much wider connotation. It can denote simply the rearing or upbringing of the child. It gives us the phrase, 'the nurture of the Lord', understood as training: education in the Christian way. That is probably its primary meaning in this context. In Hebrews 12:5–13, it is used of the kind of discipline which can be painful but which nevertheless expresses love and makes one strong and persevering in the face of the challenge of evil. It can also denote the condition which results from this process and promotes the process in others: something close to 'culture'.[6] 'Bring them up in the culture of the Lord' . . . Christian education is never to be reduced to mere instruction or content of knowledge. It is contextualized within a com-munity of faith and worship which demonstrates its faith, hope and love as it communicates its story and lifestyle.

Paul leaves the Corinthian Christians in no doubt that worship, offered to God and inspired by the Spirit, has an important educational and instructive function (cf. 1 Corinthians 14). It must 'edify' the community. It must stimulate and encourage, offering some aspect of revelation, enlightenment, prophecy or instruction. But there is an ambivalence about worship. It can so easily fail to achieve all its purposes. The charismatic worship at Corinth reduces to the cult of the individual; it has little or no benefit in terms of building up the community's

[6] Cf. W. Jaeger's classic study, *Paideia: The Ideals of Greek Culture*, 3 vols., Oxford 1943–45.

understanding or communicating the gospel of Christ.
Unworthy expressions of worship invalidate the activity itself
and send out the wrong signals. Divisions in the Corinthian
communities result in their meetings becoming counter-
productive (1 Corinthians 11:17).

> The result is that when you meet as a congregation, it is not
> the Lord's Supper you eat; when it comes to eating, each of you
> takes his own supper, one goes hungry and another has too much
> to drink . . . Can I commend you? On this point, certainly not!
> (1 Corinthians 11:20–22)

Paul goes on to insist that the story of the Last Supper be taken
as the model for the Lord's Supper in Corinth. Here we find an
important indication not only of the place of story but the place
of *significant story* in the life of worshipping community.[7] *It recalls
the faith community to its true being.* The story has consequences
for action: not only in terms of appropriate liturgical action,
important as that is, but in terms of the kind of community that
is fit to recall, celebrate and act out this story in its social life. In
other words, the culture of the community must be such that it
communicates its faith as it remembers, celebrates and
proclaims the events which have shaped it. This is the secret of
its *paideia*.

   The recalling of significant story is at the heart of the ethos of
the Churches and therefore forms an essential part of the
instruction of young and old. It is an important part of the
reading of the scriptures – in New Testament terms, the
scriptures of Israel, however defined – which are significant
both as a witness to Christ (cf. John 5:39) and for the guidance
of the faithful.

> All inspired scripture has its use for teaching the truth and refuting
> error, or for reformation of manners and discipline in right living,
> so that the man of God may be capable and equipped for good
> work of every kind. (2 Timothy 3:16–17, NEB)

But it is only within the ethos of Churches open to the spirit of
Christ that the necessary discernment will be found. Searching
the scriptures can itself lead to error if the conditions for all its
interpretation are not set by a Christ-centred faith and a Christ-
centred ethos. Like Jesus' opponents in the Fourth Gospel, we

---

[7] On this, see S. Hauerwas, *A Community of Character*, Notre Dame 1981, pp.
66–69.

may search the scriptures for the secret of eternal life yet refuse to come to him to receive that life (cf. John 5:40).[8]

Much more could be said about the importance of community for *paideia*. It is not mere convention which leads Paul to strike the note of thanksgiving when addressing many of his churches, nor to emphasize the importance of prayer. The 'psalms and spiritual songs' also played a part. It is clear from the *Haustafeln* in particular that the household community was considered to have a particular role in Christian nurture. Here again, ethos plays an important part. True, certain duties are expected and inculcated: obedience and 'honour' to parents – the secret of a long and prosperous life, as the commandment put it! (cf. Ephesians 6:1–2). But if the child had duties towards the parents, the family ethos imposed mutual responsibilities on the parents. Fathers particularly must not 'goad' their children 'to resentment'. What is being suggested is a supportive, if demanding, relationship, which fits well with 'the culture of the Lord'.

The Church as a Community of Nurture

Induction

Christian education and nurture, integral as they are to the life of the churches, are intimately involved in the process of induction into the community of faith. Preparation for baptism involves the candidate of maturer age, and the parents and sponsors in the case of infant or paedo-baptism. A rigorous system of preparation was proposed by Hippolytus in Rome about AD 200. Those seeking entry to church membership had to be sponsored by a church member of good standing. Careful enquiry had to be made about lifestyle and occupation, many occupations being for Hippolytus inconsistent with the Christian faith. Slaves had to have their master's consent before they could be admitted. In all cases, good character was essential. It should be noted that Hippolytus was attempting to reinforce the separation of the church ethos from that of the world. He was living at the time of the first great influx of outsiders into the church: a development which, however satisfying in terms of church growth, brought the danger of importing worldly standards into the church. Hippolytus

---

[8] See above, chapter 4, pp. 58–69.

proposed a time of preparation and study lasting up to three years, although some candidates might progress through it more speedily. A gradual induction into the life and worship of the church was envisaged. The catechumens would gradually progress to the hearing of the Word, but baptism, anointing and first Communion were reserved for the Easter celebration. Hippolytus' scheme was idealistic and never fully implemented. He tended to glorify the apostolic age and to believe that things had gone from bad to worse ever since! But he signalled some important aspects of Christian education and nurture as induction into the worshipping community. How do you identify the boundary between church and world? At what stage in personal development do you admit to baptism and first Communion? What is meant by a Christian lifestyle, and what is excluded?[9]

In answering these questions, churches have chosen many different procedures. For example, if adult baptism is taken as the norm, Christian nurture is essentially preparation for baptism. If infant baptism is practised, Christian nurture refers to upbringing within the culture of the church as worshipping faith community. A more detailed investigation would enter many qualifications. While Roman Catholics may receive first Communion in childhood, much weight is attached to ongoing catechetical instruction and confirmation at a later stage. Many churches adjust their practice according to their perception of earlier maturation in young people. Some evangelical congregations admit children freely to fellowship meals but delay baptism until maturity. There has long been pressure on Reformed Churches to allow access to the Lord's Supper at an earlier stage, particularly in the context of family worship. Thus, Horace Bushnell, in his classic work, *Christian Nurture*, wrote in 1861:

> I must also speak of another and more general mode of dis-
> couragement, in what may be called the holding back, or holding
> aloof system, by which children are denied an early recognition of
> their membership in the Church, and an admission to the Lord's
> table . . . What I now refer to, more especially, is the negatively bad
> or discouraging effect thrown upon their piety, by these methods
> of detention, or exclusion. The child, giving evidence, however
> beautiful, of his piety, is still kept back from the fellowship and

[9] On Hippolytus, see Gregory Dix (ed.), *The Apostolic Tradition of St Hippolytus*, London 1968, pp. 23–43; also, the General Introduction, pp. xi–li.

table of Christ, for the simple defect of years. As if years were one
of the Scripture evidences of grace.[10]

The strongest argument for such alteration in practice relates
to nurture. If the sacraments are indeed 'means of grace', then
all adherents who could conceivably benefit from them should
be able to do so in the context of a supportive faith community.
Such policies would give expression to Bushnell's dictum that
the child born into a Christian family should never know
himself or herself to be other than a Christian from earliest
years. They would also place a premium on good communication in Christian worship and teaching. The thoughtful reception of the sacrament – 'what is the meaning of this rite?' (cf.
Exodus 12:26) – should be in context with thoughtful use of
the Bible, the source of the Church's story, and learning to
participate meaningfully in prayer and worship. Even the
disciples asked Jesus to teach them how to pray.

Instruction

The Christian tradition has always had a prominent instruc-
tional emphasis, which it inherited from ancient Judaism.
Instruction, however, involves methods as well as content. In
his parabolic teaching, Jesus instructed in a creative way,
projecting a world in which his hearers were invited to
participate, yet that created world also impinged on the world
of their own experience and so opened up new possibilities
of belief and action.[11] Augustine used the group dynamics of
his community at Cassiciacum to develop active learning.[12] He
also emphasized the importance of the moral and spiritual
quality of the teacher in the educative process and stressed
the importance of recognizing and responding to the learner's
limitations and difficulties. Yet, like other Church Fathers,
Augustine was inevitably concerned with the content of
instruction. He mapped out a biblically based catechetical
programme, designed to impart the fundamentals of the
Christian story. He also provided a Christian-centred
curriculum for use in schools. All these features are involved

---

[10] H. Bushnell, *Christian Nurture*, New York 1861, pp. 10ff.

[11] Cf. B. Chilton and J. I. H. McDonald, *Jesus and the Ethics of the Kingdom*, London
1987, pp. 120–24.

[12] Cf. G. Howie, *Educational Theory and Practice in St Augustine*, London 1969, pp.
139–81.

in the Christian tradition of instruction, which may be considered briefly under the following headings.

- *Catechesis.* This term properly denotes the instruction given to catechumens preparing for baptism and therefore originally included the whole range of interaction between teacher and pupils. Subsequently it came to denote the content of such instruction. Catechisms were handbooks of instruction, common throughout the Middle Ages and the Reformation period. Since they characteristically contained material to be learned by heart – for example, the Lord's Prayer, the Ten Commandments and the Creeds – they were often set out in question-and-answer form and became identified with rote learning methods. As such, they were attacked – often execrated – by progressive educators from Rousseau onwards. While these critics rejected both the dogmatics and the pedagogics of the catechetical method, they operated with a variety of assumptions of their own. It is worth noting that catechetics in the early Christian centuries had a wider connotation than in later times. The catechetical school of Alexandria, particularly under the leadership of Clement and Origen, was concerned with a theological outreach to the cultured in society. In post-Reformation Scotland, the catechism had greatest impact when it operated in the context of family life in a relatively static society. In spite of idealistic defences sometimes made of the traditional usage,[13] catechisms are unlikely to be effective or accepted tools of Christian instruction today unless they are completely suited to the context in which they are used and are also much more stimulating and imaginative, in content and method, than has often been the case in past.

- *Christian schools?* In the early centuries, Christians were living in a multi-religious society in which they formed a small minority. Because of the pagan content of the school curriculum, Hippolytus regarded school teaching as a doubtful or unacceptable vocation for Christians. Christian children had to be educated at home, at least in well-off families who could include a tutor in their households. That was the kind of situation which John Chrysostom addressed. Augustine anticipated the growth of Christian

---

[13] Cf. T. F. Torrance, *The School of Faith*, London 1959, especially pp. xi–cxxvi.

schools, and his approach to curriculum influenced the monastic and other Christian schools of the Middle Ages. The Reformers strongly encouraged the national and universal provision of education, as in a celebrated section of the *First Book of Discipline* (1561).[14] But this concordat with the state ran into difficulty with the progressive secularization of society, so that – as in Scotland, for example – the school system that had its roots in the Presbyterian tradition has become 'non-denominational'. The Roman Catholic Church, after a period of difficulty, was eventually able to retain control of its religious teaching within the state sector. Such a solution is not without its difficulties. In England, the Church of England and the Roman Catholic Churches in particular operate church schools within the state provision, alongside 'non-denominational' schools which also teach religious education. Other countries – such as the Netherlands and the USA – have found different ways of dealing (or not dealing) with religion in state education. In all cases, the secularization of Christendom and the pluralistic and multi-religious nature of Western society have posed acute problems for the Churches. Some look to independent or grant-aided Christian schools for a solution. Christian teaching in a post-Christian age is problematic but is capable of being handled with integrity in both school and church settings. At any rate, it is clear that Christian formation will henceforth take place in the context of cultural pluralism (as reflected, for example, in the media), rather than in a sterilized cultural vacuum. The Churches require to face this scenario, not with mere traditionalism or sectarian isolation, but with a determined realism which gives primacy to the quality of Christian education in church and home and recognizes the need to develop a 'critical consciousness' to enable people to come to terms with an aggressive and pervasive secularism.

- *Sunday schools.* The Sunday school movement had its effective beginnings with the work of Thomas Stock and Robert Raikes in Gloucester in the latter part of the eighteenth century. As its name suggests, it met an educational need by responding positively to the question

[14] Cf. J. F. Cameron, *The First Book of Discipline*, Edinburgh 1972.

whether the children of the poor should be educated. It was essentially a lay movement, with strong social, moral and religious aims. Overcoming a variety of opposition, it spread rapidly, aided by Raikes' journalistic advocacy and planning skills. Acknowledging that literacy and good character were essential in personal, social and religious life, it served as a precursor of universal education provision, which was not established until after 1870 in England and Wales. By the end of the century, it acquired a narrower focus on religious and moral education. In spite of its undoubted achievements, its educational standards were never high, and as its influence began to wane Christian educationists demanded reform. The first major overhaul of its procedures is associated with G. H. Archibald in the early twentieth century. He instituted a programme of 'decentralization', which saw departments established to cater for the needs of particular age groups. He emphasized the need to understand the growth and development of children, and introduced lively new visual and activity methods, including outdoor activities; and he underlined the importance of the training of teachers. In consequence, the Sunday school movement experienced something of a revival, cut short by World War I. Later, attention switched to sociological issues, such as the separation of Sunday school and church, in which social class played a part. H. A. Hamilton pled for the integration of the two bodies, advocating the 'family church' concept. From baptism, a child was given a 'church friend'; families shared in worship, even in planning it; and considerable demands were made on parents and teachers. After World War II, there was a new stress on designing curricula to reflect the context of the faith community. Sunday schools were now seen as agents of Christian nurture, conveying the joy of Christian life and worship within a loving faith community. Yet in many respects the gulf between church and Sunday school was never fully overcome. Sunday schools seem unavoidably to take children out of church worship, without being able to induct them into a meaningful experience of worship which might compensate for so doing. In face of the growing secularization of society, they need to take on board the critical notion of what it means to grow up as Christian children in a world hostile or indifferent to the Christian faith. They are unlikely to be successful unless they are seen to be integral to the life and worship of the church community and a vital part of its mission, and are given human and material resources to match the demands of such a task. Sensitivity to church, child and world would seem imperative. They also need the full co-operation and involvement of parents, imaginative and dynamic leadership, staff training, and all-round commitment to effective Christian nurture.[15]

Institution

While Christian education and nurture are to be seen as vital elements in the life of churches today, they are also widely regarded as problematic. Much depends on the willingness of the church community to view itself as a nurturing, educating fellowship, and to accept that the Church is about Christian formation and should be shaped accordingly. The dilemmas discussed above reflect the dilemmas of the Church in modern society. Facing the consequences of decline in numbers and influence that affects 'mainstream' churches today, there tends to be a resort to crisis management or damage limitation. The preservation of the institution becomes a vital concern. Yet the demands of nurture and education – of Christian formation – suggest that the institution itself must change. Community rather than institution, participation rather than passivity, communication rather than wordiness, provide a basic orientation. Worship must indeed preserve – or recover! – its liturgical integrity and purpose, but it must be such as to enable young and old to participate meaningfully in it. The token prologue for children is not satisfactory, nor are 'family services' which alienate many by their sheer banality. Nor are wordy 'hymn sandwiches' which lose liturgical direction. The double question must be asked: is this worship worthy to be offered to God, and is it helpful for the Christian formation of all those who share in it? In other words, the ethos of worship must reflect the nurtural priorities of the community and must be supported by a variety of agencies, from parental groups concerned with upbringing and priorities in the modern world to adult learning programmes of a shorter or longer duration.

[15] On Sunday schools, cf. J. Ferguson (ed.), *Christianity, Society and Education*, London 1981.

One reaction might be, 'But we do all this already . . .' Check,
then, how fundamental or how peripheral it is to the life of
the church. Churches have a seemingly infinite capacity to
domesticate new initiatives within traditional structures and
practices. As Hippolytus and Augustine saw in their day, nurture
and education present a radical challenge to the faith
community. Christian formation involves the re-formation of
the Churches.

Growth and Development as Christians

Developmental studies and their significance

The twentieth century has witnessed an abundance of developmental studies. Classic students of the discipline include Piaget
in cognitive development; Erikson in emotional development;
Kohlberg (and Piaget) in moral development; and Goldman in
religious understanding. However controversial they may be,
the educational importance of such studies is beyond dispute,
as the work of an educationist such as Jerome Bruner indicates.
Studies relating to faith development are of particular relevance
to us, although only one example can be noted here and very
briefly at that.

James Fowler has done pioneering work on faith development, using stage theory to present a meaningful pattern.[16]

- *Stage 1.* Beyond the earliest stage of undifferentiated faith
  (personally important but largely beyond empirical
  research), Fowler identified the first stage, typical of 3–7
  year-old children, as 'intuitive-projective'. As they encounter the rich novelty of their worlds, imagination and
  fantasy create long-lasting images and feelings, later
  hopefully to be clarified. Egocentric and imitative, children
  at this stage are influenced by the example, stories and
  actions of adults and others to whom they primarily and
  trustingly relate.

- *Stage 2.* The 'mythic-literal' state points up the somewhat
  literal internalizing of the stories and beliefs that symbolize
  belonging to one's community. The previous fantasy-filled
  operations are now curbed by an increasingly concrete and

---

[16] James Fowler, *Stages of Faith. The Psychology of Human Development and the Quest
for Meaning*, San Francisco 1981.

realistic understanding of a more coherent and linear world: a world of people, places and events. If story interprets life, stories of a cosmic nature are interpreted anthropomorphically and are not subjected to conceptual analysis. Children are now more aware of others' perspectives. A degree of reciprocity characterizes their moral awareness; 'fairness' is the primary moral criterion. While this stage is typical of middle childhood, many adolescents and adults evince similar structures.

- *Stage 3.* As we grow up, life becomes more complicated. We are immersed in the world of people, but a number of different spheres demand our attention: family, school, peer groups, work, local community, the worlds of media – and church, if it has retained relevance to life. One has to synthesize this material; that is, to bring it into a coherent whole as part of one's identity and outlook: in short, one's faith. This is what is meant by the 'synthetic-conventional' stage, typical of adolescents and many adults. Strongly interpersonal, it is conventional in that it relates to the values and expectation of significant others. People at this stage tend to have an implicit ideology – a clustering of beliefs and values strongly but tacitly held. Authority is traditionally located or found in peer group or intimate group consensus.

- *Stage 4.* The 'individuative-reflective' stage marks a notable development, often accomplished in early adulthood or in mid-life, if at all. Personal identity is no longer simply conformity to others' expectations and values but relates to a carefully defined frame of meaning or world view which emerges through one's own reflection on life experiences and moral judgements. At the same time, it is conscious of being part of a larger or ultimate framework of meaning. Stories and symbols are now 'demythologized' into concepts and ideas. Commitment to this self-certain system of meaning and value is likely to be much stronger than awareness of the unconscious influences or sociological conditioning inherent in the view taken.

- *Stage 5.* 'Conjunctive faith' brings together image and concept, personal perception and social unconscious. There is a new appreciation of the freshness and depth of story and symbol as one reworks one's past and reclaims it as one's own. This stage acknowledges the 'deeper self', the 'social self', the 'conditioned self'. It takes failure and defeat within the compass of life's meaning, affirming their role in personal development; hence Fowler sometimes applies the term 'paradoxical consolidative' to this stage. While renewing one's awareness of one's tradition, one is also made open and vulnerable to those who find truth in quite different traditions and outlooks, as well as to new dimensions of religious truth. One's ideas of justice now acquire a universal dimension, and the promotion of others' growth and development becomes a priority.

• *Stage 6.* The final stage is found only in the spiritual giants of humanity. It embraces those who have incarnated that which is truly human and liberating, and whose lives have radiated cosmic or ultimate purpose. The power of their presence in the world has often been seen as threatening to the structures that sustain human systems of meaning, and in consequence they have often been persecuted or killed. They evince a simplicity, lucidity and grace which is of the essence of their humanity and spirituality: hence they might well point, as Jesus did, to a servant boy as the pattern of the disciple. Life is both affirmed and let go. They have an abiding significance, across the barriers of race, class, creed or gender, of which not even death can rob them.

The debate about faith development and related topics is by no means over, and the entire project has a provisional aspect. While formal aspects of Fowler's stage theory and the complexities of his analysis may be criticized, this is not the place for a detailed critique. Holistic interpretations of faith have their uses. Neither conservative nor liberal in orientation, they place us *all* on the map – and that can be a humbling experience.

Worship and faith development

Only a brief exemplification of the relation of worship to faith development is possible here. Worship is *both* offered to the glory of God *and* is of formative benefit to the individual worshipper and the congregation as a whole. In its latter aspect, it is intended to be an 'edifying' or learning experience (cf. 1 Corinthians 14). As such, it involves the participation of the whole congregation, young and old, and also engages the *whole person*. It thus involves cognitive, affective and conative responses, and relates to the whole life. The 'all age' aspect of worship suggests that young and old, rich and poor, male and female, can learn from one another. Examples may be cited briefly from each of the recognized stages.

- *Stage 1.* If young children learn from adults, can adults learn from young children? This stage provides a remarkable range of metaphors and models. 'Unless you turn round and become like children, you will never enter the kingdom of Heaven' (Matthew 18:3, REB). God hides many things from the learned and wise and reveals them to 'babes' (Matthew 11:25). The writer of 1 John addresses the congregation as 'children', because they 'know the Father'; but also writes, perhaps more literally, to 'fathers' and 'young men' (1 John 12–14). Hence, there are qualities and strengths in every stage of life, and it is the mark of the mature teacher to be able to highlight them and use them to develop spiritual awareness. Worship itself has been compared to play, the learning activity most characteristic of childhood. It combines lightheartedness with serious purpose. For example, playtime is also story-time, and for many today worship is the only time they hear the Christian story. Indeed, in worship we enact and celebrate the story, and graft together this story and our own story. Play is essential for growth and education and the development of a capacity to relate. In worship God nurtures his family, and this is most fully expressed in liturgy which is playful rather than solemn, and serious but joyful. But it is also true that when we become adult we put away childish things. The metaphors and models of childhood are helpful only so far as they promote spiritual growth.[17]

- Communication with young children is also part of congregational worship. Here the description of developmental stages is directly relevant. Following Piaget and Bruner as well as Fowler, we would underline the need to enter their world, not in a paternalistic or condescending way, but as part of a natural conversation which wins response from

[17] On worship and play, cf. T. Driver, *The Magic of Ritual*, San Francisco 1991, pp. 98–99.

them. We must accept them as the persons they are, and begin with their awareness of life. We must stimulate their interest and involvement, widen their horizons, which can only be achieved through their co-operation and involvement, and thus (without lecturing or moralizing!) convey a worthwhile message. This is the stage of *enactive learning*, which puts a premium on involvement, participation, imagination and spontaneity. But it is not designed simply for the entertainment of the adults, although their sympathetic participation is also part of the learning situation. Enactive representation is a set of actions for achieving a certain result. The speaker must therefore have in view a clear objective which is capable of realization with this particular group in the time available.

- *Stage 2.* Fowler's use of the term 'mythical literal' points to the *iconic* or pictorial nature of the 'stage 2 world' and perhaps underlines its limitations. Piaget described it as the 'concrete operational' stage; reality consists of people, places, events, stories of life, experiments, explorations; in short, the material, tangible, empirical world. Worship does not lack iconic elements: bread, wine, Bible, pulpit, choir, organ, worshippers ... Bruner described iconic representation as a set of summary images or graphics that illustrate or stand for a concept without fully defining it. Metaphors are derived from this stage: such as Jesus' indication of the servant boy as the image of humble service and 'greatness'; and Paul's use of the race, or armour. Parables are grounded in such images. The challenge for the communicator is to encapsulate the message in such images while leaving the door open for further development in understanding. It cannot be emphasized too strongly that this iconic representation is the mode of communication central to the tele-visual age, and the need to express the faith in such terms is of overriding importance. Such an emphasis is in line with the insistence that worship should be grounded in 'real life'.

- *Stage 3.* The sheer conventionality of this stage is a threat to worship. It represents a conformity to the accepted social ethos of congregations. But while worship is our offering of ourselves to God as we are, it is also an encounter with God which changes us. Stage 3 tends to domesticate the divine word and make it subordinate to an ideology formed largely of conventional elements. There is even a tendency – a temptation, perhaps – for churches to nurture such attitudes, for many prized virtues – loyalty to the institution, reliability, commitment – coexist within the limitations of this group and are seen as vital to institutional life. Social bonding is, of course, important both for adults and adolescents. The absence of adolescents from many congregations demonstrates the importance of the peer group for this age-group and its relative distrust and rejection of the adult (or childish) ethos discerned in churches.[18] Education and nurture alike depend on rebuilding structures of trust and acceptance, encouraging participation, giving opportunities for talking about real life issues and emphasizing the personal and inter-personal strength of Christian community. In the cases of adolescents and adults alike, the goal is to create possibilities of moral and spiritual growth and insight, not least through a deeper understanding of, and more meaningful participation in, worship itself.

- *Stage 4.* The 'individuative reflective' stage may partly reflect a maturation beyond the conventional stage. It is characteristic of the 'thinking person': one who is not afraid to let the Word intersect conventional values and transform them. At its best, this stage encapsulates response to the prophetic word in worship and to the leading of the Spirit. Intelligent worship promotes religious and moral discernment. Yet the dangers – as Paul found in the 'enlightened' party at Corinth (cf. 1 Corinthians 8) – lie in individualism and a lack of humility. Conventional stage 3 values may be superseded not by Word and Spirit but by an individualistic ideology that owes more to a kind of complacent, intellectual or even religious self-satisfaction. Self-awareness needs to be fostered as part of pastoral care. Hence it is important that the worshipping community both encourages critical thinking and also remains in dialogue with its searching spirits. To be sure, Paul is all too well aware of the dangers of 'knowledge', insisting that one must, in love, consider the effect of one's attitudes and actions on others. This brings an essentially Christian

---

[18] Cf. L. Francis, *Teenagers and the Church*, London 1984.

perspective to bear on personal and social development and modifies individualistic values. Thus, dialogue and discussion – in association with worship if not actually part of it – are essential if worship is to be a creative force in the lives of participants and in the life of the world.[19]

- *Stage 5.* By its very nature, worship deals with the deep things of God. It can therefore draw the worshipper into the mysteries of life and eternity, good and evil, alienation and redemption. To some it is given to see further than others, and they are able, in the spirit of understanding, to share their perceptions with others. Like Paul, they can demonstrate in their lives the paradoxes of mature faith: commitment to truth, yet tolerance of others; awareness of suffering, yet affirmation of God's love; respect for doctrinal statements, yet awareness that the reality is much greater than the formulae. Paradox occurs even in the notion that one's deepest perceptions are, in fact, *given* through relationship with others and with the Other. Here is a maturity which overcomes the limitations of conventional or individualistic religious attitudes, and which serves as an inspiration for others. Yet the possibilities of growth towards such maturity are implicit – occasionally explicit – in the experience and the substance of worship.

- *Stage 6.* Christian worship centres on Christ, the Word made flesh. He incarnates cosmic purpose and divine salvation – in his life and ministry, death and resurrection, abiding presence and transcendent glory. He is mediator and model, high priest and atonement. The rich symbolism of Christian worship points to him as God with us and for us. He represents for us the full stature of humanity, but that humanity is transparent upon the nature and purpose of God. Stage 6, if we adopt such a convention, is thus more than the high point of human development. We look to Christ as the goal of our personal and spiritual development, and we press on towards the goal in company with the faithful in heaven and on earth. The goal transcends what we are; it is eschatological, the ultimate point in our pilgrimage. Yet that ultimate point was expressed in human

---

[19] Relevant here is the work of Oser: cf. Oser and Reich, 'Moral judgement, religious judgement, world view and logical thought: a review of their relationship', *British Journal of Religious Education* 12, 1990, pp. 94–101, 172–81.

terms in Christ, who therefore showed us the new humanity, lived out in faith and transfigured by hope and love. Christ is therefore more than one of 'the spiritual giants of mankind', although what he expresses is inherent in God's creation. God in Christ affirms and enhances life. Worship is similarly life enhancing, radiating the joy of life made whole.

Arguments will continue about the strengths and weaknesses of patterns of faith development such as that outlined above. Discussion of that nature, however, should not divert us from the challenge of their insights. For example, the recent convert loudly proclaiming that he has 'found the Lord' may be little more than stage 2 in faith development. The traditionalist who constantly exhorts the church to 'take a strong moral line' or to 'get back to the Bible', like literalists and legalists of all hues, is probably no higher than stage 3. The liberal, appealing to rationality and enlightened conscience, and insisting on the need to demythologize ancient scriptures, evinces stage 4 characteristics. Stage 5, so elusive for most of us at least on a consistent basis, is positively required of the Christian who would work for community and racial harmony in a multi-religious society. And what about parish ministry and church life? Are they geared to sustaining people at the level of conventional attachment and institutional survival rather than committed to faith development and Christian witness in an alien world? Christian education is a parody of itself if wholly domesticated to institutional requirements. Its nature is to be deeply challenging. Christian formation is an on-going process of growth and development, for individual and community.

Christian formation involves life-long learning. The focus of this learning is the faith community itself, with its worship and sacraments which enhance our remembrance of the Church's story, relate it to our life-stories and engender spiritual renewal and transformation. Learning takes place by a variety of means: hearing the Christian proclamation and story; participating in worship and sacrament; sharing in the life of the faith community; learning from others' example, widening one's contacts with other Christians and the work of the Churches in the wider world; and attempting to bear a quiet witness in the world of work, business or community. Learning is not about

sitting in a classroom all day! To be sure, adult learning classes
have their place, as do Christian education centres and distance
learning. But the main factor is to establish that the Christian
life is itself a learning process, fed by many streams. We need to
take seriously the fact that 'disciple' means 'learner'. The
language of Christian spirituality suggests an on-going process
– becoming more than one presently is. It is a living of the
Christian story as our story; a more complete turning to the
goal or vision which Christ sets before us.

As we have seen, Christian growth and development are
eschatological; their goal is mature personhood, 'measured by
nothing less than the full stature of Christ' (Ephesians 4:13).
But the peculiarity of Christian eschatology is that it is not
simply reserved for 'the last days' but vitally intersects life here
and now. Eschatology presents the goal, the vision. Looking to
Christ, 'the originator and perfecter of our faith', we have a
stable faith yet one which is always growing towards its ultimate
goal, which is also its inspiration. And this change and
development takes place in organic unity with 'the body of
Christ', which is a spiritual rather than an institutional concept
but one earthed in the community of faith. Thus

> we are to maintain the truth in a spirit of love; so shall we fully grow
> up into Christ. He is the head, and on him the whole body depends.
> Bonded and held together by every constituent joint, the whole
> frame grows through the proper functioning of each part, and
> builds itself up in love. (Ephesians 4:15–16, REB)

FURTHER READING

J. Astley and L. J. Francis (eds.), *Critical Perspectives on Christian
Education*, Fowler Wright, Herefordshire 1994.

H. Bushnell, *Christian Nurture*, New York 1861.

J. Ferguson (ed.), *Christianity, Society and Education*, London
1981.

J. Fowler, *Stages of Faith. The Psychology of Human Development and
the Quest for Meaning*, San Francisco 1981.

T. H. Groome, *Sharing Faith: A Comprehensive Approach to
Religious Education and Pastoral Ministry*, San Francisco
1991.

J. Hull, *What Prevents Christian Adults from Learning?*, London
1985.

F. K. Schweitzer, G. Faust-Siehl, B. Krupka, K.-E. Nipkow, 'Religious Development and the Praxis of Religious Education', *Journal of Empirical Theology* 8, 1995, 1.

FOR DISCUSSION

1. How fundamental to Christian formation are learning and identifying with the Church's story? How does one learn to identify with it? Are there strengths and weaknesses in this kind of approach?
2. Is the perspective of religious development the key to understanding Christian formation? If it is important, what place does worship have in it, and what are the consequences for worship?
3. Has the Sunday school had its day? If not, what contribution can it make to Christian formation in future? If it is outmoded, what can replace it as the agency for the Christian nurture of the young?
4. Why do so many Christian adults find it difficult to progress in religious understanding?

CHAPTER 9

THE MEAL FOR THE LIFE OF THE WORLD

The Meal in the Upper Room

Jesus, on the evening of his arrest, gathered his disciples together for a meal in an upper room in the city of Jerusalem. The earliest written account of that meal which we possess is in Paul's First Letter to the Corinthians 11:23–26. Here Paul speaks of having given the Corinthians, on his first arrival the tradition, the story, of this meal, which he had himself earlier received from the Lord. Paul was first in Corinth about the year 51, and he must have received this account at the time of his conversion. Thus, we have here a story which goes back to the very early days of the Church, indicating a conviction that the Church's obedient following of the command and example of the Lord in taking the bread and the cup was vital to its life and worship and witness.[1] Paul was insisting that the Church's meals must have been seen as continuous with the supper in the upper room on the night of Jesus' betrayal; he is imposing a 'Last Supper' motif on a variety of existing practices. The synoptic gospels were written later than 1 Corinthians, and each has an account of the Last Supper. These passages agree with 1 Corinthians 11 and with each other in the broad outlines of what happened in the upper room, but they differ in numerous details, some of which we will notice later (Matthew 26:26–38; Mark 14:22–24; Luke 22:17–19). John's Gospel has, in chapter 13, an account of the Last Supper which differs substantially both from Paul and from the synoptic stories. In John there is nothing about the bread and the cup, or Jesus' sayings about them; instead there is the narrative of the

[1] Cf. I. Howard Marshall, *Last Supper and Lord's Supper*, Exeter 1980, pp. 32–33.

168

footwashing and a discussion between Jesus and the disciples about service, the coming betrayal, and the destiny of Jesus, leading into the farewell discourses of chapters 14–16 and the prayer of chapter 17.

All the sources are agreed that Jesus met with his disciples for a familiar ceremonial meal on that fateful night. The disciples were a mixed bunch; former zealots together with a reformed quisling; a handful of fishermen; Peter who was going to deny in a few hours' time having had any involvement with Jesus; and Judas, who was about to betray him to the authorities for a paltry fee. None of them were excluded from fellowship with Jesus as he approached his ultimate crisis. It was in a way a family occasion; Jesus and his family of disciples gathered for the ritual meal just as every pious Jewish family came together for such festivals. Despite the gathering clouds, it was in paradoxical fashion a festive occasion, and a ritual so familiar to the disciples that they must have found security in the midst of stress as they heard the familiar words and took part in the well-remembered actions, so rich with associations and speaking so powerfully of the things of God.

Jesus took this comfortingly familiar rite, and he must have startled and disconcerted his disciples by giving it a new meaning and a quite unexpected and puzzling significance. When he performed the traditional ritual of taking the bread he said (whether it was in addition to, or instead of, the customary words we are not told; Jesus' words made such an impression that they alone were remembered and passed down), 'This is my body which is for (or, broken for) you.' And when he took the cup he said, 'This is my blood of the new covenant which is poured out for many.'[2] In doing and saying these things, Jesus was linking together in the strongest and most dramatic of ways what happened at the Supper and what was to happen on the cross the next day. The two events interpreted one another and remain indissolubly linked. In the Supper, Jesus proclaimed to his disciples that the death on the cross was to be the inauguration of a new covenantal relationship between God and his people; that he was to die for the disciples and 'for many' – a term which must be understood in the inclusive rather than exclusive sense as meaning 'everyone'.

---

[2] There is no space here to go into the variations in the words of Jesus in the various sources. For detailed discussions the reader is directed to J. Jeremias, *The Eucharistic Words of Jesus*, London 1966; and I. Howard Marshall, *op. cit.*

He is giving up his life for them; they are to be nourished unto eternal life by his broken body and outpoured blood. The rite of the footwashing, which takes the central place in the Johannine account, should be understood as another way of describing the linkage between the Supper and the Death. The footwashing speaks of the servant-role of Jesus. The narrative is not simply exemplary – though it is that: 'If I, then, your Lord and Teacher, have washed your feet, you also ought to wash one another's feet. For I have given you an example, that you also should do as I have done to you' (John 13:14–15). It may well have awakened associations with the Old Testament figure of the Suffering Servant and passages such as Isaiah 53 may have come to mind, along with sayings of the Lord like, 'The Son of man . . . came not to be served but to serve, and to give his life as a ransom for many' (Mark 10:45). Thus, the Lord's Supper and the Lord's Sufferings were linked permanently and closely together, so that each lights up the mystery and the significance of the other, and neither can be properly understood in isolation.

The accounts of the Last Supper in 1 Corinthians, Luke and John all suggest that in the course of the Supper Jesus indicated to his disciples that they should regard what he did and said at that time as an example to be followed frequently; in Paul and Luke it is an explicit command to take the bread and the cup, in John it is the suggestion that the disciples should serve one another in days to come as Jesus had served them by symbolically washing their feet in the upper room. And both the New Testament and other sources for the practice of the early Church make it quite clear that the regular and distinctively Christian mode of worship was the repeating of the Supper that the Lord had celebrated with his disciples, thereby being obedient to his explicit command, becoming aware of his continuing presence with his people, and being nourished and sustained by his body and blood signified and conveyed in the bread and the wine.

The repetition of the Supper was to be 'in remembrance of me' (*eis ten emen anamnesin*). This phrase is more difficult to interpret than it might seem at first sight. While it clearly includes the idea of remembering Jesus and what he did, the Lord's Supper has never been a commemoration of a dead Jesus, or a wake for a dead God; it has always been a celebration of the living presence of the resurrected Lord. Perhaps a better translation into modern English would be to speak of 'recalling' Jesus and his work, for in the Supper he is present according to his promise, and the fruits of his self-offering are given to his people.[3]

Was the Last Supper a Passover meal, or some other kind of ritual fellowship meal? The Passover was an annual feast, celebrated whenever possible in Jerusalem, but throughout the *diaspora* as well, in small groups, and typically in the family. It commemorated and symbolized God's deliverance of his people from death by the blood of the passover lamb smeared on their lintels and doorposts, and their hasty departure from Egypt and safe passage through the Red Sea. The synoptic accounts suggest that the Last Supper was indeed a passover meal; John, however, indicates that it took place *before* the Passover, and Jesus was crucified as the Passover lambs were being sacrificed; while the epistles do not indicate whether it was understood as a Passover feast or not. The argument is complex, but not of crucial importance for our understanding of the Lord's Supper.[4] As we have argued earlier, the Last Supper, the crucifixion and the resurrection were tied together intimately and inextricably, and all the sources are agreed that this three-sided event took place at Passover time and must be understood in the light of the Passover. The Jesus who gave himself on the cross for his people and who gave and gives himself to them in the Supper may be understood as the Passover lamb: 'Christ our Passover lamb has been sacrificed for us; therefore let us keep the feast', cries St. Paul (1 Corinthians 5:7). Christ died for the deliverance of all: this was a 'new exodus', the fulfilment and completion of the old. In Luke's account of the Transfiguration, Moses and Elijah spoke with Jesus of his '*exodus* which he was to accomplish at Jerusalem' (Luke 9:31). It is thus clear that the Supper, whether its origin was a Passover feast or not, must be understood along with the death and resurrection of Jesus in the light of the Passover – i.e. that it relates to a sacrificial death through which liberation is achieved, and through this Supper the people of God participate in the fruits of the sacrifice, in the liberation that has been won for them. They

---

[3] For Jeremias' controversial interpretation of the *anamnesis*, see *The Eucharistic Words of Jesus*, pp. 237–55.

[4] Readers may follow the argument in Jeremias, *op. cit.*, pp. 15–18; and I. Howard Marshall, *op. cit.*, chapter 3.

encounter God's purpose for all humankind and respond
with joy to his call.

If the Lord's Supper inherited from the passover tradition an
emphasis on looking back to Christ's acts of sacrifice and
liberation which were real once again in the rite, it also took
from the Passover the idea that the Supper looked forward, not
just to the cross and resurrection but to the culmination of
all God's purposes. Just as the Passover nourished and aroused
a thirst for freedom and a longing for God's future, so the
Lord's Supper looked forward with eager anticipation to a
future which was often described by the image of the messianic
banquet: 'On this mountain the Lord of hosts will make for all
peoples a feast of fat things, a feast of wine on the lees, of fat
things full of marrow, of wine on the lees well refined' (Isaiah
25:6). The synoptic gospels record that Jesus at the Last Supper
looked forward to renewing the festivities with his disciples in
the kingdom: 'I tell you I shall not drink again of this fruit of
the vine until that day when I drink it new with you in my
Father's kingdom.'[5] From the beginning, then, the Lord's
Supper has been a feast of hope and expectation, pointing to
the future, a kind of appetizer (*antepast*) for the messianic
banquet. Thus, the Lord's Supper should be seen as stimulating
a thirst, a longing, for the immediate presence of God and an
eagerness for the Kingdom and its justice. It therefore is also an
act of commitment to the work of the Kingdom, the work of
justice, liberation and peace. To share the bread and the cup is
to share a destiny.[6]

Eating with Jesus

Other memories of Jesus enriched and fertilized the early
Christians' understanding of the Lord's Supper; indeed it is
possible that as these memories influenced the way the early
Church celebrated the Supper, so the liturgical experience of
the writers may have shaped the way certain gospel narratives
were committed to writing. It is, first, necessary to remember
that Jesus ate many times with his disciples before the supper in
the upper room on the night of his betrayal. Many of these

---

[5] Matthew 26:29; cf. Mark 14:25, Luke 14:16, 17. For detailed discussion of these
texts, see Jeremias, *op. cit.*, pp. 218ff.
[6] On this paragraph, see Geoffrey Wainwright, *Eucharist and Eschatology*, London
1971.

earlier meals would certainly have had a ritual element in them. They were celebrations of friendship, in which the disciples learned the meaning of love. It should not be necessary to argue that it matters a great deal whom one eats with and the way eating is organized. A radically segmented society like Hindu India had multitudinous strict rules concerning who could eat what with whom, rules which preserved the segmentation of the society by ensuring that people from castes far apart in the social hierarchy could never meet as friends around the one table. Commensalism, eating together, is a sign and a source of friendship. If a family, or a group of friends, always 'eat on the trot', never sit down around a table to eat, and drink, and talk, they have lost one of the greatest sources of friendship and caring.

Jesus ate often with his disciples. He got a reputation as one who enjoyed eating and drinking, not at all a gloomy ascetic: 'This man's a drunkard and a glutton', they said, scandalized that eating and drinking should play so large a part in his life. But what really shocked the religious people of the time was not that Jesus enjoyed eating and drinking with his disciples, but that he was willing to share table-fellowship with all sorts of people. He received prostitutes and quislings and other notorious sinners, the outcasts of society, at his table. He refused to put up the fences that were so beloved of pious Jews. 'This fellow welcomes sinners and eats with them' (Luke 15:2 NEB), they said in horror. For them the idea that a devout believer should eat with Gentiles, or with known wrongdoers, was unthinkable; the very possibility aroused deep-seated fears not very different from those of a high-caste Hindu afraid of the pollution incurred by sharing table-fellowship with an untouchable. But Jesus mixed freely with all sorts of people and was generally considered to keep the most undesirable of company at his table. He welcomed people who were known wrongdoers or had the most dubious of reputations.

The example – the shocking precedent – of Jesus' table-fellowship was only established in the early Church after bitter controversy. Jewish Christians found it desperately difficult to share at the Lord's Table, or at the common table, with Gentile Christians. Many of them said that the issue did not matter, that separate celebrations of the Supper for Jews and Gentiles would in no way compromise the Gospel. But Paul thought otherwise. For him the universality of the Gospel and the work of Christ in tearing down barriers among people must be displayed in celebrations of the Lord's Supper at which there was no discrimination, no recognition or sanctioning of the old-age suspicion and hostility between Jew and Gentile. He withstood Cephas to his face because he had equivocated on this vital issue (Galatians 2:11ff.). Paul battled on until he won. And the controversy was of no little moment; henceforward, wherever the Church was established, there was to be one common table at which all, as equals, received and shared the things of God. And this principle of eucharistic commensalism shaped not only the Church but the whole of Western society, as Max Weber recognized.[7]

Not that it has been sustained consistently within the Church; the tradition in the Reformed Churches to 'fence the tables' in order to exclude the unworthy seems strange when measured against the practice of the Lord himself. And the refusal of one denomination to allow believers of another to join them at the Lord's Supper contrasts glaringly with Jesus' welcome to his table of a whole assortment of disciples, including the one who lost faith in him and betrayed him, and the one who denied any knowledge of him when the going got rough.

The narratives of the feeding miracles and the account of the Last Supper also shed light on one another. Consider, for instance, this narrative:

> As he went ashore he saw a great throng, and he had compassion on them, because they were like sheep without a shepherd; and he began to teach them many things. And when it grew late, his disciples came to him and said, 'This is a lonely place, and the hour is late; send them away, to go into the country and villages round about and buy themselves something to eat.' But he answered them, 'You give them something to eat.' And they said to him, 'Shall we go and buy two hundred denarii worth of bread, and give it to them to eat?' And he said to them, 'How many loaves have you? Go and see.' And when they found out, they said, 'Five, and two fish.' Then he commanded them all to sit down by companies on the green grass. So they sat down in groups, by hundreds and by fifties. And taking the five loaves and the two fish he looked up to heaven, and blessed, and broke the loaves, and gave them to his disciples to set before the people; and he divided the two fish among them all. And they all ate and were satisfied. And they took up twelve baskets full of broken pieces and of the fish. (Mark 6:34–43)

[7] Max Weber, *The Religion of India*. Translated by Hans Gerth and Don Martindale, New York 1958, pp. 37–38.

We may note the resonances between such an account as this, the narratives of the Last Supper, and the Church's celebrations of the Lord's Supper. For instance, the context of the feeding, and its immediate prelude, is teaching; it is not isolated, but must be understood as the consequence of the teaching, the two having a very significant linkage. Here we see quite clearly a theme we discussed in chapter 4 – the complementarity of Word and Sacrament and their inseparability the one from the other. Both the teaching and the feeding are instances of Jesus' care for the people, but neither on its own is an adequate expression of that boundless compassion. Next, the relation between Jesus and the disciples in the story must have reminded the early Christians of the activities of the various ministers at the Lord's Supper, suggesting both that the host is always Jesus, and that even faithless and mundane disciples have an important function in the distribution of the Lord's largesse to his people. The companies sitting in orderly fashion may have reflected more accurately than the image of the twelve disciples with Jesus, gathered around the table, the actual experience of the Lord's Supper in the churches in which the Gospel was read. But the most impressive similarity between this miracle and the Last Supper was the action of Jesus: he took the food, blessed it (*eulogesen*), broke the bread, and gave it to the people. These are precisely the four actions at the heart of the accounts of the Last Supper, and the actions repeated from the very earliest days every time Christians have celebrated the Supper of the Lord. There are differences, of course, and they are of no little importance. Fish are mentioned in the narrative along with the bread, and there is no wine; there is no explicit connection with the sufferings of Jesus, or suggestion that the bread is his body. But some of the differences give a new depth to the under-standing of the Lord's Supper. There is, for example, a strong emphasis on the lavishness of God's gracious provision for his people; there is wondrously enough food to satisfy everyone, and when the food had been shared among the multitude the remaining plenty was not wasted or thrown away but gathered together in baskets – sufficient for all Israel, enough for the whole world.

Similar light is cast upon the Lord's Supper by the Johannine story of the marriage at Cana of Galilee: Jesus is present at a festive occasion, a party, and he miraculously provides abundant wine as his contribution to the celebration. Here the emphasis is not so much on the meeting of human needs as on the importance of festivity and new life. And in the sixth chapter of John after a miracle of feeding, Jesus speaks of himself as the bread that comes down from heaven to nourish a pilgrim people just as the manna was given in the wilderness. God provides for the material and spiritual needs of his people with infinite and wonderful generosity.

Finally, the Lord's Supper has been interpreted in the light of the meals which the resurrected Jesus had with his disciples, recounted in Luke and John. The story of the Emmaeus road (Luke 24:13–32) stresses the hidden presence of the Lord with the two disciples on their way, and how when 'he took the bread and blessed, and broke it, and gave it to them . . . Their eyes were opened and they recognized him' (vv. 30–31). Once again, we have the four actions, and table-fellowship with the Lord so that 'he was known to them in the breaking of the bread' – an experience which has been repeated countless times down the ages as the Church has broken the bread in obedience to her Lord's command and example. Another instance of recognition of the risen Lord in the context of a meal is the breakfast on the lakeside recounted in John 21:12–13. As they ate together, 'none of the disciples dared ask him, "Who are you?" They knew it was the Lord' (v. 12). In a meal, the presence of the risen Lord is recognized; this table-fellowship of the first disciples is continued every time the Church celebrates the Supper of the Risen Lord.

The Lord's Supper in the Early Church

And so it was from the beginning of the Church. In Acts we hear that the early Jerusalem Christians 'devoted themselves to the apostles' teaching and fellowship, to the breaking of the bread and the prayers' (2:42). Almost certainly this indicates the main features of the early gatherings for worship, which appear to have taken place alongside attendance at the Temple, and very frequently, in the homes of the Christians rather than in any special buildings (Acts 2:47). It is suggested later in Acts that the Breaking of the Bread, the name in all probability for the Lord's Supper (and still used as such by sects like the Brethren), was the normal way of marking the first day of the week, the feast of the Resurrection. This frequency is at first sight a little strange, particularly if the Last Supper had been a

Passover, for the Passover was celebrated only once a year. But in view of the influence of Jesus' regular table-fellowship on the understanding of the Lord's Supper, and the fact that from very early indeed the Christians observed the first day of the week as the feast of the Resurrection, weekly or even more frequent celebration is easy to explain, despite the Passover connection.

In 1 Corinthians 11, Paul is commenting on a situation where the Lord's Supper – a rite involving bread and wine and specifically connected with the death and resurrection of Jesus – is part of a full meal for the congregation. This meal has become scandalous and divisive because the better-off Christians were bringing plenty of food to eat themselves and refusing to share with the poorer Christians who went hungry. Hence Paul proclaims that 'when you meet together, it is not the Lord's Supper that you eat' (v. 20). For the rich despise and humiliate the poor and divide the Body of Christ, making a parody of the sacred rite, a practical denial of its significance. (This may illumine the meaning of v. 29: 'For any one who eats and drinks without discerning the body eats and drinks judgement upon himself.') 1 Corinthians 11 and other Pauline passages, along with the references in Acts, remind us that the Lord's Supper was in fact a real meal, not an isolated ritual whose association with meals, or with the continuation of table-fellowship with Jesus, had been forgotten. This point remains valid even if Paul was insisting on a distinction and even separation between the Eucharist and the *agape* meal. The emphases in the Acts and the Pauline accounts are rather different, but they seem to be complementary descriptions of a form of worship which was in essentials the same. Acts does not connect the Breaking of the Bread explicitly with the death of Jesus and makes no mention of wine, but sees the supper as a festive continuation of the table-fellowship the disciples enjoyed with Jesus before his death and after the resurrection. And it is worth remembering that the author of Acts also wrote the Gospel of Luke which has a special interest in Jesus' meals, and contains the story of the supper at Emmaus. In Paul we see the connection with the Last Supper and the linking with the dying of Jesus spelled out in very explicit terms. The interests of Paul and Luke may be slightly different, but they both enrich our understanding of the early and perennial forms of the Supper, without fundamental conflict.

As we move out of the New Testament period, we find evidence that the Churches strove to follow the command and example of the Lord as closely as possible, celebrating the Lord's Supper weekly or more frequently, to recall Jesus and his death, to rejoice in his resurrection, to continue a real fellowship with him and with one another around the table, and to nourish faith and hope and love. Writing about the year 110, Pliny the Younger, who was a Proconsul in Asia Minor, reported to the Emperor Trajan on the activities of the strange new sect of Christians. Among their suspicious activities was the fact that they met together on a fixed day each week – clearly Sunday – for a common meal. This must have been the Lord's Supper, or the Eucharist or 'Thanksgiving' as it became increasingly commonly called, and which is mentioned in other early Christian sources. The *Didache* (probably early second century) gives evidence of weekly eucharistic worship:[8]

> On the Lord's Day of the Lord, come together, break bread, and give thanks, having first confessed your transgressions, that your sacrifice may be pure (chapter 14:1).

There is an account of a common meal with explicit sacramental practices. Thanks is given over the cup as follows:

> We give thanks to you, our Father, for the holy vine of your child David, which you made known to us through Jesus. Glory to you for evermore.

Then thanks is given over the bread – the order is rather unusual:

> We give thanks to you, our Father, for the life and knowledge which you have made known to us through your child Jesus; glory to you for evermore. As this broken bread was scattered over the mountains, and when brought together became one, so let your Church be brought together from the ends of the earth into your Kingdom; for yours are the glory and the power through Jesus Christ for evermore (chapter 9).

After the meal there follows a magnificent prayer of thanksgiving. The motifs are participation in the vine of David, gratitude for the life and knowledge and immortality which believers have received through Jesus, the 'sacred name' which is lodged in the hearts of the faithful, and the eschatological

---

[8] Cited from R. C. D. Jasper and G. J. Cuming, *Prayers of the Eucharist – Early and Reformed*, London 1975, pp. 14–16.

gathering together of the church. The strange thing is that there is no mention of the passion or the resurrection, of the body and blood of Christ, or of the Last Supper. Accordingly some scholars regard this passage as an account of an *agape*, or perhaps a very eccentric Eucharist. The *Didache*, primarily a very early product of Jewish Christianity, should remind us of the rich plurality of theme and imagery which goes into the making of the Christian eucharistic tradition.

Justin Martyr was converted to Christianity about the year 130, and his *First Apology* was probably written about 150. Here he gives two accounts of the Lord's Supper. In the first, a baptism is followed by prayers of intercession, the 'kiss of peace', and

> Then bread and a cup of water and of mixed wine are brought to him who presides over the brethren, and he takes them and offers praise and glory to the Father of all in the name of the Son and of the Holy Spirit, and gives thanks at some length that we have been deemed worthy of these things from him. When he has finished the prayers and the thanksgiving, all the people present give their assent by saying, 'Amen'.
>
> ... And when the president has given thanks and all the people have assented those whom we call deacons give to each one present a portion of the bread and wine and water over which thanks have been given, and take them to those who are not present.[9]

The second account relates to an 'ordinary' Sunday celebration – incidentally making it quite clear that the Eucharist was the main Sunday service. On this occasion the service starts with the reading of 'the records of the apostles or writings of the prophets', followed by a homily. Thereafter the service proceeds much as before, except that there is no kiss of peace, it is mentioned that the president prays 'to the best of his ability', i.e. he is not tied to a text, and there is a collection for the needy.

Hippolytus' *The Apostolic Tradition* was probably written in the early third century. It contains the earliest text of eucharistic prayer and comes before the development of the varied families of liturgies in East and West. Its account of the Eucharist is closely similar to that of Justin, but there is considerably more detail. The text of the eucharistic prayer was probably a specimen rather than a mandatory form and it has been highly influential on all modern liturgical revisions. It contains all the

[9] First Apology, 65, 3: cited in Jasper and Cuming, *op. cit.*, pp. 18–19.

major sections and emphases which most scholars regard as important in a eucharistic prayer. The Eucharist follows the consecration of a bishop with the Peace and the offering of gifts, on which the new bishop 'with all the presbytery' lays hands and gives thanks:

Greeting
> The Lord be with you.
> And with your spirit.

Sursum Corda
> Lift up your hearts.
> We hold them towards the Lord (Greek: Let us pray to the Lord).
> Let us give thanks to the Lord.
> It is worthy and right.

Thanksgiving
> We give thanks to you, O God, through your beloved servant Jesus Christ, whom in the last times you sent to us as saviour and redeemer and messenger of your will; he is the Word inseparable from you, through whom you made all things, and on whom your favour rested. You sent him from heaven into a virgin's womb; he was conceived, made flesh and revealed as your Son, born of the Holy Spirit (and a virgin). As he gave full expression to your will and created for you a holy people, he stretched out his hands in suffering in order to free from suffering those who put their trust in you. And after he was handed over to suffering, which he freely accepted, that he might destroy death and break the bonds of the devil, tread down hell and give light to the righteous, fix the limit and manifest the resurrection.

Narrative of Institution
> he took bread, gave thanks to you and said, 'Take, eat; this is my body, which is broken for you.' Likewise also the cup, saying, 'This is my blood, which is shed for you; when you do this, do it to remember me.'

Anamnesis, or Remembrance
> We remember therefore his death and resurrection, and

Oblation
> we offer to you the bread and the cup, giving you thanks because you have accepted us as worthy to stand before you and serve you.

Epiclesis, or Invocation of the Holy Spirit

And we ask you to send your Holy Spirit upon the offering of your Holy Church; to unite all your saints, and to grant them, as they partake, that they may be filled with the Holy Spirit and that their faith may be confirmed in the truth;

Doxology

so that we may praise and glorify you through your servant Jesus Christ, through whom be glory and honour to you, to the Father and the Son with the Holy Spirit, in your Holy Church, both now and for ages and ages.

Assent of the People

Amen.[10]

All these early sources indicate that while there was a good deal of flexibility in the way in which the Supper was conducted and no form of words was mandatory, there was a close similarity in the *shape* of the rite, clearly determined by the intention of following the command and example of the Lord as closely as possible in taking, blessing, breaking and sharing. The great prayer was always one of thanksgiving over the elements and commonly, but not universally, included a narrative of the institution – as the story of the Last Supper tends to be called. The connections with the cross and with the resurrection are clearly affirmed by the explicit linking of the elements with the death of Jesus and the fact that the most appropriate day for the Lord's Supper was recognized to be Sunday, the weekly celebration of the resurrection.

Some Developments

We cannot here give more than the sketchiest of outlines of the development of the Lord's Supper. Readers who wish to know more are referred to some of the books listed in the bibliography. Certain developments which took place gradually over a period of centuries require, however, to be noted.

1. As we have suggested above, the Lord's Supper became disjoined from the common meal of the congregation, and the latter apparently disappeared in most places. The kind of

---

[10] Hippolytus, *The Apostolic Tradition*, chapter 4. Translated from text L, taking into account text E, in B. Botte's, *La Tradition Apostolique de saint Hippolyte*, Paris 1963, pp. 12–16.

situation of which we read in 1 Corinthians 11 was no longer to be found; perhaps partly because in other places, as in Corinth, the meal had become an occasion for disorder, gluttony, drunkenness, and faction in the church. It is also difficult to see how, as the size of congregations increased, a weekly or even more frequent common meal could have been sustained. With this change there went a change of title: the Lord's Supper, which clearly connotes a meal at which the host is the Lord himself, became known as the Eucharist, a word which quickly became a technical term for a rite. Whereas the earliest Church had seen one of the marks of distinction between itself and the pagan cults of the ancient world as being that the church had no altar but a table around which they met for a meal, the way was now open to the Eucharist being understood as a sacrifice on an altar rather than a meal at a table.

2. We have seen earlier that the death of Jesus was interpreted, among other ways, as a sacrifice in the New Testament period, and that there was from the beginning a very intimate connection between the cross and the Lord's Supper. There was thus a necessary link between the Supper and the sacrificial death of Christ, and the Supper could never be freed from sacrificial connotations. But the precise relationship between the Supper and the Sacrifice needed to be spelled out. At the beginning the Lord's Supper was never referred to as being itself a sacrifice, but gradually in the second century it became common to refer to it as a sacrifice. Justin Martyr refers to the Eucharist as the sacrifice of the Church, and Tertullian describes it in terms of a sacrifice at an altar. This development may have been partly in response to an environment where a religion meant to most people a sacrificial system, and Christians had to be able to point to their sacrifice or be despised as atheists. It is a vast leap from this, but one that the Church found it fatally easy to make, to regard the Eucharist as a repetition or continuation of the sacrifice of Christ, under the control of the Church and implying some sort of incompleteness in what Christ did on the cross. No adequate interpretation of the Lord's Supper is possible without recourse to the language of sacrifice; but this language has to be used with a discretion and care that was not always obvious, particularly in popular understandings of the Eucharist; and if the category of sacrifice is given so prominent a place in the

understanding of the Supper that other complementary concepts are all but forgotten, a radically distorted understanding ensues.

3.   In 1 Peter and in Revelation the community of believers is referred to as a royal priesthood, and the term used for pagan or Jewish priests was never applied in the New Testament to anyone in the Church. The Church was regarded as a corporate priesthood, but it had no individual priests who could act in isolation from, or on behalf of, the community. The whole body of believers had access through the blood of Christ to the holiest of all, and needed no other intermediary. But the Church as a whole stood in a priestly relationship to the world: they represented God to the world and the world to God, on the grounds of the Church's participation in the sacrifice of Christ. Accordingly worship, and especially the Lord's Supper, was seen as an activity of the community of believers, in which each had a role to play; and that role was priestly. As, however, the corporate priesthood of the whole body of believers was gradually overshadowed by a new understanding that there were individual priests within the community whose primary responsibility for worship was strongly stressed, the people tended to become more and more passive in worship. Two indications of these processes are the fact that after the early Christian centuries until the Reformation, the people 'heard Mass', but communicated only once or twice a year. In other words, the people watched and listened to a priest doing and saying intricate and unintelligible things, and only very infrequently participated as far as to receive communion. And when they did receive communion, they were denied the wine; only the priest received in both kinds; the people were disfranchised by being made passive observers, or partial participants.[11]

4.   There was an increasing tendency to concentrate attention on the elements of bread and wine rather than the rite as a whole, and to narrow down the understanding of Christ's presence by affirming his presence in the bread and wine and underplaying his presence as the host and master of the feast; his presence, according to his promise, whenever two or three are gathered together in his name; his presence in the Word;

---

[11] On this see especially J. A. Jungmann, *The Early Liturgy*, London 1960, chapter 2: 'The Church as a Worshipping Community.'

his presence in his Body, the Church; and his presence in the needy neighbour. And this concentration on the bread and wine led to people asking about 'the moment of change' – when the bread and wine ceased to be what they appeared to be and became the Body and Blood of Christ. The two commonest answers – that the moment of change is when the words 'This is my body' and 'This is my blood' are said by the priest, or that the elements change at the *epiclesis*, the invocation of the Holy Spirit to bless and sanctify the elements – make one suspect that the question itself is inappropriate, and remind us of the dangers of a magical and mechanical understanding of the sacrament.

5. From early days the Lord's Supper has commonly been called the Mystery or the Holy Mysteries – a useful reminder that every encounter with God must be mysterious and that Rudolph Otto was right in defining the Holy as *mysterium tremendum et fascinans*. But in the case of the Lord's Supper it is possible for the authentic and necessary mystery to be obscured by a contrived and misleading kind of mystery. As elaborate ceremonial and ritual gathered around the Lord's Supper, particularly after Christianity became the official religion of the Roman Empire under Constantine, the structure which tied the Lord's Supper to the Last Supper and conveyed the authentic Christian mystery often became obscured. It was not only the steady proliferation of additional rituals and the inclusion of all sorts of extra prayers and private devotions which hid the structure of the rite, but also the fact that the Mass was said in Latin, at crucial points in an inaudible murmur, which reduced people's involvement in, and understanding of, the service and encouraged stupid or superstitious misunderstandings. In addition it was impossible for the people to see what was happening; in the East because the major part of the service was performed behind an elaborate *ikonostasis* (or screen covered with pictures of the saints) totally obscuring the view, and in the West at a distant altar and often behind a heavy screen, the priest standing with his back to the people.

The Reformation saw itself, in worship as in doctrine and ethics, as endeavouring to recover the beliefs and practices of the New Testament Church. In the Lord's Supper, the Reformers tried to strip away what they regarded as the distortions of practice and doctrine and the accretions of ritual which obscured the true nature of the sacrament instituted by the Lord. Like the earliest Christians, they tried to follow, as simply and directly as possible, the command and example of the Lord, and as a consequence they recovered something of what had been lost. They sought a simple, biblical shape for the sacrament: they believed it should always be allied with the preaching of the Word, for Word and Sacrament were seen as complementary and neither could stand on its own; they wanted the full participation and communion in both the bread and the wine of all present; and they wished the Supper to be frequently celebrated, and certainly every Sunday. Calvin spoke of the custom, which had arisen in the Middle Ages, of annual communion as a 'veritable invention of the Devil', for 'The Lord's Table should be spread at least once a week for the assembly of Christians'.[12] So also Bucer wrote, 'I could wish that all would communicate at the Table of the Lord every Lord's Day.' And Richard Baxter, the great English Puritan pastor and divine wrote, 'The Lord's Supper is a part of the settled order for Lord's Day worship, and omitting it maimeth and altereth the worship of the day.'[13] Indeed, the 'right administration of the sacraments' which the Calvinist Reformers saw as one of the three marks of the true church must certainly be seen as including frequent celebrations of the Lord's Supper.

The Reformation was a corrective to what it denounced as 'the idolatry of the mass'. Like most correctives, it went too far, so that many Protestants tended to see the Lord's Supper as no more than a commemoration, to deny the real presence, and to refuse to consider any sacrificial or eschatological connotations whatsoever. In practice the Protestant Churches were not able to carry through the changes that they wished and became, despite themselves, captives to the mediaeval traditions. For example, strong resistance from the people made frequent communion impossible in most situations. From the Reformation until recent times the Protestant and Roman Catholic traditions of eucharistic theology and practice tended to polarize and, as is common in such situations, each pole represented an unbalanced, one-sided and partial under-standing and practice of the Supper which Jesus had commanded his disciples to keep.

[12] *Institutes*, IV.17.46.
[13] Cited in G. W. Sprott, *The Worship and Offices of the Church of Scotland*, Edinburgh 1882, p. 99.

The Lord's Supper Today

The twentieth century has been a period of remarkable convergence in eucharistic theology and renewal of eucharistic practice in almost all branches of the Church. The roots of the liturgical movement lie in the nineteenth century, but there is no space here to tell the fascinating story of its development and spread. Both in theology and in liturgical practice recent developments have arisen from the determination to get back to fundamentals. It has been realized on all sides that relevant liturgy must be faithful to the Church's Lord and take account of historical continuity. But this does not mean getting stalled in the debates of the Reformation, or the Enlightenment, or the Middle Ages, or absolutizing the doctrine and practice of the Council of Trent, or Thomas Aquinas, or Calvin or Luther. The asking of more fundamental theological questions in the now much broader ecumenical context has led to the careful development of a truly remarkable theological consensus in the understanding of the Lord's Supper. The most notable fruit of this process is probably the document produced by the World Council of Churches' Faith and Order Department as a result of some forty years' work by a large number of theologians, including many Roman Catholics, *Baptism, Eucharist and Ministry.* This was published in 1982 and sent to the Churches for comment, but already it indicates a very broad-based agreement.

In this document the Eucharist is seen, first, as Thanksgiving to the Father for all his goodness and mighty acts, in which the Church offers through, with, and in Christ a sacrifice of praise on behalf of the whole of creation. The Lord's Supper thus 'signifies what the world is to become: an offering and hymn of praise to the Creator, a universal communion in the body of Christ, a kingdom of justice, love and peace in the Holy Spirit'. It is, secondly, a memorial of Christ: 'the living and effective sign of his sacrifice, accomplished once and for all on the cross and still operative on behalf of all humankind', and thus the proclamation of God's mighty acts and promises. The Church recognizes 'Christ's real, living and active presence' in the Supper. Thirdly, the Eucharist is seen as the Invocation of the Spirit who sanctifies, renews, leads into justice, truth and unity, empowers the Church for mission, and gives a foretaste of the Kingdom. Fourthly, the Eucharist is communion with Christ and within the body, in which the true nature of the Church is made manifest and a 'hunger and thirst after righteousness' is stimulated. It is, therefore 'a constant challenge in the search for appropriate relationships in social economic and political life'. And, finally, the Eucharist is the meal of the Kingdom, which brings into the present age a new reality. It 'is precious food for missionaries, bread and wine for pilgrims on their apostolic journey'. Other notable recent statements of agreement on the Eucharist include the Windsor Statement of the Anglican-Roman Catholic International Commission in 1971, and the 1967 American Lutheran and Roman Catholic Statement on the Eucharist as Sacrifice.

Along with the development of a theological consensus has gone a remarkable convergence in eucharistic practice. Much impetus was given to this by the measures of liturgical renewal laid down by the Second Vatican Council, but many of the non-Roman Churches had already produced new liturgical orders, much influenced by new work on theology and the liturgical studies of scholars such as Dom Gregory Dix and J. A. Jungmann. The Liturgy of the Church of South India (1951) was one of the most interesting and influential of the new wave of liturgies. Since then almost all new eucharistic liturgies have virtually the same structure and although there is much diversity in language and in theological emphasis there is a strong common tendency to greater simplicity, more participation by the people, a proper balance between Word and Sacrament, and much greater flexibility and variety than was common in most traditions. But the eucharistic liturgy is essentially an integrated whole, moving through all or most of these elements, with some variety as to the sequence and emphasis:

Hymns of praise
Act of penitence
Declaration of Pardon
Proclamation of the Word of God
Confession of faith
Intercessions for the Church and the world
Preparation of the bread and wine
Thanksgiving to the Father for the marvels of creation,
    redemption and sanctification
The Words of Christ's institution of the sacrament
The *anamnesis* or memorial of the great acts of redemption,
    passion, death, resurrection, ascension and Pentecost
The invocation of the Holy Spirit on the community and the
    elements of bread and wine

Consecration of the faithful to God
Reference to the communion of saints
Prayer for the return of the Lord and the definitive
    manifestation of his Kingdom
The Amen of the community
The Lord's Prayer
Sign of reconciliation and peace
The breaking of the bread
Eating and drinking in communion with Christ and with each
    member of the Church
Blessing and sending.[14]

In every conceivable situation in every land men and women seek to obey the Lord's command by taking, and blessing, and breaking and sharing the bread and the wine. Outwardly there is immense variety in the ways they do this, but basically it is always the same: a festival of praise and thanksgiving for God's great love in Christ, a celebration of our fellowship with Christ and with one another, nourishment for a pilgrim people, and stimulus to seek God's ways of justice and of peace. Here we encounter God in Christ; he gives himself to us, and we to him. He gives himself for the life of the world.

FURTHER READING

Alasdair Heron, *Table and Tradition*, Edinburgh 1983.

Josef A. Jungman, *The Early Liturgy*, London 1960.

I. Howard Marshall, *Last Supper and Lord's Supper*, Exeter 1980.

Joachim Jeremias, *The Eucharistic Words of Jesus*, London 1966.

W. Rordorf and others, *The Eucharist of the Early Christians*, New York 1978.

Nicholas Lash, *His Presence in the World*, London 1968.

Geoffrey Wainwright, *Eucharist and Eschatology*, London 1971.

Louis Bouyer, *The Eucharist*, Notre Dame 1968.

J. Fenwick, *Eucharistic Celebration*, Bramcote, Notts 1982.

---

[14] Slightly adapted from *Baptism, Eucharist and Ministry*, Geneva, World Council of Churches, 1982, pp. 15–16.

FOR DISCUSSION

1. How do you understand the presence of Christ in the Lord's Supper?
2. Is it important that the bread and wine rather than, say, tea and biscuits are used in the Lord's Supper?
3. How should we understand the Eucharist as a *memorial* of Christ?
4. Should the Lord's Supper be an experience of liberation?
5. Can we speak of the Lord's Supper as 'the feast of the future'?

CHAPTER 10

WORSHIP AND PASTORAL CARE

Introduction

Worship and pastoral care – here, surely, we have two central activities of the Christian Church, two indispensable aspects of Christian praxis. The two are interdependent, and each illumines the other. When Christians treat worship as an escape from caring for the neighbour and being responsive to the needs of the world, when worship becomes an alternative to the doing of justice, when clergy attempt to avoid the role-ambiguity of the pastor by affirming their professionalism as 'experts in liturgy', then worship is being radically distorted by the dissolution of the necessary partnership between liturgy and pastoral care. The two share a whole range of common themes: grace, guilt, forgiveness, new beginnings, dialogue, communication, fellowship, reconciliation, healing are obviously the concern both of worship and of pastoral care. In its own fashion, each attempts to help men and women to cope with reality, open themselves to truth, and grow towards a mature relationship with God and their fellows. Of course they overlap and flow into one another; they are complementary – and more, for it would be fair to say that liturgy is a dimension of Christian pastoral care, and pastoral care is a dimension of Christian worship.

We are not suggesting that there is in worship *nothing but* pastoral care going on, and certainly not that pastoral care can be absorbed entirely into worship. There is more to worship than pastoral care, and *vice versa*. Worship is not just a kind of group therapy or corporate pastoral counselling, but none the less it plays an important, perhaps indispensable, part in the processes of healing, restoring, reconciling, purifying, growing, and forming fellowship. In other words, there is a highly significant overlap between the two activities; worship has a pastoral dimension and pastoral care has a liturgical dimension.

We are not arguing that worship is a good thing because it is psychologically beneficial or socially useful. It may well perform such functions, well or ill, but that is not the reason why people worship. We glorify and praise God because 'it is our duty and our joy', not because we seek some personal or collective benefit. That such benefits can flow from worship and are promised in worship should not be forgotten. But that is not the point of worship, and it would become mechanical if such expectations were to come to the fore. Worship used simply as a means of psychological hygiene or emotional manipulation is perverted and loses its authenticity; but we should expect participation in the worship of God to affect profoundly the deepest levels of our personality and emotions and relationships, and to shape and disturb the life of the worshipping community. Yet these fruits of worship are not its justification.

There is more to worship than the pastoral dimension – that is most certainly true. But if that element is lacking, worship is defective and inadequate. And likewise with pastoral care; there must be a dimension of worship or its integrity as *Christian* pastoral care has to be called into question.

The Pastoral Dimension in Worship

'For centuries', wrote J. A. Jungmann, a leading Roman Catholic liturgical scholar, 'the liturgy, actively celebrated, has been the most important form for pastoral care'.[1] One could demonstrate the truth of this remark by drawing up a list of the rites and elements in worship which clearly have a significant and necessary pastoral content: penance, confession, funerals, baptism, confirmation, the 'Peace', marriage, and so on. But Jungmann means more than that; the pastoral should be a dimension in all worship, not simply a characteristic of certain moments or types of worship. Because the church, the community which worships, is a pastoral fellowship, pastoral care should be the context, content and consequence of its worship. The God who is worshipped is the Shepherd of his people, and it is as Shepherd that he deals with his people in worship,

[1] *Pastoral Liturgy*, NYC 1962, p. 380.

enabling them to exercise a mutual pastoral care and outreach to all mankind.

This mutuality in pastoral caring deserves some emphasis. Worship considered as a human activity is something in which the whole people of God participates actively; it is not the acts and speech of 'professionals', of experts, which the people observe and listen to passively and without personal involvement. Similarly, the pastoral care that takes place in worship is not provided by the priest, pastor or minister for a passive people, but something in which every worshipper should participate both as provider and as recipient. And in the reciprocity of this kind of worshipful pastoral care, God's people encounter his care through their care for one another.

There is such a thing as a *pastoral* theology of worship, reminding us of the important fact that in worship God is dealing with *people*, both as individuals and in their collectivities. As soon as this is lost sight of, and the pastoral dimension in worship is neglected, worship becomes mechanical and impersonal and ultimately degenerates into magic. But such worship is defective in that it does not express God's concern for the individual and his communities, God's care for people, and the Christian fellowship's reflection of that care.

In worship that is authentically Christian, believers should experience God's loving care in and through the mutuality of caring within the fellowship, and find resources of insight and sensitivity to deepen and enrich their care. Those who encounter the Lord in worship should learn there how to discern his presence in the neighbour and in the needs of the world.

The Liturgical Dimension in Pastoral Care

When worship and pastoral care become separated from one another, pastoral care easily becomes secular, theologically empty and rooted in the latest theories of psychotherapy without reference to the Christian tradition. A kind of individualism takes over, suggesting that pastoral care has nothing to do with the flock or the fellowship, but takes place in one-to-one therapeutic sessions or small encounter groups. The pastor then becomes the expert, whose skills disable mutual pastoral care within the fellowship. The emphasis is increasingly on crisis intervention: care is less and less seen as an ongoing process of support, encouragement, learning and growth, and more and more as the solving of problems, the healing of sickness. These medical or psychiatric models can only take over if worship is pushed to the periphery.

It is easy for pastoral care to conform to secular models of counselling and therapy so that clergy are regarded – and sometimes see themselves – as counsellors and therapists and a great gulf opens between what happens in the counselling session and what happens in worship. It is even possible to find clergy who regard what goes on in the worship of the Christian community as an anachronistic distraction from the 'real business' of counselling individuals. There is in such cases a theologically suspect split between the sanctuary, which takes on the quality of a museum, and the study, office, or vestry, which is regarded more and more as a clinic. In the one the community gathers for rituals which its leaders no longer believe significant; in the other the weak, bruised, or sick individual meets the professional problem-solver or therapist.

The liturgical dimension protects three particular emphases in pastoral care. First, it expresses and reminds us of God's primary role in caring for people. Pastoral caring, in other words, has to do with grace; the pastoral activities of the Church, like its worship, involve participation in the ongoing work of God. Secondly, we are reminded that the whole community is in-volved in caring, as it is involved in worshipping. Pastoral care is not something that can be delegated to a few or monopolized by an elite within the Church. When caring is concentrated in the person of the pastor and the community becomes dependent on his skills and competence, we have a new kind of sacerdotalism, which like all sacerdotalism deprives the People of God of their true functions and responsibility, reducing the laity to the status of 'clients' or 'patients' of a falsely professionalized clergy. Pastoral care is a responsibility of the whole household of faith which constantly interacts with worship, the central praxis of that fellowship. Thirdly, it follows that there must be an ongoing dialectical interaction between theology and pastoral care. Pastoral care dare not cut loose from theology and attempt to root itself exclusively in psychological and sociological theory. Nor is it merely the application of an already established theology. Pastoral care which is Christian must both listen to theology and ask theology hard questions which arise out of the caring experience.

Worship is a collective activity, something that the Christian fellowship does. More than mutuality is involved here: the members of the community of faith care for one another and for their needy neighbours, that is true, but this care must also concern the structures of society which so deeply affect people's lives and happiness. Thus, there is a necessary interaction and movement between the pastoral and the political. Since the Church may aptly be described as the sacrament of the unity of all humankind, we should not be surprised that the Church's worship is full of signs of those structures of community which sustain fraternity and harmony. In other words, Christian worship is a political act, making statements and symbolic demonstrations concerning the nature of the Kingdom. Worship is prophetic to the world; it expresses the nature of Christian community, and thus proclaims what true fellowship is and what society should be. It makes the Gospel clear and visible. When Christians exchange the sign of Peace, or share the bread and the cup, or offer themselves to God, they are symbolically affirming God's care for them, their responsive caring for one another and the care for the world God loves, which is at the heart of mission.

Pastoral Themes in Worship

(i) Fellowship

In worship fellowship is both expressed and strengthened. The symbols which we use effect what they express, like the kiss which simultaneously shows and confirms love. In worship God and his people open themselves to one another in love and service, so that worship involves mutual commitment to one another and to God, the whole being grounded on the self-giving of God in Christ. And worship is a pledge, a binding commitment to God and his people and purposes. In worship we enrol anew in the household of faith.

Worship is meeting, encounter with God and with our fellows. In worship fellowship is made, sustained, confirmed. Karl Barth was right when he said, 'It is not only in worship that the community is edified and edifies itself. But it is here first that this continuously takes place. And if it does not take place here, it does not take place anywhere'.[2] The Church is edified by the

[2] Karl Barth, *Church Dogmatics* IV/2, Edinburgh 1958, p. 638.

Word encountered and received in worship, by the challenge, strengthening, encouragement, enlightenment, affirmation, direction, forgiveness, hope, conviviality received in worship, and above all by the awareness mediated through worship of acceptance and incorporation into a supportive, understanding and purposive community. Worship gives us a sense of belonging.

Worship is also concerned with the restoration of fellowship. There has recently been a recovery of the understanding that sin is primarily a breach in relationship with God and with one's fellows, rather than violation of law. Sin divides people from God and from one another; forgiveness means reconciliation, the healing of estrangement and the restoration of fellowship: 'where sin has divided and scattered, may your love make one again', runs part of one of the prayers in the new Roman *Rite of Penance*. In worship, or sometimes as part of the preliminaries to worship, sin is recognized and confessed, and with forgiveness the worshipper knows himself to be accepted fully and without condition into fellowship with God and the Church. General confession and absolution have a place in almost all forms of worship. In the Middle Ages these corporate acts of confession became increasingly overshadowed by an even more complex system of individual sacramental confession in which penances were carefully allocated to particular sins, and the performance of these penances was the condition for the receiving of absolution. The wilder shores of penance, particular the system of indulgences, attracted the wrath of the Reformers, and they attacked the system as legalistic, sacerdotalist (because of the power of the priest over the penitent) and shot through with justification by works rather than grace. To replace the individual penitential process, the Reformers emphasized two things: corporate confession as an indispensable part of congregational worship and the system called by the Calvinists 'ecclesiastical discipline'. The former frequently developed into a repetitive and verbose part of the service of worship, the emphasis often being more on long catalogues of sins than on God's gracious forgiveness. The latter, as developed in Geneva, Scotland and other Calvinist countries, involved the minister and elders having special responsibilities for the oversight of morals. Offenders were brought to trial before the Session or Consistory, and a whole range of penalties from private admonitions to excommunication were available to help to bring offenders to repentance. The more heinous offences involved several appearances in church as the 'stool of repentance', there to be publicly rebuked before forgiveness was proclaimed. In the form for Public Repentance used in Scotland in the sixteenth and early seventeenth centuries, absolution is pronounced with great authority and the penitent is then received back warmly to the congregation:

> The minister shall say, in manner of absolution: If thou unfeignedly repent of thy former iniquity, and believe in the Lord Jesus, then I, in his name, pronounce and affirm that thy sins are forgiven, not only on earth, but also in heaven, according to the promises annexed with the preaching of his word, and to the power put in the ministry of his Church.
>
> Then shall the elders and deacons, with ministers (if any be), in the name of the whole Church, take reconciled brother by the hand, and embrace him, in sign of full reconciliation.[3]

Although in such exercise of discipline the whole congregation is encouraged to join in confession and seeking forgiveness, the system quickly became legalistic and hard, often becoming a public spectacle in which some of the 'godly' rejoiced at the discomfiture of the sinners. The note of solidarity sounded clearly in Knox's Liturgy, ceased to be heard: 'We all here present join our sins with your sins; we all repute and esteem your fall to be our own; we accuse ourselves no less than we accuse you; now, finally, we join our prayers with yours, that we and you may obtain mercy, and that by the means of the Lord Jesus Christ.'[4] Instead, self-righteousness, judgementalism and gossip were engendererd.

The remnants of 'ecclesiastical discipline' and the practice of private sacramental penance have been very properly criticized by those who seek a renewed and living expression of confession and forgiveness in the life and worship of the Church. Alastair Campbell, for instance, argues that the fact that 'we rightly shy away from an *imposed* penitence, from a heavy-handed judgement on others which reduces them to the status of errant children requiring interrogation and hard discipline . . . should

---

[3] *The Liturgy of the Church of Scotland, or Knox's Book of Common Order*, John Cumming (ed.), London & Edinburgh 1840, p. 150.

[4] *Ibid.*, p. 145. Cf. today the *Book of Common Order of the Church of Scotland*, Edinburgh 1994.

not prevent us from pointing the way and leading the way to a positive form of penitence, which goes *through* the complexity of human motivation not away from it.'[5] Justifiable impatience with the neat distinctions and tidy classifications of the older penitential system led to its sharp decline in modern times. All Christian traditions are now seeking, with variable success, to encourage communal and flexible rites of confession and reconciliation as integral parts of worship, and more informal and personal ways of confession, counselling and mutual support.[6] Through reconciliation and forgiveness, fellowship is restored.

(ii) Wholeness

Precisely because it engages the whole personality, worship has a role to play in the integration of the personality. Worship can help in the overcoming of the great splits engendered by our culture, between reason and the emotions, the body and the spirit; but sadly it sometimes reflects and accentuates these cleavages.

If worship speaks to the heart as well as to the head, if it communicates to the feelings and plays a part in what John Macmurray called 'the education of the emotions'[7] there should be an accepted place for the expression of emotion in worship. Take for instance, grief. In Western cultures it is often felt that strong emotion should not be expressed in public, that even at a funeral service it is 'not done' to weep. This attitude persists despite the increasing popular awareness that bottled-up grief is often destructive, and shows itself in other ways which can be persistent and disabling. Even among Christians many would see public grieving as a sign of emotional instability or spiritual weakness and inadequacy. But the Gospels record that Jesus wept over Jerusalem, the city that he loved, and over his dead friend Lazarus.

It is similar with the split between body and spirit. Although views which depreciate the body have been repeatedly labelled heretical, and William Temple could speak of Christianity as the most materialistic of all the great religions, despite the fact that Christians believe that the Word became flesh, that in Jesus God was embodied, the body has often been despised. But in

---

[5] *Rediscovering Pastoral Care*, London 1981, p. 8.
[6] See, for instance, the Roman *Rite of Penance*, 1974.
[7] *Reason and the Emotions*, London 1935.

authentic Christian worship the body is accepted as an integral
and splendid aspect of the person: spiritual worship is also, and
necessarily, bodily worship, in which the body is an agent of
celebration in harmony with mind, spirit and heart.

(iii) Liberation

Listen to James Cone speaking of the significance of worship
for American Blacks:

> The eschatological significance of the black community is found in
> the people believing that the spirit of Jesus is coming to visit them
> in the worship service each time two or three are gathered in his
> name, and to bestow upon them a new vision of their future
> humanity. This eschatological revolution is ... a change in the
> people's identity, wherein they are no longer named by the world
> but named by the Spirit of Jesus ... The Holy Spirit's presence
> with the people is a liberating experience. Black people who have
> been humiliated and oppressed by the structures of white society
> six days of the week, gather together each Sunday morning in order
> to experience a new definition of their humanity. The transition
> from Saturday to Sunday is not just a chronological change from
> the seventh to the first day of the week. It is rather a rupture in
> time ... which produces a radical transformation in the people's
> identity. The janitor becomes the chairperson of the Deacon
> Board; the maid becomes the president of the Stewardess Board
> Number 1. Everyone becomes Mr. and Mrs., or Brother and Sister.
> The last becomes first, making a radical change of self and one's
> calling in the society. Every person becomes somebody, and one
> can see the people's recognition of their new found identity by the
> way they walk and talk and 'carry themselves'. They walk with a
> rhythm of an assurance that they know where they are going, and
> they talk as if they know the truth about which they speak. It is this
> experience of being radically transformed by the power of the spirit
> that defines the primary style of black worship. This transformation
> is found not only in the titles of Deacons, Stewardesses, Trustees
> and Ushers, but also in the excitement of the entire congregation
> at worship. To be at the end of time where one has been given a
> new name requires a passionate response with the felt power of the
> Spirit in one's heart.[8]

All round the world, in all sorts of contexts, one finds this
exhilarating experience of Christian worship as liberating.
Polish shipyard workers, striking for free trade unions and free

---

[8] J. H. Cone, cited in Geoffrey Wainwright, *Doxology: The Praise of God in Worship,
Doctrine and Life*, London 1980, p. 419.

expression in an authoritarian society, were sustained in their search for liberty by daily celebration of the mass in the yards. Groups of victims of dictatorship in South Korea found that their thirst for freedom and justice was totally dependent on regular meetings together for prayer – and for those in prison, the knowledge that their brothers and sisters prayed for them gave them new courage.[9] In Latin America even traditional forms of piety such as the stations of the cross have often come to be regarded as protests against oppressive regimes which deny liberty to the people. As the sufferings of Christ are remembered the words, 'As you did it to one of the least of these my brethren, you did it to me', come to mind.[10] That Archbishop Romero of El Salvador was murdered while presiding over the worship of the people of God was no accident, for he and the Church he led had often shown that worship was central to their concern for the oppressed, at the same time a protest against oppression and the nourishing of a thirst for liberty.

Enough has been said to show that in our day there has been a remarkable recovery of the experience of Christian worship as liberating. But one must enquire as to the authenticity of this understanding of worship. Is it, perhaps, that people turn to worship for the stimulant or tranquillizer most in demand at any given time, and in an age of liberation movements fighting for political emancipation, or women's liberation, and gay liberation, and so on, naturally seek liberation in worship? Are we in danger of speaking not of worship in the Spirit, but of worship in the *Zeitgeist*? The question is a real one, but the answer is quite clear: what has happened is, in fact, the recovery of a central emphasis of Christian worship which has in the past often been all but lost.

It is not, of course, as if worship as such, in isolation as it were, is liberating. Christian worship is the re-presentation of God's mighty deliverance of his people, the recapitulation of salvation history, in which the people of God appropriate and enter into the salvation or liberation wrought by God himself, express their gratitude and delight in freedom, are nourished to work for liberty and stimulated to yearn for freedom's final consummation. It is God who is the liberator; in worship we respond to his act, enter into the freedom he has given us, and

[9] Julio de Santa Ana (ed.), *Towards a Church of the Poor*, Geneva 1979, pp. 11–12.
[10] J. Moltmann, *The Crucified God*, London 1974, p. 53.

are nourished to share in his continuing work of deliverance.
As the psalmist puts it:

> When the Lord delivered Sion from bondage,
> It seemed like a dream.
> Then was our mouth filled with laughter,
> on our lips there were songs.
>
> The heathens themselves said: 'What marvels
> the Lord worked for them!'
> What marvels the Lord worked for us!
> Indeed we were glad.
>
> Deliver us, O Lord, from bondage
> as streams in dry land.[11]

Passover above all was the celebration of God's liberation of
his people. The rite expressed, and continues to express, the
present liberty of God's people, reclining as free men and
women around the table, as totally dependent on God's
gracious act of deliverance. Had God not acted, Israel would
still be in bondage, not yet a People (*laos*), without name or
dignity. The rite repeats and re-enacts the story, reminding the
people of their roots, of their dependence upon God, of their
dignity, and celebrating the liberty they have been given. And it
does more than represent a past deliverance; it gives the
resources for living as free men and women now, and provides
an appetiser and a foretaste of the joys of the fully con-
summated liberty that is to come. Each Passover points forward
– 'Next year in Jerusalem' – and beyond that to the messianic
banquet.

It is hardly surprising that Passover became a time when a
peculiarly intense thirst for liberty was commonly in the air, a
time when Jews were usually liable to protest or revolt against
contemporary oppression, being nourished at the feast of
liberty. And it was this rite that Jesus took, re-shaped and
attached for ever to the 'exodus' that he was to accomplish in
Jerusalem. In the Lord's Supper, at the centre of Christian
worship, there is accordingly this inescapable focusing on
liberation. We remember, recapitulate, and participate in the
liberty won and given to us by Christ. Here we receive food for
living as free men and women, and a thirst for the banquet in
the Kingdom of heaven when many will come from north and
south and east and west and sit down with Abraham and Isaac

---

[11] Psalm 126, Grail Version.

and Jacob. And in this Supper not only do we receive liberty and a thirst for liberty, but our understanding of liberty is clarified and refined, our vision enlarged and our hope stimulated.

Authentic Christian worship, then, cannot be separated from a concern for liberation, for this would be to detach it from its rooting in the mighty acts of the God who delivers his people from bondage. For freedom Christ has set us free; in worship we appropriate, enjoy, proclaim and express this freedom; and the freedom celebrated in the cult must infect the life and structures of society if we are to avoid a quite blasphemous separation between the sacred and the secular.[12]

In this chapter we have been arguing that there is a pastoral dimension in the whole of Christian worship. But some forms of worship have a heavier 'pastoral loading' than others. Notably those services which may be reckoned as 'rites of passage' have particular pastoral significance. A rite of passage is a ritual which invests with meaning an individual's change of status, gives public recognition to the new situation, supports those going through a crisis of change, and proclaims the community's understanding of the significance of what has happened.[13] Rites of passage are associated particularly with birth, puberty, marriage and death. Elsewhere in this book we deal with baptism and confirmation, the two central rites of Christian initiation. In this chapter we will say something about marriage and funerals, two rites of passage which clearly require to be discussed in a pastoral context. They are also by far the most popular Christian rituals in secularized Western societies.

Marriage

(i) Theories of Sexuality

'Sexual intercourse', said St. Jerome, baldly stating the dominant view for centuries in Christendom, 'is impure.'[14] A strongly negative attitude to sexuality, borrowed initially from the Stoicism of late antiquity which saw sexual intercourse as 'a little epilepsy', flourished in a Christian setting, so that Origen

---

[12] Cf. Peter Berger, *A Rumour of Angels*, London 1970; and J. G. Davies, *New Perspectives on Worship*, London 1978, chapter 1.

[13] The classic treatment of rites of passage is Arnold Van Gennep, *Les rites de Passage*, Paris 1909; E.T., *The Rites of Passage*, London and Chicago 1960.

[14] Jerome, *Ad Jovinianum*, 1.20: PL 23.238, cited in E. Schillebeeckx, *Ministry: A Case for Change*, London 1981, p. 88.

could say that during intercourse the couple lost the Holy Spirit, for 'the matter does not require the presence of the Holy Spirit, nor would it be fitting'.[15] This belief in the impurity of sexual intercourse led to the assertion of celibacy as a superior and purer state, and the gradual development in the West of compulsory clerical celibacy.

It also made more difficult a positive assessment of marriage. Gregory of Nyssa dismissed marriage as 'a sad tragedy',[16] while Jerome could find little positive to say about marriage save that it was necessary for the production of virgins![17] Augustine's theory that original sin was transmitted through sexual intercourse was widely held. Marriage was seen by many as a kind of compromise through which lust could be controlled. Even Luther could speak of marriage as 'a hospital for incurables, which prevents its inmates from falling into graver sin',[18] although elsewhere he takes a much more positive view of marriage.

Such grudging admission that marriage may be acceptable for Christians as a lesser evil than fornication and promiscuity, as a recognition that many people are incapable of sustaining a life of celibacy, as a way of disciplining sinful passions, as necessary for the procreation of the human race, jars strongly with the main thrust of the Bible's teaching. Little is left of the Song of Songs' magnificent celebration of sexual love, or even St. Paul's daring analogy between Christ's love for the Church and the love of a husband and wife. As Jack Dominian writes: 'The sexual union with its own physical and temporal limitations cannot exhaust the mystery of Christ and his Church. But by making this particular analogy, Paul continues the familiar symbolism of marriage between God and his people found in the Old Testament and thus brings the sexual union into the very centre of the history of salvation.'[19]

(ii) Theologies of Marriage

There have been two types of theology of marriage in the Church – sacramental and non-sacramental. The sacramental

---

[15] *Homilies on the Book of Numbers 6*, cited in J. Martos, *Doors to the Sacred*, London 1981, p. 408.
[16] Cited in J. Dominian, *Christian Marriage*, London 1968, p. 26.
[17] *Ibid.*
[18] *Collected Works*, vol. 44, pp. 1–14, cited in A. V. Campbell, *op. cit.*, p. 74.
[19] *Op. cit.*, p. 119.

interpretation stems from Augustine, who built on the Pauline analogy between marriage and the relation between Christ and the Church. Because marriage reflected this profound and permanent unity between Christ and the Church, it was of its nature indissoluble. Augustine also built on the occurrence of the word *sacramentum* in the Vulgate translation of Ephesians 5:32 to argue that like the soldier's *sacramentum* or pledge of loyalty, marriage involved an irrevocable commitment to one another on the part of the bride and groom. Prominent among the blessings of marriage were children, the others being fidelity and the indissoluble sacramental bond. The relation between these three - *proles, fides* and *sacramentum* – was much discussed. Thomas Aquinas laid down his position as follows:

> Marriage has as its principal end the procreation and upbringing of children, which end belongs to man by reason of his generic nature and hence is common to other animals; in this way we get offspring as the blessing attached to matrimony. But as a secondary end, as Aristotle says, we have in man alone a common sharing in tasks which are necessary in life, and from this standpoint, husband and wife owe faith to each other, and that is another blessing attached to matrimony. Marriage, as it exists among believers, has yet another end, and this consists in its significance of the union between Christ and the Church and thus we get the sacrament as a matrimonial good. Hence the first end is found in human marriage, in as much as man is an animal, the second in him precisely as man, and the third in his *qua* believer.[20]

The sacramental view gradually gained wide acceptance in the Church. Interestingly, the ministers of the sacrament were, and are, the couple themselves; the priest does no more than bless a sacrament which they perform, and declares publicly that they have entered into the married state. A strength of the sacramental understanding of marriage is that it founds the relationship of husband and wife on an objective basis, *ex opere operato*, rather than upon feelings or the subjectivity of the couple: but a consequence is the absolute indissolubility of a sacramental marriage – a rigidity which raises serious pastoral issues.

The Reformers attacked with great vigour the sacramental understanding of marriage. For a rite to be a sacrament they required dominical institution, and concluded that there were

[20] S.T. III (Suppl.) q. 65 art. 1, cited in Dominian, *op. cit.*, p. 30.

only two true sacraments – Baptism and the Lord's Supper. The exegetical basis for a sacramental interpretation based on Ephesians 5:32 was easily demolished. Sacraments are means of grace, but, Luther argued, 'It is nowhere written that he who takes a wife receives the grace of God.'[21] Marriage remained an ordinance of God, a permanent commitment of a man to a woman, providing the ideal context for companionship and the procreation of children. In certain extreme cases of breakdown in relationship, divorce became a possibility. A Christian marriage is a parable rather than a sacrament of the love which Christ has for his Church. There may, according to the Reformers, be a distinction of quality between a Christian marriage and marriage as such, but there is not a difference of kind. Marriage is, therefore, basically a secular thing, subject to the civil law; it belongs to the order of creation, worldly, but at the same time a divine institution.[22]

The contrast between the two types of theology of marriage must not be overstressed; they share a remarkable amount in common, and are different ways of saying similar things: that marriage involves a permanent, exclusive and unconditional commitment to one another on the part of husband and wife; that this is the proper context for the full expression of sexual love; that it provides the most secure environment for the upbringing of children; and that God's blessing is good, if not essential, for a Christian marriage. In marriage people encounter the love of God, whether they recognize it as such or not, and a Christian marriage may be a demonstration of the reality and power of that love, a sign of the love of God.

(iii) The Pastoral Context of Marriage

The observant reader will have noticed that our discussion of the theology of marriage moved to and fro between consideration of marriage as a prolonged relationship between a man and a woman, normally terminated only by the death of one of the partners, and the wedding service, the initiation, blessing, and celebration of that relationship. The two belong together, of course: the wedding is the rite of passage into the married state. Accordingly, even in a book on worship, we should not go

---

[21] *Babylonish Captivity.*
[22] For more detailed discussion, particularly of Luther's position, see H. Thielicke, *Theological Ethics*, vol. 3, pp. 125ff.

very far in talking about wedding services without asking questions about the understanding of marriage that is expressed and
confirmed in a particular rite. But it is also true that the
wedding service has a specific role to play in the Church's
pastoral care for married couples. Sometimes couples are
married in church with minimal or non-existent preparation
for marriage, and preliminaries to the service consisting of the
legal formalities, the choosing of hymns, and an indication of
how much should be paid to whom. Even when a more personal
approach is taken and the couples are given opportunities to
discuss the meaning of Christian marriage and explore their
relationship as well as participating in the planning of the
service, that is sometimes the total of the church's pastoral care
directed to them as the married couple or a Christian family.
Jack Dominian, the lay Roman Catholic psychiatrist, argues that
compared to the preparation and continuing support given to
the celibate religious, the married have been profoundly
neglected. He traces this neglect of care for marriage as an
unfolding relationship to 'the conceptualization of the sacrament as an entity which was complete in the exchange of rights
over each other's bodies followed by sexual consummation'.[23]
The wedding service accordingly ought to be from the pastoral
point of view one moment, and an immensely significant
moment, in an ongoing process of care and support for the
growth of love and marriage. And it is only thus that the
wedding service can proclaim an adequate understanding of
marriage.

(iv) Wedding Rites

The early Church combined considerable concern with
Christian marriage with a singular lack of interest in wedding
rites. A marriage was initiated by the couple entering into a
contract which was regulated by the civil authorities rather than
by the Church. Churchmen might criticize legal possibilities
of divorce or other details of the law, and when the Roman
Empire began to break down, the Church took an increasingly
detailed interest in the regulation of marriage. But still a
wedding was regarded as basically a legal affair. That is not
to say that rituals might not appropriately be appended to
the legal marriage: according to Tertullian, for instance, a

---

[23] Jack Dominian, *Marriage, Faith and Love*, London 1981, p. 119.

blessing and a celebration of the Eucharist were appropriate in weddings.[24] Sometimes the bishop's consent to betrothal was sought, and many ceremonies of secular or pagan origin became associated with the weddings of Christians – e.g. the giving of a ring and dowry, the crowning of one or both parties and the veiling of the bride. The giving of a blessing by priest or bishop was considered something of a special honour; Christians were often married without the presence of a priest. From about the fifth century in various parts of Christendom the clergy began to be more regularly involved in the conduct of weddings, and a variety of local rites gradually emerged. These rites were legally recognized as valid marriages, but for centuries it remained optional even for Christians whether they should have what we would today call a 'church wedding' or a purely civil ceremony. Only with the Council of Trent did a uniform wedding service come into use in the West.

Prolonged confusion about what is essential in a Christian wedding service has not yet been satisfactorily resolved. The sacramental interpretation of marriage, stemming as we have seen from St. Augustine, gradually heightened the liturgical significance of the wedding service (or the service, together with the subsequent consummation) so that it stood on a par with the other sacraments, particularly baptism and the Lord's Supper. Almost all traditions, whether or not they regard marriage as a sacrament, would today view this kind of 'liturgical inflation' of the wedding as a mistake. At the heart of rites of matrimony lies the public commitment of a man and a woman to one another, the public recognition of their net status, God's blessing on their relationship, and the celebration of their love for one another. Around this core prayers, scriptural readings, exhortation and the celebration of the Eucharist are appropriately arranged, together with the use of symbols such as the ring which, while not specifically Christian, are apt, evocative and sanctioned by long usage.

Funerals

(i) The Pastoral Context

Strictly speaking, there is no such thing as a theology of funeral services, but just as behind wedding services there lies a theology of marriage which relates both to the rite and to the

[24] Ad. Ux. 2.6.

pastoral care of which it is a central expression, so funeral services relate to a theology of death and resurrection on the one hand, and to the church's care for the grieving on the other. In the New Testament one finds much material on death and eternal life, and discussions about grieving and the Christian hope, but no indication whatsoever that the early Christians had some kind of distinctive burial rite. Since virtually all religions have a solemn rite of passage to mark the fact that a death has taken place and to dispose of the body reverently, we may suppose that the early Christians also had something of the sort, but it does not seem to have had importance enough for it to have left its mark on the pages of the New Testament. We do have evidence from the early centuries that Christians had funeral rites which were essentially Jewish or pagan rituals adapted to express the Christian belief in resurrection. Services of prayers, praise and Bible readings took place around the body, usually in the home, but sometimes in church. The cortege to the place of burial took place in daylight, with the Christians dressed in white robes with lights and palm branches, singing psalms of triumph and hope. All this was in stark contrast to the sombre funerals of classic paganism, which took place in darkness because death was regarded as an ill-omened threat to life. From quite early on the Lord's Supper was often associated with funerals – a reminder of the reality of continuing fellowship with the departed.

These practices continued well into the Middle Ages, although the atmosphere of hope and joy was gradually super-seded by a strong emphasis on sin, judgement and purgatory, all reflecting an uncertainty about the destiny of the departed soul, well expressed in the *Dies irae*. It is hardly surprising that, particularly in the popular mind, the main intention of the funeral was seen as earning some remission for the departed in Purgatory, or some easing of the awful judgement. All such attempts to influence the fate of the dead were strongly resisted by the Reformers, Anglican, Lutheran and Calvinist. Masses for the dead, vigils, requiems and virtually all the mediaeval funeral observances were dismissed by Luther as 'papistical abomina-tions', but both Lutherans and Anglicans quickly developed purged funeral services which omitted prayers for the departed and quite clearly had a pastoral intention – to speak to the mourners of the hope of the Gospel. For Luther, the intention of a funeral was to 'strengthen our faith and encourage the people to true devotion. For it is right and fitting that a funeral should be performed honourably, to the praise and honour of the joyful article of our faith, the resurrection of the dead'.[25]

The Calvinists went far further. They saw a pressing need to prepare people for death, but when all superstition had been swept away from funeral rites and Scripture consulted for guidance, they found virtually nothing left, or permissible, by way of funeral services. In Knox's *Liturgy*, for example, after a long and impressive section on the Visitation of the Sick, itself a striking instance of the pastoral use of prayer and worship, the whole section on burial is as follows: 'The corpse is reverently to be brought unto the grave, accompanied with the congregation, without any further ceremonies; which being buried, the minister, if he be present, and required, goeth to the church, if it be not far off, and maketh some comfortable exhortation to the people, touching death and resurrection.'[26] Nearly a century later, the *Westminster Directory for the Publick Worship of God* (1645) advocates a similar paucity, indeed absence, of ritual at the time of burial:

> And because the custom of kneeling down, and praying by or towards the dead corpse, and other such usages, in the place where it lies before it be carried to burial, are superstitious; and for that praying, reading, and singing, both in going to and at the grave, have been grossly abused, are no way beneficial to the dead, and have proved many ways hurtful to the living; therefore let all such things be laid aside.

But even where all burial ceremonies and funeral services were explicitly rejected, they soon came back, and probably never entirely disappeared. There seems to be a very basic need for this particular rite of passage. And as an act of worship relating to death, a funeral service is a time when the Church affirms her beliefs about death and the hope of eternal life; and expresses her pastoral care for the bereaved.

(ii) Theology of Death

Death is a problem to which Christianity gives no slick or simple answer. But it is also a problem that Christianity does not evade. The apostle Paul, who speaks of death as a friend, so that we

---

[25] WA 35, 479, cited in J. G. Davies (ed.), *A Dictionary of Liturgy and Worship*, London 1972, p. 102.
[26] *Knox's Liturgy*, p. 105.

long through death to put on our heavenly dwelling, is also aware of the bitterness and threat of death 'the last enemy', even for those who know that Christ has given us the victory over death. A general theodicy does not always help in explaining this particular death – and all deaths are particular and specific. C. S. Lewis's *The Problem of Pain* has much clear, reasoned Christian discussion of death and suffering; but his later *A Grief Observed*, written while he was himself mourning the death of his wife, has a profundity which many people find more helpful, for in it his Christian hope has been shaped and forged on the anvil of experience.

Death is the completion of life. This is most easy to accept in the case of the death of one who is full of years and honour, who welcomes death as a goal and fulfilment, who sees worldly finitude as something to rejoice at. 'Do not seek death,' wrote Dag Hammarskjöld, 'Death will find you. But seek the road which makes death a fulfilment.'[27] Yet death cannot always be seen as the natural completion of life; death is a foe, bitter and destructive, to be feared as 'the wages of sin', to be resisted and rebelled against. Here we may note the contrast between the death of Socrates and the death of Jesus. For Socrates, death was to be embraced, a liberation from the tomb of the body, as the beginning of real life; it was to be accepted with equanimity and without fear. Jesus, on the other hand, prays in agony in the garden that the cup may pass from him, and finally dies in anguish, alone, forsaken ('My God, my God, why have you forsaken me?') and with loud cries. Here we see how terrible death can be – and how God could draw its sting and set us free from its power. Thus, Christians believe that Christ has triumphed over death, and they have cause for rejoicing and the opportunity of entering into eternal life now, an adventure which has its culmination beyond the grave.[28]

(iii) Grief

Christians have a strange ambivalence in face of death, well expressed by Thomas Becket in T. S. Eliot's *Murder in the Cathedral*: 'Beloved, as the World sees, this is to behave in strange fashion. For who in the world will both mourn and rejoice at once and for the same reason?'[29]

[27] *Markings*, p. 136.
[28] This paragraph is indebted to an essay by Dr. Alan Lewis.
[29] T. S. Eliot, *Murder in the Cathedral*, London 1968, p. 51.

A death means grief and mourning for those who are left behind. Commonly grief goes through stages such as these. First, shock, when the initial impact of the loss often leads to erratic and uncharacteristic behaviour Secondly, control, a short period, usually ending with the funeral, in which there is a socially recognized and accepted pattern of grief behaviour. Thirdly, regression, pretending that nothing has changed, desperately trying to recover the past – a time of acute loneliness. Fourthly, adaptation: life must be taken up again, but now the pattern must be changed. Grieving takes time – far more time than many people recognize. And grieving is commonly accompanied with strong and discordant emotions; anger, remorse, recrimination, fear, regret, emptiness. Pastors must learn to respond appropriately to a range of deep feelings, and to support people throughout the time of grieving.

The funeral is a stage – and a vital stage – both in the grieving process and in the pastoral care of the mourners by the community. It is worship addressed to God, in which the community hold up the bereaved before god, and it is also a part of an ongoing process of pastoral care, exercised by the community as well as by the pastor. The mourners are held in fellowship, accepted in their new status by the community. Their grief is expressed, shared, publicly recognized, accepted. And thus the funeral plays its part in care, comfort and healing. The death of someone close to one is commonly experienced as a threat to the meaning of one's own life and disturbs structures of support and significance on which one has come to rely. The reverence for the body and the memory of a dead companion which is expressed in the funeral service helps to assure the mourners of their own worth. Christians can be realistic in the face of death, because its awfulness and its finality is understood in the context of hope. Christians do not 'grieve as others who have no hope' (1 Thessalonians 4:13). But Christians do and should grieve, even as they hope. And at the funeral service they are reminded not only of the grace and mercy of God, but also that there is a fellowship which cares for them and will mourn them when they come to die.

FURTHER READING

William H. Willimon, *Worship as Pastoral Care*, New York 1979.
Alastair V. Campbell, *Rediscovering Pastoral Care*, London 1981.
Jack Dominian, *Marriage, Faith and Love*, London 1981.
J. Spiegel, *The Grief Process*, London 1978.
David Lyall, *Counselling in the Pastoral and Spiritual Context*, Buckingham and Philadelphia 1995.

FOR DISCUSSION

1. In what ways can worship stimulate and encourage personal growth?
2. Is Christian worship defective if it is not experienced as a liberation?
3. How effectively may marriage or funeral services perform their pastoral function?

CHAPTER 11

WORSHIP IN THE MODERN WORLD

The Crisis of Worship

'There is a crisis of worship', proclaimed the Uppsala Assembly of the World Council of Churches in 1968. Since that time there has been a deeper and more widespread conviction that something unprecedented is happening to worship , particularly but not exclusively in the industrialized countries of the West. Quite simply, societies seem to be emerging in which worship of any sort occupies only a marginal position, in which many people regard worship as an optional extra, hardly more than a hobby for the small minority of people who 'like that sort of thing'. Are we perhaps seeing the emergence of societies in which there is no place for worship, of people who have no need or inclination to worship?

We must be careful, not to overstate things. There have been crises of worship before. To mention but three examples: some of the Old Testament prophets launched devastating onslaughts on the pattern of worship of their day; Jesus' attitude to the Temple and its cult was, to put it mildly, ambivalent; and the Reformation denounced 'the idolatry of the Mass' and virtually the whole apparatus of mediaeval worship. But all these protest movements saw the issue as a choice between true and false worship; they did not envisage the possibility of having no worship at all. They did not look benignly on worship *as such* – false worship, they suggest, is worse than no worship at all, but true worship is of vital importance to individuals and to societies. In itself, worship is regarded as problematic and constantly liable to perversion; it is not seen (as it is by many modern sociologists) as something necessary, good and useful for the smooth and proper functioning of societies and individuals. False worship is harmful and destructive and immoral; true worship is a duty and a delight – and probably useful in all sorts of ways as well, but its utility is merely a by-product of its truth.

The contemporary crisis of worship arises from the fact that so many people see the acids of modernity eating away all kinds of worship, true and false, useful and harmful, so fast that soon only vestiges will remain. There is no doubt that many people in Western societies look on any manifestation of worship as quaint, disposable and infantile, an irrational activity from which increasing numbers of people are successfully emancipating themselves. All worship, in this view, is false. Grudgingly it may be admitted that for a time at least, and for some people, worship may be useful or necessary. But worship belongs to the nursery, and the human race has come of age.

Like all such problems, this crisis penetrates deep into the life of the Church. There is genuine puzzlement about the place of worship in the Christian faith and life. Even in the Christian scheme of things, worship appears to occupy a far less significant place than it did in the past. A gap has opened in many places between theology and the practice of worship; it is forgotten that in the past worship generated much of the problematic of theology and provided one criterion of theological truth. Some of the best and most thoughtful of Christians, as Charles Davis has pointed out,[1] have withdrawn from participation in worship because they find it archaic, formal and unrelated to the context in which they are endeavouring to live out their faith. Others continue to attend worship, but find it jarring or quaint rather than enlightening, stirring and relevant.

The crisis is no superficial or transient matter, capable of being solved by tinkering with liturgical forms. Doubts about the principles and meaningfulness of liturgy are integrally connected with the modern crisis of faith, and this in its turn cannot be separated from the contemporary cultural, social and intellectual confusion and uncertainty. 'If worship constitutes a problem in our secularized society', writes Raymond Panikkar, 'the principal reason is not that the liturgy is outmoded or boring (it was almost equally so 200 years ago), but rather that

---

[1] Charles Davis, 'Ghetto or Desert: Liturgy in a Cultural Dilemma' in *The Temptations of Religion*, London 1973, p. 125.

the principles of the liturgy are themselves in crisis. Fashion or boredom are not in the main obstacles, but the fear of meaninglessness. All too often theological reflection about this problem remains superficial, considering it mainly as a practical or pastoral problem, while basically it is theological.'[2] Great issues are at stake, and it is important that we should try to understand in some general way at least what is happening. Worship, after all, is concerned with the search for meaning, with renewing, affirming, re-ordering our view of reality, of God, the world, and our relations with our neighbours. Worship is therefore necessary for the sustaining and proclamation of the Christian vision, because it is an encounter with the living God, that is, with Reality. And that is why the crisis of worship has to be taken with the most profound seriousness.

The Changing Place of Worship

The most obvious and easily documented change in recent times is the decline in attendance at worship. This type of data is easily quantifiable and although there are problems in interpreting its significance, and dangers that a decline in attendance at public worship should be seen as necessarily indicating a decline in religious belief or commitment, the trend in almost all industrial societies is unmistakable; there has been a prolonged, very substantial and probably unparalleled decline in participation in public worship over the last century or so. This decline has not been uniform over time; it has tended to accelerate since the middle of the twentieth century. It is more marked in urban than in country areas, among the working classes than the middle classes, and among Protestants than among Roman Catholics. All these factors suggest some kind of incompatibility between worship and modern industrial society. Exceptions to this rule which have been suggested include the United States of America and Poland. In the case of the United States it is true that attendance at worship is markedly higher than in most West European situations, but even there religious observance has been declining since the 1950s. In Poland the close association of national sentiment and the Catholic Church complicates the picture, but here, too, attendance at worship has been

---

[2] Raymond Panikkar, *Worship and Secular Man*, London 1973, p. 16.

decreasing – or was, prior to the conflict between the Solidarity trade union and the government. In most of the less industrialized countries, attendance at worship remains high, but falls off markedly as industrialization makes itself felt.[3]

Certain types of worship, however, survive more strongly than others in an industrial, secular society and continue to attract large numbers of people. For instance, even in situations where attendance at the 'normal Sunday service', whether that is Mass, Parish Communion, 'hymn sandwich', or a sermon with preliminaries, is low, surprisingly large numbers of people wish to be married in church bring their babies for baptism, and want a Christian funeral. Motivations in this matter are clearly complex and do not directly concern us at this point. But the resilience of these *rites of passage* is such that strongly antireligious regimes feel the necessity to provide secular alternatives.

The rituals of folk religion also continue to flourish and even increase in popularity, existing in an increasingly uneasy and often confusing symbiosis with Christian worship. Folk religion has to do with locality and the soil, with one's sense of belonging in a particular place and a specific community; with bonding to neighbour, and home, and a particular history. It is a religion of sacred places, sacred buildings, and special communities. Sometimes folk religion takes the form of a religion of national identity, as in Poland, or Scotland where some perfervid patriots are presbyterian atheists. The church building often is a focus of primordial sentiments shared by many who never worship there; it is good to have it there to stay away from; the existence of this sacred space within the area confers some unspecifiable benefit upon the community! When a church building is closed, vandalized or demolished it is not only those who worshipped there who are disturbed, but many others as well often show signs of uneasiness that this reassuringly physical presence is no longer securely among them. Subconsciously the building and what goes on within it are felt to continue to play a vital role in the folk religion of social cohesion and social continuity; a focus for the sense of belonging. The harvest festival is an example of a rite of folk religion, part harvest home, part fertility ritual, which has in modern times by popular demand becomes one

---

[3] Documentation and discussion of the points made in this paragraph may be found in S. S. Acquaviva, *The Decline of the Sacred in Industrial Society*, Oxford 1979.

of the main peaks of the church's years for many – even in city churches where the most that any member of the congregation cultivates is a back garden. Christmas, the pagan mid-winter festival long-since Christianized, is well established as by far the most popular Christian feast, but to judge by the tone of many sermons on Christmas it is in danger of reverting to its pagan, folk-religious origins. Be that as it may, amazing numbers of people go to church to worship at Christmas time, and if one counts, as one must, hymns and carols as forms of worship, each Christmas is a veritable bonanza of worship, much of it combining in subtle and significant ways elements of folk religion and more explicitly Christian forms. Christian worship and the rituals of folk religion have mingled and grown together so closely through many centuries that it is hard to disentangle them from one another and often difficult to distinguish what is Christian and what is folk religion in a particular act of worship. It is fairly clear that as soon as Christianity became the religion of the majority, or even of a substantial proportion of the people, it had to fulfil the functions of folk religion, and baptize at least some of its rituals. The interaction between the two over many centuries has left its mark on each so that one may reasonably argue that the two are now interdependent. Interestingly enough, one line of criticism of the Anglican liturgical reforms represented by the Alternative Service Book has been that the attempt to produce theologically and liturgically more adequate forms of worship endangers the delicate balance between Christianity and English folk religion in which the Book of Common Prayer has, rather strangely, become the pivot. In other words, the endeavour to make worship more explicitly and unambiguously Christian in a modern idiom makes it less capable of being a vehicle of folk religion as well.

The rites of civil religion flourish exceedingly, probably increasingly, in a secular context. These rites (like civil religions as a whole) legitimate, sacralize and conserve the authority of a society; they encourage and extol the civic virtues such as patriotism; and they assuage concern about the propriety of the behaviour of governments and the society as a whole. Some form or other of religion is the most widespread agency of legitimation, and where there is no recognized, established or suitable religion to hand for these purposes, a quasi-religion has to be developed. Since Constantine, Christianity has played the role of the civil religion in most of Europe. Macchiavelli recognized long ago that Christianity by its very nature does not make a wholly satisfactory civil religion, and he yearned to exchange it for the lustier religion of ancient Rome. But, for all that, Christian worship has doubled as the ritual of civil religion, and continues to do so. Armistice Day, now Remembrance Sunday, in Britain fulfilled and continues to fulfil a variety of needs – to recollect those who have died in the service of their country, to revive memories of the camaraderie of the forces, to give thanks for deliverance from enemies, and also to set at rest doubts about the wasteful carnage of war and questions about the justification of it all – by a ritual which at its worst becomes a celebration of chauvinism rather than of Christianity. Compulsory chapel in boarding schools, whatever the actual content of the worship, often gives the pupils the impression that worship is good for one in some rather unspecific way, like other compulsory items of the lifestyle: cold baths, cross-country runs, and the Combined Cadet Force. It is hard for it is not to be seen as a rite of civil religion, the celebration and sanctification of the public school ethos and the kind of society that ethos is intended to sustain.[4]

Civil religion and its rituals have been as unpopular with the theologians as they have been central to many sociologists' concerns. The theologians have regarded civil religion with suspicion because of the belief that the liberal *Kulturprotestantismus* of nineteenth-century Germany led directly to the sacralizing of blood and soil under Hitler and the difficulty many Christians found in disengaging themselves from Nazism. The sociologists, on the other hand, see the provisions of what Peter Berger calls a 'social theodicy' as a primary function of religion, and if Christianity cannot or will not provide what is necessary, an alternative must be found. Typical of such an alternative was the staged ritual of viewing Lenin's embalmed body in his tomb in Red Square in Moscow. As the long queue edged forward reverently towards the tomb one knew that one was observing a ritual of civil religion, a rite which has a significant function in the Soviet atheistic scheme of things.

[4] Civil religion has been a central concern of sociologists at least since the time of Durkheim. The most interesting current discussion concerns American civil religion. See Robert N. Bellah, *The Broken Covenant: American Civil Religion in Time of Trial*, New York 1975; Russell E. Richey and Donald G. Jones (eds.), *American Civil Religion*, New York 1974; and Gail Gehrig, 'The American Civil Religion Debate', *Journal for the Scientific Study of Religion* 20, 1981, pp. 51–63.

The accusations that Stalin encouraged 'the *cult* of personality' denotes at least an incipient awareness that ritual has a place in politics, or tends to return surreptitiously whenever it is cast out.[5] One could hardly wish for a better instance of civil religion than this account of a rally in China which appeared in *China Reconstructs* in 1976:

> At ten o'clock in the morning, to the majestic strains of 'The East is Red', Chairman Mao, the reddest, reddest sun in our hearts, appeared on the Tien An Men rostrum. 'Chairman Mao is here! Chairman Mao is here!' Thousands of emotion-filled eyes turned towards Chairman Mao! Thousands of people waved their gleaming red *Quotations from Chairman Mao Tse-tung* and shouted again and again: 'Long live Chairman Mao! Long, long live Chairman Mao! Oh, our respected and beloved Chairman Mao, how we have longed to see you. It is you who have given us new life. It is you who have lighted the flame in our fighting youthful hearts. It is you who have led us from victory to victory. We knew that just one glimpse of you would give us greater wisdom and courage – and today our wish has come true!'[6]

Peter Berger is probably right in suggesting that when the Christian world-view is no longer generally accepted, a specifically Christian legitimation of the social order cannot be maintained for long.[7] But that is not to say that the Church may not continue to be used as an agency of civil religion, increasingly evacuated of Christian content. Problems also arise in situations of religious pluralism, of which the United States is probably the classic instance. Here, as Will Herberg showed in his classic *Protestant–Catholic–Jew* (New York, 1955), there has emerged a kind of 'establishment' of the three types of mainstream religion. It is this triple religion which interacts so closely with the American Way of Life, and performs the functions of a civil religion. In countries like England and Scotland where there are established churches in situations of increasing religious pluralism, it is notable that in recent times on great national occasions – coronations, royal weddings and the like – the established Churches have given up their monopoly and the other main Churches share in the service, suggesting a gradual move in a similar direction to that already taken by the

---

[5] On political ritual in the Soviet Union, see Christel Lane, *The Rites of Rulers: Ritual in Industrial Society – The Soviet Case*, Cambridge 1981.

[6] Cited in Bruce Read, *The Dynamics of Religion*, London 1978, p. 107.

[7] Peter Berger, *The Social Reality of Religion*, Harmondsworth 1973, p. 86.

States. In the more ecumenical atmosphere of today the rituals of civil religion suggest an establishment of Christianity rather than of a particular denomination. This is almost inevitable, because the rites of civil religion must express unity rather than division and partiality. They are a matter of adaptation, compromise and alliance between Christianity and civil society's need for ideological support and ritual articulation.

The importance of the rites of civil religion may help us to understand why most Western societies have attempted, until modern times, to enforce uniformity of worship. Diversity of cult was seen as politically dangerous as well as theologically suspect, and the uneasiness about a variety of forms of worship being tolerated reflected an awareness of the need for one particular denomination to be the civil religion of the state; other cults were potentially or actually seditious. Diversity of worship was seen as theologically unacceptable, socially divisive, and politically disruptive. As time went by the conviction that worship makes a vital contribution to social order and the legitimation of authority was not abandoned, but the limits of tolerance were gradually extended: first, in northern Europe, Protestant worship in any of its major forms became acceptable; then any mainstream mode of Christian worship; and now secular as well as religious ritual is seen as capable of performing the functions of a civil religion. This expansion of tolerance has gone *pari passu* with a decline in the significance generally attributed to worship and with the increasing religious pluralism of society. In addition to the rich variety of Christian sects and denominations, most cities today have places of worship for the major world faiths, and also for some of the huge and ever-changing diversity of cults and groups of devotees. But large numbers of people, including many who seldom if ever darken the doors of a place of worship, continue to believe that worship, whatever the kind, is in some very general way 'a good thing'. Worship has become a matter of choice and not compulsion: there are no Acts of Uniformity or of Conformity remaining on the statute books; and there is much to be said for this 'free market' in forms of worship. But undergirding the new pluralism is a general public assumption that all worship is really the same thing, and rather a good thing at that; in such relativistic atmosphere it becomes rather bad form to speak in terms of true and false worship any longer. Liturgical syncretism, patching together ersatz forms of worship

without any coherent theological rationale out of the nicest and
most moving bits collected from every quarter, or liturgical
fundamentalism, rigid adherence to a specific denominational
tradition, so that worshippers may continue in the comfortable delusion that nothing has changed, nothing has been
challenged, are the two easiest responses to pluralism. Each is a
trap, and fortunately there are far more exciting possibilities of
mutual enrichment, theological rediscovery, and a refreshing
of worship presented by the modern diversity of forms of
worship.

Worship occupies a less central place in the life of most
modern societies. There is less of it and fewer people
participate. But worship is not dispensable. If people are
deprived of the traditional forms of worship, or find they have
gone moribund, they seek alternative forms for creating and
sustaining meaning and solidarity, they find surrogates for
worship. Mary Douglas, the social anthropologist, writes:

> If ritual is suppressed in one form it crops up in others, more
> strongly the more intense the social interaction. Without the letters
> of condolence, telegrams of congratulations and even occasional
> postcards, the friendship of a separated friend is not a social reality.
> It has no existence without the rites of friendship. Social rituals
> create a reality which would be nothing without them ... It is
> impossible to have social relations without symbolic acts.[8]

The prevalence of worship surrogates, sometimes of rather
bizarre sort, at a time when worship seems to be in decline
suggests the continuing existence of a fundamental human
need which is not being met adequately by the worship of the
Churches. The vacuum is filled by a strange medley of rituals
which attempt to convey meaning and significance to human
existence. Astrology, with its suggestion that the details of
earthly life are governed by the stars and given significance
thereby, occupies at least as much space in the popular press as
'serious religion'. The occult, spiritualism, even witchcraft and
black magic seem not only to continue but to flourish in secular
societies where organized religious worship declines in significance. Some worship surrogates are essentially debased and
suspect quasi-religious forms; others, like the rituals of the
football match or the political demonstration are avowedly
secular (although hymns are sometimes sung by football

[8] Mary Douglas, *Purity and Danger*, London 1966, p. 62.

crowds!). Television commercials not infrequently exude an unction or an awe which might suggest that they are central rites of the acquisitive society. And some religious programmes on radio and television, notably *The Daily Service* and *Songs of Praise*, are clearly intended to fulfil a felt need for worship on the part of many people who may have only the faintest connection with the organized Churches.

Some worship surrogates appear to be ethical alternatives to the worship of the Churches. Bodies such as Amnesty International, the Anti-Apartheid Movement, CND, and many other radical or idealistic groups, attract to their rituals – demonstrations, marches, rallies, petitions and so forth – many who feel that Christian worship has been caught in a 'culti trap' of ethical and political irrelevance. Their criticisms, implied or explicit, should be listened to by the Churches, as should the feelings of those who, despairing of Christian worship, have sought in the rites of Eastern religions a truer encounter with the mystery of the holy than they have found in their home Churches. For authentic Christian worship must be simultaneously a meeting with the holy living God and an alignment with his call for justice, compassion and peace.

Some contemporary theologians, supported by numerous sociologists of religion, have argued that religion in the modern world has been 'privatized' and this process has deeply affected the nature of worship. Privatization means that religion is removed from the public realm and concerns itself almost entirely with the individual and domestic activity. Religion and worship, it is suggested, have capitulated to modern individualism and become, in fact, 'what a person does with solitariness', with a strong emphasis on personal morality and family life. On the face of it, this privatized worship should seem incompatible with the still flourishing worship of civil religion, but the contrary is in fact the case: the two fit together very neatly in societies dominated by the idealogy of bourgeois individualism. 'Extremely privatized religion', writes the German Roman Catholic theologian Johann Baptist Metz, 'has been, as it were, specially prepared for the domestic use of the propertied middle-class citizen. It is above all a religion of inner feeling. It does not protest against or oppose in any way the definitions of reality, meaning or truth, for example, that are accepted by the middle-class society of exchange and success. It gives greater height and depth to what already applies even without it.'[9] Peter Berger's argument that privatized religion can no longer provide a comprehensive structure of meaning for social life because it has evacuated the public realm and only addresses itself to minor enclaves, particularly the domestic, needs to be qualified.[10] The very fact that organized religion now makes few, and not notably successful, attempts to intervene in the public sphere, makes it more amenable to being used to legitimate and sanctify the practices of the public realm. This is why privatization is a trap for Christian worship. Privatized worship is partial and unprophetic and distorted; its concern with issues of personal morality and domestic life goes happily with conferring an outward veneer of religious respectability on the proceedings of the public realm. But true Christian worship is a matter both for individual and community, both for the public and the private realms.

Closely associated with privatization is the belief that worship is not about participation in outward, objective realities, but concerned only with inward, subjective, individual and ultimately incommunicable truths. The 'historicizing' of the worship of Israel and of the Church which led to worship being understood as the celebration and renewal of an encounter in history between God and humankind was not exactly reversed – that would have been to focus worship on the cycles of nature rather than the events of history.[11] Cross, resurrection, incarnation, if they are events at all, are seen as events within the individual's subjectivity and existence; it is the inner, rather than the outer, drama with which worship is concerned. So Angelius Silesius the hymn-writer could sing:

> Though Christ a thousand times
> In Bethlehem be born.
> If he's not born in thee
> Thy soul is still forlorn.

> The cross on Golgotha
> Will never save thy soul
> The cross in thine own heart
> Alone can make thee whole.[12]

[9] J. B. Metz, *Faith in History and Society*, London 1980, p. 45.

[10] Peter Berger, *Social Reality*, pp. 137-38.

[11] On this, see Eugene H. Maly, 'The Interplay of World and Worship in the Scriptures', *Concilium* 2, No. 7 (1971).

[12] Johann Schefflet, otherwise known as Angelus Silesius, a seventeenth-century German hymn-writer, quoted in George Appleton, *Journey for a Soul*, London 1974, pp. 37–38.

This emphasis leads to a considerable reserve towards communal worship; it is in danger of losing its *raison d'être* as a result of the extreme subjectivizing of faith.

The decline in the numerical strength and influence of the Churches together with the linked processes of privatization and subjectivization leads not uncommonly to worship becoming sectarian. Congregations who know themselves to be, in Berger's term, 'cognitive deviants' have a strong temptation to withdraw to the security of operating as inturned sects, striving for their own survival and without a basic concern for the world 'outside' or for the broader community. The existence and worship of such congregations, which are hardly more than religious clubs, gatherings of the like-minded, are tolerated and indeed encouraged even in societies which are inherently irreligious, just as the Roman Empire tolerated various *religiones licitae* on the grounds that they did not interfere with the rites of the civil religion and did not press any disturbing universal claims, or proselytise too vigorously. The early Church found that it could not operate within the limits imposed upon a *religio licita*, and called down persecution upon itself. Nor could it go along with the social divisions of society, in particular that between Jew and Gentile, because to do so would be a denial of the universality of the Gospel and would have allowed the Church to fragment into a variety of little sects the boundaries of which followed the social divisions of the time. William Temple's belief that the church exists for the sake of those who never darken its doors is also true of the church's worship, and worship can never provide an adequate sense of meaning if it allows itself to degenerate into being the self-conscious and contrived ritual of a club.

Interpretation

Most of the developments and problems which we have outlined in the previous section are symptoms or effects of the pervasive social process called secularization. Put baldly, secularization is the process whereby religion and religious ideas and rituals come to play a less and less significant role in the life of a society. The influence of the Church is dramatically reduced, particularly in the economic, political and cultural spheres; in matters of personal morality it sometimes continues to have a greater say, for a time at least. Religious interpretations of reality come to have less and less formative influence on people's consciousness, and decisions are taken increasingly without reference either to religious authorities or to theological notions. As Peter Berger puts it, 'Probably for the first time in history, the religious legitimations of the world have lost their plausibility, not only for a few intellectuals and other marginal individuals, but for the broad masses of entire societies.'[13] The world has been evacuated of the sacred, or the sacred only lurks here and there in dark crevices. In Max Weber's terms, the world has been disenchanted, and any approach which puts the holy or the sacred at the centre of its concern, as does Christian worship, finds itself in an invidious situation of uncertainty and confusion. The secular person has 'come of age': free from clerical, churchy, or religious control, and accepting a new responsibility for shaping their world and guiding its progress into the future. Starting in Western Europe, the process of secularization has spread throughout the world and affected almost all societies and cultures to a greater or lesser extent. Even in the United States, where the Churches continue to occupy a far more significant and central role than is the case in Europe, they have only managed to do so, the argument runs, because they have themselves become secularized. We may suspect that some secularization theorists want to have it both ways, and would most willingly acknowledge that any case – Poland, for instance – could falsify their theory. This is not the place to enter into the contemporary discussion about secularization among sociologists, important as it is; it is enough for our present purposes to note that the displacement of religion and worship from the centre of the stage in most societies since the Enlightenment raises hard questions for worship: in particular, how can worship survive in a society in which the majority of people find it meaningless, objectionable, or simply quaint?[14]

For long it was assumed among Christians that secularization was unambiguously antagonistic to the Christian faith and therefore to Christian worship. This belief in an inherent opposition and incompatibility between Christian worship and

---

[13] Berger, *Social Reality*, p. 130.

[14] On secularization, see David Martin, *A General Theory of Secularization*, Oxford 1978; Bryan Wilson, *Religion in Secular Society*, Harmondsworth 1969; David Lyon, *The Steeple's Shadow*, London 1985; Steve Bruce, *Religion in Modern Britain*, Oxford 1995.

secularization depended on some fundamental, and seldom examined, assumptions about the nature of Christian worship. Foremost among these assumptions was this: Christian worship depends on a religious *a priori*, a general agreement within a society and culture that religion is an important dimension of life, and worship a major manifestation of religion. Christianity then proceeds to press its specific claims against those of the other religions on offer, and Christian worship tries to assert its claim to be the truest, or best, or purest form of worship. Christianity belongs to the class of religions, and claims to be the crown of all religion: Christian worship is one among many forms of response to the Holy, but claims to be 'worship in spirit and in truth' while the other kinds of worship are more or less defective in comparison. But when religion is regarded as an optional matter of no great importance, and worship a peculiar, eccentric and perhaps infantile activity in a world come of age, we are involved in a different ball-game. The first response on the part of Christian theologians was to see secularization as the great enemy, which must be met by the various religions and their forms of worship standing shoulder to shoulder against the assaults of secular modernity. Once secularization was repulsed, there would be an opportunity to give renewed attention to the differences between the various faiths and their cults; meanwhile they were allies in a struggle against the common foe.

The growth in the 1930s and 1940s of what is rather loosely called 'dialectical theology' led many theologians to look with suspicion on 'religion' and oppose very sharply Christianity and the religions. Religion, Karl Barth proclaimed, is unbelief, it is false, it is human striving to reach God. Christianity is misunderstood if it is seen as a religion; its essence is God's gracious reaching out for human beings in Christ. It belongs to a separate category entirely from 'the religions'. Theologians such as Gogarten and Bonhoeffer, in addition to Barth, spoke of the temptations, dangers and distortions of religion, perhaps influenced more than a little by their experience of the religious pretensions of Nazism in Germany. This suspicion of religion on the part of deeply committed Christian theologians opened the way for them to begin a much more positive theological assessment of the secular. So far from being the irreconcilable opponent of all religion and all worship, secularization comes to be seen as the ally of Christianity in its conflict with false religion and false worship. Secularization is capable of purifying and reforming worship. Arendt Th. van Leeuwen in his book *Christianity in World History* (London, 1964) argues that secularization is rooted in the Judaeo-Christian tradition, its effects are fruits of the Gospel, and its spread throughout the world is continuous with the Christian mission. Others, most notably Harvey Cox in *The Secular City* (London, 1965), saw secularization as something which should be welcomed, encouraged, celebrated and spread as an inherently Christian movement of liberation and maturing. Because secularization is understood as making possible a more human and responsible life for people before God, because it opens up new perspectives, and presents new opportunities for Christianity, but above all because it is interpreted by thinkers such as Cox and van Leeuwen as the work of God in history, it should be welcomed with confidence and Christians should ally themselves with the process of secularization.

All that glitters is not gold, and the sparkle which attracted some theologians to pronounce that secularization carried the divine hallmark has now become tarnished; even Harvey Cox has long ceased to celebrate the Christian mysteries of the secular city. More discriminating and chastened judgements of secularization are now being made. But even those who continue to give a more or less unqualified welcome to the new secular age acknowledge that the place of worship is highly problematic in a secular society and that this raises crucial questions for the Church.

In an important article, 'Ghetto or Desert: Liturgy in a Cultural Dilemma'[15] Charles Davis argues that the problem of worship in the modern secular age is unsolved. Modern culture is dynamic and aggressively secular; worship is at the margin, irrelevant to the fundamental concerns of the society, out of date in a culture that is no longer Christian. Davis suggests that public worship as we know it presupposes a common culture, shared by all, and is itself 'a rich cultural form' which brings to focus a unified living culture. But today Christian worship – or any form of worship, for that matter – is at variance with the culture in which it is set. Worship is a nostalgic anachronism, harking back to the time when it was the expression of a rich and lively Christian culture. It finds it impossible to relate to

---

[15] In Charles Davis, *The Temptations of Religion*, London 1973, pp. 93–125.

the dominant secular culture, which is more vigorous, fruitful and open by far than the deviant and atavistic Christian (or religious) sub-culture. Secularization has produced a form of society which has no place for worship; particularly for those Christians who gave an unqualified welcome to the process, this involves a profound theological and practical dilemma; is it possible to envisage a form of the Christian faith which has no place for worship, or can Christian worship take on a shape which is relevant and appropriate to a secular society? Underlying this dilemma is the problem of the relation between culture and society on the one hand and Christian worship on the other. We will shortly have to raise some questions about Charles Davis's formulation of this relationship, but few would disagree with his argument that the place and nature of Christian worship in a secular age is a major problem for Christians, and one which admits of no easy solution.

Response

Charles Davis suggests that there are two, and only two, responses possible to the crisis of worship in a secularized society. These he labels 'the ghetto' and 'the desert'.

1. *The Ghetto.* Since liturgy has to have a social and cultural setting to which it is integrally related and it is impossible for it to be 'some kind of pure expression of the Christian faith', it may remain central to the life of small deviant and anachronistic communities, largely cut off from the dominant secular culture and devoting a great deal of their energies to the process of boundary maintenance. Such ghetto religious communities exist – for instance, the Amish people in Pennsylvania, or the Closed Brethren in north-east Scotland – nourishing a world-view, a lifestyle, and a form of worship radically at variance with those of the surrounding community, with which they have as little contact and interaction as possible. Davis finds this option unattractive. Christian culture, he believes (making an astoundingly unqualified judgement), is now decadent and inferior to secular culture, in crucial respects *less Christian* than its secular setting. Rather strangely, Davis does not press beyond his somewhat dubious identification of Christianity and a lively culture to examine other theological and practical objections to the ghetto – that a ghetto existence involves an abdication of responsibility for the life of the world,

a repudiation by implication of the universality of the Gospel, and a sinful obsession with group survival. Nor does he consider the alternative notion of the 'counter-culture' as developed by writers such as Theodore Roszak,[16] and put into practice into Europe and America in such a bewildering variety of ways, some of them bizarre, but others of considerable importance. What Davis might dismiss as a ghetto, turned in on itself and engrossed with questions of its own survival, may turn out, on closer acquaintance, to be quite different; a counter-cultural community, passionately concerned for the world and its life and culture, not cutting off communications with the world but witnessing *to* and *against* the society and culture in which it is set. This model of a group which deviates from the values and assumptions of the dominant culture but is dedicated to the transforming of the world rather than conforming to the world may be an attractive alternative to the ghetto.

2. *The Desert.* Davis's preferred possibility is the desert, the situation in which the believer finds himself an almost isolated wanderer in a cultural desert. The Christian culture of the past is dead; the future Christian culture has yet to be born; meanwhile the believer has no appropriate cultural forms in which to express his faith and worship. Liturgy, or public worship, is impossible, but impossible because Davis has defined it as an expression of a generally accepted cultural and religious synthesis which no longer exists. The believer in the desert longs for the future, when liturgy becomes possible once again because a new and lively synthesis of Christianity and culture has emerged, when 'the present secular culture will be redeemed and rendered open to Christian faith'. Meanwhile the believer lives between the times, wandering in the desert, without liturgy or public worship, until a return to the promised land becomes possible. But although there are no appropriate forms of liturgy available, the believer cannot live without worship, so privately and in small groups believers will soldier on, sometimes using antiquated or despised forms inherited from the past, sometimes developing a variety of experimental forms of worship for themselves. And in all this the dominant motive is the search for a new synthesis of culture and worship, which is certain to be substantially different from any earlier

---

[16] Theodore Roszak, *The Making of a Counter Culture*, London 1970, and *Where the Waste Land Ends*, London 1973.

synthesis. 'The movement for the renewal of worship', he writes, 'coincides with the mission of Christians to transform secular culture, preserving indeed its proper character and its gains, but opening it to a higher level.'[17]

The central problem raised in Davis's analysis is the relation of worship and culture. Clearly they are connected, and sometimes in history it is clear that worship has indeed been a major vehicle and shaper of culture. But the relation is not as direct and simple as Davis suggests. Although there have been periods when liturgy has been a vital and central cultural expression, and other periods when there has been a creative and conscious interaction between culture and worship, for much of its history and particularly at the beginning, Christian worship has been structured and practised as the way of giving glory to God, and any cultural role it may have had has been regarded as of little consequence. Neither the second-century Christian participants, nor the pagan official Pliny, nor the Emperor Trajan to whom he was reporting could have thought early Christian worship a *cultural* form – Pliny regarded it as a 'superstitious contagion' posing a very minor threat to the official cult because the Christians regarded the civil cult and culture as basically idolatrous; the Christians themselves probably regarded it as their duty and delight.[18]

Most forms of Christian worship have been shaped in detail and in general primarily by the attempt to be faithful – to the God who is worshipped, to Scripture, to theological orthodoxy. They have not been understood as expressions of cultural responsibility. Liturgical reforms which are primarily attempting to be up-to-date, or 'with-it', are not misguided because they are seeking a premature and superficial synthesis between Christian worship and contemporary culture, as Charles Davis would suggest, but because they have been seduced into giving cultural considerations priority over the Christian integrity of worship.

Davis's argument is spoiled by his assumption that there is, or can be such a thing as a 'Christian culture', and by his nostalgia for the mediaeval synthesis and for the idea of Christendom which is now irrecoverable. What we are saying is this: the effect of liturgy upon culture is vast and varied, but for the most part indirect, unconscious and unintended. And although it is

[17] Davis, *The Temptations of Religion*, p. 124.
[18] *The Letters of Pliny the Younger*, book 10, especially 97.

obvious that culture influences liturgy very deeply it must not become simply a cultural expression. Christian worship must always combine catholicity – the sense of being the worship of the one Church all down the ages and throughout the globe – with indigenization – the sense that Christian worship has a home, albeit a temporary camp for a pilgrim people, in every culture, society and age. The way forward, we would suggest, is neither that of the ghetto nor the desert, but the attempt in faithfulness to the tradition and its sources and sensitive interaction with the culture and the political, social and intellectual issues of today, to seek ways of giving glory to God which are appropriate to *this* time and *this* place.[19]

Davis picks up Peter Berger's argument that Christians have become a marginalized minority of 'cognitive deviants', Religion, he accurately reports 'has been relegated to the margins. It has no real part to play in thinking and decision-making even in quite minor matters'.[20] The 'plausibility structure', which used to sustain mass Christianity, has collapsed. To be a group of deviants at the margin of things is not easy; subtle and threatening pressures to conform are there all the time; and uncomfortable sense of loneliness and isola-tion from the mainstream of things is a common experience; it becomes increasingly hard to sustain beliefs, values and practices which diverge from those of the majority and are commonly regarded as quaint and unimportant – and almost certainly false as well. But the margin is not a strange place for Christians; it is not only a problem, but a place of opportunity too. Indeed, one could argue that the margin is a more proper place for Christians to be, than at the centre of things. After all, Jesus himself was a marginalized person, who 'suffered outside the gate in order to sanctify the people through his own blood' (Hebrews 13:13). The margin, it would appear, is the place of illumination, revelation, insight, the place where we can discern the depth of what God is doing in the life of the city or the camp. It is also the place of redemption, the place outside the city from which the salvation of the city flows. And the Letter to the Hebrews suggests that it is the place where we meet the Lord and share in his work – and keep the company he keeps, for he chooses to associate particularly with those whom society

---

[19] A useful critique of Davis' essay to which the above paragraphs are somewhat indebted is J. G. Davies, *Every Day God*, London 1973, pp. 253–46.
[20] Davis, *The Temptations of Religion*, p. 97.

has marginalized: 'therefore let us go forth to him outside the camp, and bear the abuse he endured. For here we have no lasting city, but we seek the city which is to come. Through him then let us continually offer up a sacrifice of praise to God, that is, the fruit of lips that acknowledge his name' (Hebrews 13:13–15).

Christian Worship Today and Tomorrow

Christian worship is today in a state of crisis. This is the situation which we have tried to analyse in this chapter. Some see nothing but the acids of modernity eating away the substance of worship, leaving only some flakes of rust behind. Others believe that the crisis is a challenge to renewal, in which worship may be liberated, renewed and purified. As in all crises, there is both danger and opportunity, and the Christian is called to respond in faith asking what God is doing and saying to his Church in the modern situation. The prophetic tradition reminds us that God may reject and destroy forms of worship when they become covers for injustice, meaningless survivals from the past or impersonal routines. But destruction goes often with purification and renewal. The same process that challenges and erodes forms of worship opens up the possibility of the recovery of vital but long-forgotten elements in the worship tradition, the rebirth of long dormant symbols and images, and the development of new and living symbols, words and forms. A crisis is no time for timidity, and Christians should be adventurous in their worship, confident that God is at work amidst the threats and opportunities of the modern age.

In a secular society Christians see worship as continuing to perform vital functions. In the first place it is a way in which life is given meaning, and depth. Worship does not belong in a separate order from everyday life, and does not provide a bolt-hole from the pressures of existence. It must be rooted in ordinary life, providing an interpretation of that life which sustains and invigorates it by giving it depth. And worship is the celebration of life. In Christian worship the vertical – our encounter with God – and the horizontal – our encounter with the neighbour – are held together. To emphasize one at the expense of the other is to distort the cruciform shape of Christian worship. But worship which holds together the vertical and the horizontal is capable of transforming life. As Panikkar puts it:

People eat. It is the eating that has to be transformed by the sacramental presence and thus the Eucharist has to regain its symbolism of being a meal. People dance and amuse themselves. Christian worship has here again to recover its aspect of celebration and festivity. People are born, come of age, get married, adopt a profession and die. The sacraments have to sanctify and consecrate these most universal and elemental human acts. The sacraments of Initiation, Maturity, Marriage, etc. must not be simply ceremonies and traditional ritualisms, but have a real bearing and meaning for these important moments of human existence; in a word, they must really shape them ... Worship has to permeate human life once again and render it more meaningful, enhancing the significance of those acts and also giving the necessary strength (grace) for one to live up to such a human calling.[21]

Only too often, however, the actuality of worship conveys precisely the contrary message to that intended – 'celebrations' expressing gloom and solemnity rather than joy, the Lord's Supper less a symbolic fellowship meal than a parody of the cafeteria, food eaten in haste and isolation from the community. Some worship neither soars to the heights nor penetrates to the depths but skates nervously over the surface of life. The sign of these distortions is the driving of a wedge between worship and life. When worship is safely confined in a strange and unreal world of its own, boxed into a special compartment from which it cannot impinge on the rest of life, it quickly dies of asphyxia.

But worship does not sanctify things as they are. It is not a way of conforming to the world but of transforming the world. It is not in the business of maintaining the social equilibrium or sacralizing the social order. Worship disturbs the *status quo*, it is a standing challenge to the injustices and oppression of the earthly city because worshippers are looking to the city whose builder and maker is God, and in worship they are already anticipating the life of that city.

Worship provokes the quest for understanding. It does not simply reflect experience, but formulates, modifies and interprets experience in the light of the encounter with the living God. As Mary Douglas puts it:

Ritual is not merely like the visual aid which illustrates the verbal instructions for opening cans and cases. If it were just a kind of dramatic map or diagram of what is known it would always follow

[21] Panikkar, *Worship and Secular Man*, p. 59.

experience. But in fact ritual does not play this secondary role. It can come first in formulating experience. It can permit knowledge of what would otherwise not be known at all. It does not merely externalize experience, bringing it into the light of day, but it modifies experience in so expressing it.[22]

The trouble is that we have such trivial understandings of what worship is – as if it were 'instructions for opening cans', or a controlled way of passing on a self-contained and satisfactory pattern of theological understanding or a device for conserving a religious culture, or a means for solidifying patterns of community, order and authority. But worship is the encounter with the living God! Michael Polanyi, chemist and philosopher, speaks of Christian worship as a 'continual attempt at breaking out, at casting off, the condition of man, even while humbly acknowledging its inescapability'. Worship fosters, as it questions, Christian practice within the context of a fellowship that is both pastoral and prophetic; it stimulates a thirst for the Kingdom of God and his righteousness by providing an authentic anticipation of that Kingdom; it makes worshippers dissatisfied with themselves and society; it mediates the forgiveness and grace upon which effective and purposive action depends; it sustains that vision without which the people perish and alerts us to attempts to subvert that vision; it nourishes those who live as pilgrims seeking that city whose builder and maker is God.

FURTHER READING

Raymond Panikkar, *Worship and Secular Man*, London 1973.
Peter Berger, *The Social Reality of Religion*, Harmondsworth 1973.
J. G. Davies, *Every Day God*, London 1973.
Tom Driver, *The Magic of Ritual*, San Francisco 1991.
Steve Bruce, *Religion in Modern Britain*, Oxford 1995.

FOR DISCUSSION

1. How would you assess the impact of secularization on worship?
2. In what ways may Christian worship relate to the rituals of civil religion?

[22] Mary Douglas, *Purity and Danger*, p. 64.

3. 'There is no modern form of worship, because worship itself is outdated in the modern world and Christian faith a state of deviancy from contemporary culture' (Charles Davis). Discuss.

4. Is there a 'crisis of worship' which undermines nurture within the faith community? If so, how does it manifest itself in practice? What steps can be taken to counteract it?

INDEX OF PROPER NAMES

INDEX OF SUBJECTS